35 Dead

ONE SURVIVOR

How I Became the Sole Kidnapped and
Raped Survivor

of the Casanova Serial Killer

(Paul John Knowles)

Barbara Mabee Abel

Edited, additional content and cover designed by

Laurel L. Galvan

35 Dead

ONE SURVIVOR

How I Became the Sole Kidnapped and Raped Survivor of the Casanova Serial Killer
(Paul John Knowles)

By Barbara Mabee Abel

Edited, additional content and cover designed by
Laurel L. Galvan

This book is a work of nonfiction. Some of the names have been changed to protect their identity and privacy.

The errors: historical, typos, grammar, and all mistakes otherwise are mine alone.

Printed in the United States of America

ISBN-13: 978-0-578-24471-6

Author's Bridge Publishing
320 Mamie Cook Road
Boone, NC 28607-7784

35 Dead

ONE SURVIVOR

How I Became the Sole Kidnapped and Raped
Survivor

of the Casanova Serial Killer

(Paul John Knowles)

By Barbara Mabee Abel

Edited, additional content and cover designed by

Laurel L. Galvan

Author's Bridge

PUBLISHERS

TABLE OF CONTENTS

DEDICATION

Beverly Jean Mabee, my beautiful twin sister, you are my angel. I realize you are up in Heaven now, after dying from a rare form of cancer, but you are not suffering any longer. You knew how important you were to me all these years. Even up until the end, you still smiled through your pain with not only cancer but being born with Cerebral Palsy. Dale Tucker, my son, even though you were six years of age when I was taken from you for a short time, you are a part of my life forever and I am proud of how you have grown as a young man. Your strong faith in our Lord, Jesus Christ, brought us through the bad times because we never gave

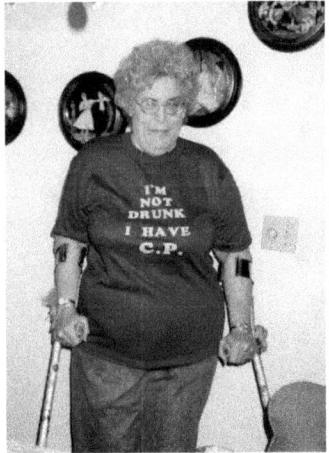

Beverly Mabee - 1992

up on each other! You both have been with me through this entire process and helped me find the courage to write this book. I hope it will help other victims of crime.

PREFACE

How does one survive a serial killer that claims to have killed 35 people? He NEVER leaves a witness alive. He is so deranged that his chosen victims are as young as a set of sisters 7 and 11 years old and a senior woman as old as 63, raping and strangling them to death. The senior woman choking to death while being gagged as this monster burglarizes her home. He rapes and kills men, women, and children. He slays them by strangulation, stabbing or shooting them. His victims even include a state trooper.

This man's Jekyll and Hyde personalities surface without warning. A man that is so well-spoken, good-looking, with wonderful manners and great intelligence, could instantly flip his personality into a vicious, homicidal maniac. This killer crosses through 40 states, covering over 20,000 miles in six months, just to seek out victims to kill. His goal is to become the most infamous serial killer in history.

What are your chances of survival? Can it make you stronger? Not only can it strengthen your faith in God and life, but it can give you the courage in your soul to defeat so many of life's challenges...if you let it.

A LOVE STORY

Mother and father were loving parents who raised four children in a Christian home. It was a beautiful two-story grey wood shingled home with white trim. The large screened in front porch spanned the front of the house in downtown Detroit, Michigan. Growing up in a safe neighborhood was wonderful. You could leave your doors and windows open without worrying about crime.

Mama was born in Burlington, Canada, and Daddy was born in Toronto, Canada, two cities that were 36 miles apart. Years later fate, or God's divine wisdom, would lead them to find each other.

Mama learned French in high school, which helped her in her senior play *Kicked Out of College* playing Mademoiselle Mimi Fleurette, a French customer. Strangers in the audience were deceived as to her nationality. Numerous people in the audience declared that she must be Parisian. In her high school yearbook, it was written: "As the Sara Bernhardt of the senior class, she possessed a spark of talent, which may one day place her in a high rank of dramatic achievement, should she choose to follow that vocation."

Mama and Daddy each moved to Detroit at different times. Daddy was in the Navy for several years, while Mama began working as a saleswoman at a department store downtown. Even though she made a decent living, her dream job was to apply at Macy's. But she realized she would need more experience to qualify for a job at such a prestigious store.

Once every few months, her sisters would pick her up, then drive to Canada, to visit with their parents. Mama never had the desire to learn how to drive and nobody knew why.

She loved going out dancing with her friends on weekends to the local bars. One night, her friends took her to Toby's Detroit Bar located right in the heart of downtown. It was there she met the man who would turn out to be the love of her life. As Matilda, my mom, stumbled while entering the front door, her friend grabbed her by the arm before she fell. The nightclub was so dark inside you had to adjust your eyes by gazing at the tables with candles.

A short time later, a man entered. As his eyes adjusted, he thought he was dreaming. Here were his friends with one of the most beautiful women he had ever laid eyes on in his life.

"Well, hello, what's your name?" he asked.

"Matilda, but my friends call me Tillie," she answered.

He struggled to remember what to do next, she affected him that fast. The orchestra began playing Frank Sinatra's hit *Night and Day*, which gave him his chance to recoup. "May I have this dance?" he stammered.

"Yes, I love to dance."

As he guided her out onto the dance floor and the light shown on her face, he gasped at her beauty. She was a tall, statuesque full-bodied woman with beautiful shoulder length wavy black hair, beautiful sparkling hazel eyes and lips he wanted to kiss. Her perfume was not overpowering, but subtle and refreshing.

After dancing and gazing into her beautiful eyes he was mesmerized. He was hooked, it was love at first sight. Once the evening was over, he walked her to her friend's car. He stopped, took her face in his hands, and lightly kissed her on the lips. He knew she was the one for him. Now he had to convince her. And he would in time. I loved hearing stories like this from Mama and Daddy.

Almost a year after dating and falling head over heels in love they married. They had a small wedding at the local church with friends and family. Matilda's two sisters helped pick out her wedding dress weeks ahead of time.

When *The Wedding March* music started, Earl, my dad, began to tear up when he saw the love of his life walking down the aisle toward him. She was in a flowing floor-length satin wedding dress with long sleeves and pearls lining the bodice and sleeves. Her black shiny hair was curled, and pearls outlined her veil that flowed past her waist. Everything matched from the top of her head to the beautiful white satin covered heels. The whole picture was magical as she stopped in front of her husband to be.

The preacher began the wedding vows. "Do you take Earl to be your lawfully wedded husband?" he began.

"Yes, I do," she answered.

Then it was Earl's turn.

When it was over, the preacher said, "You may now kiss the bride!"

They both beamed quirky smiles at each other when Earl leaned over to give Tillie a passionate kiss. Then they walked hand-in-hand down the aisle. "I love you," he whispered as they headed towards the door to have pictures taken before leaving for their reception at the local clubhouse. They were now husband and wife.

They returned from their amazing honeymoon on the beach in Miami, Florida, a few weeks later, to face reality. They needed to find jobs. They both wanted to have children later, but in God's time.

Daddy took a job as a salesman who sold caskets at the local funeral home. He made a very good living being the top salesman. Mama fulfilled her dream by working at Macy's Department store and became one of their top saleswomen.

"Mrs. Rutenberger that dress fits you like a glove. Midnight blue is your color because it matches your gorgeous blue eyes," she would tell one customer. If she could not find the right dress, she had let them know when the new shipment would arrive. Her bosses loved her competitive attitude towards selling dresses to cranky customers. She always charmed the worst customers into buying a dress that would make them look and feel marvelous. It was easy to see they both loved their jobs.

A few months later, Mama was making breakfast when the smell of the bacon spattering in the pan got to her. She almost doubled over trying not to throw up.

"Earl, honey please finish frying the bacon. I have to run to the bathroom," she called out to him. He got the fork to turn the bacon as she dashed out of the kitchen.

When she returned, he noticed the washcloth in her hand. "What's happening darling?" he asked.

"Oh, it's nothing. I threw up, must be the beginning of the flu." He was not buying it.

"I want you to make an appointment with our doctor. It doesn't look like the flu to me," he said.

A week later they went to the doctor together and received the good news.

"You're going to have a baby, Matilda," the doctor said.

Earl grabbed his wife and kissed her in front of the doctor and the nurse. Everyone was thrilled. Their first baby would arrive in nine months. It was okay for Mama to quit her job after the baby was born if she wanted. Daddy would let her make up her own mind.

As the months whizzed by, Earl would lay his head on Matilda's huge belly and listen to the heartbeat of their soon-to-be born baby. "I'm as excited as you are to have this baby, darling," he whispered to the love of his life. The following week Matilda was rushed to the hospital to give birth.

"Her name will be Jacqueline," Mama said to her husband, as the nurse handed the precious baby to her for the first time. "Honey, I can't believe how tiny she is. Look at the top of her head. She has dark auburn hair. Oh, look how tiny her little hands and feet are. Thank you, God, thank you for sending us this beautiful daughter from Heaven," she said.

Mama had black hair and Daddy had red so it was understandable that their first born would have auburn hair. It did not matter at all. All that mattered was she was healthy, weighing seven pounds, and 19 inches long. The pink blanket wrapped around her had pink daisies on the corners. Matilda was beside herself with joy as she welcomed her little bundle from heaven. She always loved other people's children and babies and now she had been blessed with a child of her own. Our grandparents, aunts, uncles, and friends spoiled Jacqueline rotten.

Mama did quit her job, and became a stay-at-home mother who cooked and baked, and took care of the house and baby.

Daddy could not wait to get back home to his wife and baby each day after work. He adored them both. Mama's cooking was another thing. Heaven only knows who taught her to cook because she was terrible. She baked the same old tuna noodle casserole on a weekly basis. If she cooked chicken in the oven, it would be dry and yucky. But Daddy never complained and always complimented her meals, praying one day she would get better at cooking. At least she knew how to bake delicious, yummy, and scrumptious desserts.

Being Catholic meant no birth control for Mama. After giving up on having more children, five years later our brother, Gary, was born. She felt like he was their miracle baby. He had coal black hair, like Mama, hazel eyes, weighed eight pounds and was 20 inches long. As Mama held Gary in her arms, she instantly loved him with all her heart.

Jackie was six years old and was thrilled to have a baby in the house. She welcomed him with open arms. She came to love and adore her baby brother. She became a great help to Mama and Daddy after she learned how to take care of him. Her two best friends thought he was so cute and wanted to sit on the couch and hold him. "Nope, not yet, he's too tiny. Only I can hold him for now," she told them, as she picked Gary out of the bassinette to show him off. He meant the world to her.

Just when they thought that was the end of having more children, Mama was pregnant again. They looked forward to making room for a new baby nine months hence.

Mama was rushed to the hospital in April 1943, with excruciating pain. As the ambulance raced to the hospital, Daddy held her hands praying that baby and Mama would be alright. It was too early to have her baby because she was only seven months pregnant. He knew they had to leave it in God's hands.

The doctor came out after the birth and told our father, "Your wife has beautiful TWIN girls and they were both put in incubators." He told Daddy we both weighed in a little over three pounds and had to get up to five pounds before going home.

TWO BABY GIRLS! Everyone in the family was shocked to hear Mama had twins. Mama's sister, our Aunt Nadine named us, Beverly and Barbara since our parents were both too stunned to come up with names on their own. They were not shocked because they had twins, but because my twin sister, Beverly, was born with Cerebral Palsy.

We both had blue eyes. Beverly had straight white hair and mine was strawberry blonde. We were fraternal twins who knew instinctively when one or the other was hurting, as we got older.

Some of our parents' friends told Mama and Daddy to give Beverly up and have her institutionalized because she was disabled. They felt she would become a burden later in life. Our parents never gave her up but loved and spoiled her throughout the years when she had to go in and out of hospitals due to complications with Cerebral Palsy.

GROWING UP

Gary, Mama "Tilley", Jackie & Barbara - Canada 1949

Grandma and Grandpa, on Mama's side, lived in Burlington, Ontario, Canada. Daddy drove us through the tunnel from Detroit into Canada to visit every few months.

Grandma and Grandpa raised a few goats and chickens. I was not the country girl-type. Grandma served oatmeal with goat milk and it made me sick to my stomach. Yuck, I never had it again. I was happy to grow up in Detroit and be a city girl.

When I was a kid, I dreamed of becoming a movie star. I took rose petals from the rose bush and put them on my fingernails with my own spit. After all, when you are five years old you want to look pretty. I tried to walk

13

in Mama's high heels shoes, but my feet were too small. In my mind, I believed I had what it took to become a movie star when I was older.

Our parents joined the Shriner's Club in Detroit. One day, the bus came right to our house with other handicapped children and picked-up Beverly to take her to the parade downtown. Mama made Beverly's favorite peanut butter and jelly sandwich, a cookie, and an apple to take for her lunch. The Shriner's supplied drinks at each event.

Mama - April 3, 1948

Why was I always waving goodbye?

As the bus pulled up to pick up Beverly, I went through the front door, jumped up and down, and screamed bloody murder. I threw myself on the front porch sobbing. I was only five.

Beverly was so overwhelmed by my terrible outburst she began to cry and dropped her lunch on the front porch. Mama came over and took both of us to the couch on the porch then hugged each of us and told us everything would be alright. She picked up Beverly's lunch and handed it to her to hold.

The bus driver left the bus to see what all the commotion was about. He left the other children in good hands, with parents who were helpers. As he walked up the steps, he asked Mama why Beverly was crying. Mama explained the situation. He listened intently, then he asked if he could use the phone to call his supervisor.

Jackie, Gary, Barbara & Beverly
1950

He went inside and called his supervisor telling him what had transpired. He got permission for me to go with my twin sister to the parade.

Yay! I won. Mama was thankful the bus driver was being so thoughtful. She thanked him then went into the kitchen to pack my lunch while he took Beverly and me to the bus. "Barbara, sit by me, please," Beverly said. Mama gave my lunch to one of the ladies and threw us kisses after telling us the family would meet them downtown at the parade.

As we drove downtown to the St. Patrick's Day Parade, I was thrilled to be riding with everybody. The bus was big. I tried to reach up to look out the window, but I was too short. But that didn't bother me. Being with Beverly as we enjoyed the St. Patrick's Day Parade was the important thing.

The Shriners Club members were thoughtful towards handicapped children and had a section blocked off with chairs for the parade. We could all sit with our families and watch the floats, bands, and people walk by in front of us. Mama, Daddy, Gary, and Jackie were seated with the other family members and waved us over to sit with them. Daddy picked Beverly up and put her on his shoulders to see the floats as they passed by. Everything was magical that day. I leaned over to hug and kiss her when Daddy sat her beside me. After that day, I often went with Beverly to other events the Shriners put on for children. Daddy made me go to bed without ice

15

cream that night, but I did not care, because I won. I did decide I wouldn't throw any more fits.

A month later, Jackie, Gary, Beverly, and I were playing with our dad in the back yard. Mama was inside cooking when she looked out the window and saw Daddy struggling to climb the back-porch steps. He was holding onto his chest and gasping for air. Daddy told Jackie to take us to the swings because he was not feeling well and was going inside to take a nap.

Earl Mabee - 1952

Our father passed away suddenly from a massive heart attack that night on the way to the hospital. Mama was devastated. So was Jackie. Gary was seven and Beverly and I were six at the time, and we did not understand death.

Mama was able to get a full-time job with Macy's that was tough on her. She did not want Jackie to have fulltime care responsibilities at her young age. "Darling are you sure you don't mind taking care of Gary and the girls after school until I get home from work?" she asked.

"No, Mama I'm a big girl now, I can handle them," Jackie said. "The only one I have a problem with is Barbie because she tries to get away with stupid stuff like not helping with the dishes, but we'll be fine."

In the weeks ahead, Jackie took over light cooking, housecleaning, and babysitting. Gary, Beverly, and I

16

helped when needed. Jackie became quite a good cook within a few months. Soon, she was way better than Mama. Praise the Lord! On a few weekends a month, Mama let Jackie stay with Aunt Nadine, our Mama's sister. That is when she really learned how to cook and bake.

THE MOVE

A couple years later, Mama's arthritis got so bad during the winter months, she and Aunt Nadine made the decision to move our family to South Florida. Daddy and Mama had come to Miami several times throughout the years for vacation without us and loved Miami. She decided on West Palm Beach, Florida because Miami was too far south, and Orlando was too cold in the winter. So, when Beverly and I were 11, mother sold the house and we moved to Florida.

She was a pioneer back then, bringing four children by train from Detroit to South Florida, not knowing a soul and never having learned how to drive. That took bravery, strength, and a lot of guts!

All our family and friends were crying their eyes out when the five of us got on the train to move to Florida. I do not know how many days it took for the big train to get all the way from Detroit, Michigan to West Palm Beach, Florida. I think we all had to change trains in Jacksonville. Gary and I were having a ball walking up and down the aisles, looking at people who were feeding babies, reading books, or talking with one another. After all, I was 11 and this was a new adventure to me. At dinnertime, Mama and Jackie gathered us from our seats to go eat supper in the dining car.

We all had to take our time walking with Beverly in front of Mama because of her crutches and braces. Jackie made sure Gary and I were together. Beverly was so excited to get out of her seat, she giggled all the way to the dining car. That is our sis, we thought as we took baby steps in front of Mama.

We thought, the waiters were fascinating to watch as the train sped through the night weaving, bobbling, and jerking at times. Jackie said, "Gary, Barbie watch the waiters. Boy they're really GOOD. They haven't dropped any food on the floor."

Mama seated the four of us and then made the mistake of asking what each wanted.

"I want a steak with mashed potatoes and gravy, heavy on the gravy, Mama," Gary squealed out.

"You're not getting steak Gary; we can't afford it," Mama whispered to her son.

Beverly and I got French fries, a hamburger, and a root beer float. Mama and Jackie got meatloaf with potatoes and some yucky looking veggies. Gary decided to get a hamburger with double fries and a soda.

"Mama, Beverly, Gary, Jackie, this is the most exciting adventure in my entire life, we are on a train and moving to Florida," I stammered, then took a bite of my yummy hamburger.

After supper we went back to our seats. It was scary going through towns in the pitch blackness of the night. I laid my head down and fell asleep dreaming of my new home and more adventures.

A few days later, we all arrived safely in West Palm Beach, Florida. Mama got a taxi to take us to the nearest motel. It was right across the street from a Howard Johnson Restaurant. Mama checked-in at the front desk. When the manager saw she had four children with her, she smiled and handed Mama the keys to a larger room. The housekeeper brought two cots for Gary and Jackie to sleep on.

After putting everything away, Mama and Jackie took us across the street to eat dinner. We were very tired, but also famished. We were so hungry we all ordered the same meal of hot dogs, fries, and sodas. I was rubbing my behind when Mama put her hand on mine to stop it. "Honey, when we get back to the room and change into our night clothes, I want to look at your behind," she said.

"But Mama you don't have to, I feel like we're still on the train," I said, after I rubbed my rear end once again to ease the pain.

Mama was smart and made me walk around the motel room when we got back after eating.

My entire body was still moving when I got to bed. I reached over to Gary and asked how he felt.

"I feel like I'm still on the train. This is weird!" he exclaimed.

Then everyone, including Mama, said the same thing. It made me laugh. My rear end felt much better and Mama did not have to check it out. That would have been embarrassing. After all, I was 11 years old.

Mama had Jackie take care of us while she looked for a place to rent. The motel was alright, but we needed an apartment or house to rent until Mama could find a good job. God was with us because she found a house within a week, and it was near a bus stop.

The home reminded me of our house in Detroit. It was a wood-shingled house with a screened-in front porch, which Mama could rent for a year until she found us a home to buy.

Kathy and Mike, our new landlords were wonderful. They lived in the apartment behind the house. Kathy drove Mama to the schools we would attend. Later she drove her to Burdines department store to apply for a job. They hired Mama immediately. She would begin full-time work a week later. Macy's Department Store in Detroit gave her a glowing recommendation.

Mama took the city bus to work each day. She brought home bathing suits after she received her first paycheck. The following weekend, Kathy and Mike took us to the beach to celebrate moving to Florida.

When we arrived on Singer Island Beach, we looked in awe at this huge beach and gasped. We had to walk forever to get to where we laid our blankets, and then walked near the ocean. None of us knew how to swim.

Jackie and Mama were careful with Beverly because she wanted to go in the water. Mike and Mama helped Beverly walk between them and took her to the edge of the water to put her feet in. She was so thrilled; it was a new adventure to her.

The day was magical. It was another great adventure seeing the Atlantic Ocean for the first time.

Everyone was sunburned after arriving home, except Mama. She made hot tea, cooled it down, and put each of us into the bathtub as she poured tea over us. It worked. We were not in so much pain afterwards.

We went to school where we were the new kids on the block. Jackie went to high school by bus. Gary and I walked to the same elementary school nearby. Beverly was handicapped and labeled "not acceptable" in public schools. She had to go to Royal Palm School on the bus that picked her up at our home. There were 15 boys and four girls in her class. The boys teased her, treated her horribly, and made her feel worthless.

As we were only 11, I could not understand why she had to go to a special school for handicapped people. Mama tried to explain that it would be a safety hazard trying to climb stairs at a regular school, but it did not make sense to me. Beverly did not have anything wrong except walking with crutches and braces.

She went to the special school for only one week when she came home crying because the boys in her class were bullying her. After Gary and I found out, we started meeting her on the front walk when her bus arrived. We gave those bullies the evil eye. Gary could beat them up; I could also, but I was becoming a teenager and had to control my redheaded temper.

A year later, Mama was promoted to top saleswoman in the Better Dress Department and decided it was time to move. Our landlords, Kathy and Mike, helped her find a two-year old home about a half mile from where we lived.

"Matilda, don't forget, even though you're moving into this darling home, we're still your friends and will pick you up for church on Sunday," Kathy said, after hugging every one of us with tears in her eyes.

The home was cute after Mama filled it with new furniture, curtains, drapes, and personal items from our rented home. It had two bedrooms, one bath, and a Florida room. The backyard was large and beautiful with two palm trees, other bushes, and flowers. I was turning 13 at the time. We were close to schools, grocery stores, and the bus stops. Mama took the four of us to the beach by bus on some weekends, which was fun. Sometimes her friends drove us, so we would not have to take the bus. We girls had to be careful of the sun because we were fair. Our brother never had that problem. Darn it. He got a beautiful tan and we got blisters.

We had a solid upbringing with an amazing mother. Mama took us to church on Sundays. Our neighbor drove us on the days, Kathy was not available. Being in church helped us to learn about religion and God. I believe this foundation in trusting God early in my life became a lifesaver in my adult life.

Learning at a young age to be good to others, not bully those less fortunate than us, and trusting in God was a wonderful gift. Our mother taught us that the love of God was number one because Jesus Christ, our Lord and Savior, died on the cross for everyone.

We saw how some people treated Beverly through the years, but we always stuck by her. She knew we would always care for her and love her.

As we grew up, each of us went our separate ways. Jackie graduated, went to work for a year and met her husband, Jimmy, who was stationed here in West Palm Beach at our Air Force Base, which is now Palm Beach International Airport.

Jackie got married and left for California in a black hearse that her new husband had rented. She had so much stuff to take with her to California she really needed a bus. We went outside to say goodbye, when some of the neighbors came over to say "Goodbye," they couldn't help but laugh after looking at the hearse and asked who died.

Gary was the only one of us to attend college. He attended Florida State University studying hotel management. After college he went in the Navy and saw the world for a few years. Later he wound up in Miami Beach, Florida at the Eden Roc Hotel as their Sales Manager.

Gary met the love of his life, Ylwa, (pronounced El-va), an airline flight attendant, at a party. He knew right away she was for him. She was a tall, thin statuesque beauty with platinum blonde hair, blue-grey eyes, and a knock-out gorgeous figure. She was from Sweden and spoke seven languages, quite a challenge for my brother. After dating and falling in love, they married a year later at one of the most extravagant weddings I had ever been to on Miami Beach in the Eden Roc hotel. Ylwa's parents flew in from Sweden along with her aunt. Jackie could not make the wedding because her husband was serving our country overseas. The wedding and reception were wonderful. Afterwards, they made their home in Miami for a few years before moving to Washington. Mama, Beverly, and I were still holding down the home front.

FALLING IN LOVE OR LUST?

After high school, I worked at Southern Bell, as a long-distance telephone operator, in West Palm Beach, Florida. While at work, a few months after being trained, I made the mistake of answering a call on the switchboard that only the Service Assistants or certain Operators could answer. I plugged my cord into the socket and said, "How can I help you?"

"This is J. Edgar Hoover from Washington and I would like to be connected to the President...."

Oops, what did he just say? I yanked the cord from the switchboard and disconnected J. Edgar Hoover, FBI Director! The service assistant was beside me in a flash and reconnected the call explaining that President John F. Kennedy was now on the line. Then she looked at me as I got down from my seat and ran into the restroom to cry. I was sure I was going to lose this job that I needed so badly.

Another day after not losing my job, I took a call from Perry Como and said, "No this isn't Perry Como!"

That is when he said, "Yes, I am, do you want me to sing you a song?"

I said, "Yes," so he sang a line from *Moon River* when a different service assistant grabbed the telephone cord from my hand. To my great relief, I was not fired. It made me feel good to know that was another learning point in my life. It certainly would not be the last time that I would make a mistake on a job. But I survived.

On Saturdays, Mama and Beverly insisted that I go out with my girlfriends to unwind and have fun. As I got ready to go dancing one evening, I picked out the new sundress I had bought. It was a multi-colored flowered dress in different shades of blue that made my blue eyes bluer. As I brushed my shoulder-length strawberry blonde hair into a style that made me look pretty, I applied makeup lightly. After finishing up with lipstick and mascara, I looked into the full-length mirror and was very pleased. I was never considered beautiful, except by Mama, but pretty.

My girlfriends picked me up and told me how great I looked. They both realized how shy I was at work, but when out having fun, I became a different person entirely. As we drove over the bridge to Palm Beach, I thought to myself, I am 19 years old and never had a steady boyfriend. I had been kissed by boys, I thought I liked, but no one ever truly impressed me. What was the matter with me? Why was I thinking about being kissed?

As we entered the darkened nightclub, after showing our ID's, because in Florida you could drink at the age of 18, the waitress sat us at a table up front near the dance floor. Two good looking men came over and asked my girlfriends to dance. As I listened to the music playing in the background, the waitress served our drinks. I ordered my favorite, rum and Coke®. As I began sipping on my drink, *Duke of Earl* began playing and the guys my girlfriends met were still dancing.

That is when I heard a voice behind me ask, "Would you like to dance?"

I turned around in my chair and looked up to see a tall good-looking man with his hand out to help me from my chair. As he guided me out to the dance floor, my mind began wondering. Is this man a hunk or what? He grabbed me by the waist and threw me into his arms as we danced and held each other close. It was as if we had known each other for years. It felt so natural. The next dance was the *Peppermint Twist* and he wanted to show off, but he learned quickly that I had as many great moves on the dance floor as he did. He was impressed. I noticed his dazzling hazel eyes and full head of wavy brown hair, but it was his smile that was truly captivating. It was as if he was bewitching me with his smile. I had never before felt chills go up my spine like I did that night.

When the evening was over, I gave him my telephone number to call me. He was an insurance salesperson and loved his job. As we both walked to my girlfriend's car, he leaned over and kissed my cheek as we said our goodbyes.

"I'll call you in a few days. I have to go up to Atlanta on business but would love to take you out to supper when I return," he said as he walked off into the night.

"Barbara, what a hunk. Has he asked you out already? Wow, you're lucky, our guys danced the evening away with us, then left. Are you going to go out with him when he calls you next week?" they asked.

"Oh, I might. I'll have to think about it," I said, knowing that, of course, I would go out with him.

James called the following week and made plans to take me over to Palm Beach to a trendy restaurant for supper on Saturday. Mama and Beverly were excited to meet James to make sure he was alright for me to go out with. They were always very protective of me.

I bought another new dress just for that evening. This time it was an off the shoulder sundress that showed off my curvy shape. Since James was over six feet tall, I made sure I wore my favorite high heels to match my outfit. I was 5'7" tall and preferred taller men when I dated.

Wow. The restaurant in Palm Beach was pretty pricey. James must be making good money in the insurance business, I thought to myself after being seated. The waiter brought our drinks after ordering one of my favorite meals, filet mignon with the works. I then ordered a Brandy Manhattan drink to calm my nerves. He took my hand in his and I about leaped from my chair. The electrical shock surprised me.

"Barbara, your mother and sister are amazing. I think they were giving me the once over. But do you approve of me?" he asked.

"Of course, I do. Mama and Beverly give everybody the third degree," I said.

The supper was delicious, the small talk was just that—small talk. Later, as he walked me to the front door, the porch light started blinking.

"You've got to be kidding me. MOM stop that!" I yelled out.

James began laughing at my Mama's antics. This was our first date. Would there be others? I thought to myself.

When the light went out, James grabbed me and kissed me. His lips touched mine and I thought I was ready for what came next. Nothing compared to this kiss. I reached up and threw my arms around him and we kissed again not wanting to stop.

As I broke away, he said, "Barbara, what are you doing to me? I've never felt this good, this fast in my life. We have to take it slow." As he left to go to his car he stopped and said, "I'll call you next week, we can go skating or something."

Once inside the door, I nearly collapsed. "Mama, he kissed me, and it wasn't like any other kiss. What am I supposed to do?" I asked.

"Darling, give it time, you'll know when you've met the right man. Beverly and I like him." She said as she hugged me goodnight.

The following months flew by and, as James and I got closer, we could not get enough of each other. He was man enough not to take advantage of me, even though I wanted this man who made my heart soar. Every time we held each other close, his body was like an Adonis and it was getting tougher and tougher not to give in.

James had been divorced for about three years before meeting me. He had two beautiful children, a girl age seven and boy four. James would get them once a month for a weekend. I adored them, but we had issues with jealousy at the beginning. In fact, his daughter told me she thought her dad was going back with their mother. Children could not make marriages work, it had to be the adults.

The following Saturday we planned to take James' children along with Mama and Beverly to the circus. As I watched James interact with his children it made me want to have a few of my own one day. Beverly and Mama were also having a great time watching the circus.

"Beverly, you'd think you were a child here at the circus, screaming and giggling," I said.

"This is fun Barbara, loosen up," she said with a smirk on her face.

"Stop it you two. Here come the elephants," Mama replied, as James' two children jumped up and down giggling along with Beverly.

A month passed and one of James' quirky friends, who owned a boat, took six of us out to fish for sailfish in the beautiful blue-green waters of the Atlantic Ocean.

Harry's wife, Eloise and I were friends and I told her that I wanted to impress James and catch a huge sailfish. I then mentioned I did not have a clue how to fish. A few minutes later James set me up with the fishing rod in a chair overlooking the Atlantic. I waited and waited and waited for what? A half hour later, when I was ready to take a snooze, I felt something tug on my line.

"Help! I don't know what this is. It's too big," I stammered as I almost flew out of the chair and went overboard. James grabbed me as I held onto the fishing rod. Fifteen minutes later, we brought in a 43-pound sailfish. We gave it to his friend to have it smoked.

He knew I did not have a clue how to fish. "See darling, now you know why I love to fish," James told me as he bent down to kiss me on the cheek.

I could not wait until the following week to meet at Harry's bar and taste sailfish for the first time in my life. When we were getting off the boat, Eloise said, "Barbara, you'd better take care of that sunburn."

What sunburn? I thought to myself.

James dropped me off at the house and reminded me to take care of my sunburn. He promised to call next week after he returned from his Atlanta trip. Then he kissed me again. As I gingerly walked in the front door, my sunburned thighs cried out for help.

"Barbara, sweetie what happened to you?" Mama said. "You look like a drowned lobster. Go in the bathroom honey while I put some tea on to brew."

I was standing naked in the bathtub when Mama came in with the warmed tea. She put ice cubes in the batch so I would not get scalded. As the tea trickled over my shoulders down my back and into places I could not mention, I let out a huge sigh. Mama was taking care of me as usual. It felt good to have her nearby. A few minutes later, I felt better and was able to dress.

We dated for almost a year and our feelings for each other never changed. He was sweet enough to ask my mother for my hand in marriage. Mama and Beverly were so excited when the pastor had a date in August available. That gave me a few months to plan the wedding. Muffin, my best friend and neighbor, helped me plan and not get anxious.

There were plenty of times I told James I wanted him sexually, but he was proud of me for being a virgin. We both decided we would wait until we were married in a few months.

James' ex-wife heard about the wedding plans and made sure she planted herself in front of my house one evening after work. "You've got to be kidding Barbara. James cheated on me during our entire marriage. He'll do the same to you," she shouted out on my front lawn.

"Stop it. James told me he cheated on you because you cheated on him. So, who is telling the truth?" I told her as I reached out to grab my purse from my car and go in to make supper. Then I turned around and said to her, "I'm in love with James and we're going to get married because I know he's a changed man."

Two months later, on August 9, 1963, Mama's present to me, the morning of our wedding, was to have my hair and makeup done by her friends in Burdines Beauty Salon. When they finished applying makeup and fixing my shoulder-length strawberry blonde hair, they handed me a large mirror.

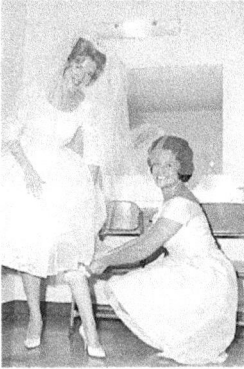

Barbara & Muffin - 1963

"Oh, my heavens, that's not me. I'm gorgeous."

"Yes, it is you darling, and baby you're stunning," Mama answered in the background.

That afternoon, we were married in the church by the pastor. I will never forget the wedding. I borrowed James' sister's wedding dress because she insisted. It had a round neckline with white lace bodice, three quarter length sleeves attached to a silk mid-length skirt. Beverly bought me a garter belt made of white lace. My headpiece was a sparkling faux diamond tiara with flowing white lace that fell past my shoulders. I felt like a princess. My bridesmaid was Muffin. She wore a pretty, light-pink, mid-length silk dress with short

Barbara Mabee and James Tucker married on August 9, 1963

sleeves that was stunning. Beverly, Mama, James' mother, two sisters and brother-in-law also attended the wedding at church, along with our friends from work.

35

The organist began *The Wedding March* as I walked through the hallway into the church and down the aisle. I was holding back the tears as I watched the love of my life, beaming with pride.

We honeymooned at the Eden Roc Hotel in Miami. I was so in love back then; I knew he would never cheat on me because our love would last forever. James picked me up in his arms and swept me off my feet as we entered our room. It was beautiful. In the center of the room was a large queen-sized bed with pillows everywhere. Champagne was chilling in ice on the table nearby, along with a basket of fruits, chocolates, and cheeses that were given to us as a honeymoon gift.

I was shy and scared since I had never made love to anyone before. I put on the most breathtakingly beautiful white lace lingerie set Mama and Beverly bought me and began feeling nervous inside. As I gazed into the mirror, I noticed that I was beautiful and would-be James' angel forever. The night was magical because he was so loving, so tender, and thoughtful when he took me in his arms, and we made love for my first time. The next morning was different. It was as if we could not get enough of each other. I never knew what true passion was. The rest of our honeymoon was amazing; I never wanted it to end.

BE CAREFUL WHAT YOU WISH FOR

Be careful what you wish for, I thought to myself after being married almost six months. James began to change that early on in our marriage. I could not pinpoint anything at the time but knew in my heart something was not right. He was too good to me if that is possible. I felt like I was in a corner. His jealousy toward me was ridiculous.

"James, you sure married a hot babe this time," one of his friends said at a party.

I thought James was going to hit him. He started to become overly possessive. I told him that if he did not change, I wanted a divorce. He pretended not to hear me.

Several years passed. James began leaving me on the weekends to party with his buddies. I worked just as hard as he did. I wanted to go out too! I was working in the traffic department doing logs for the DJ's at WPTV, Channel Five, in Palm Beach. I loved my job and even recorded a few commercials, which I enjoyed doing because I was a ham.

Suddenly, I began getting sick to my stomach at work from the fumes coming out of one of the machines.

I told management to look into it and they moved my desk.

James and I both worked five days a week. I was as tired as he was, but who did all the cooking, cleaning, and laundry? Me! I could not believe he had become so selfish, and only thought of himself. His ex-wife took him to court because he stopped paying child support.

Barbara Mabee Tucker

A week later, I was on my way home, entering the driveway with our beautiful 1967 white Mustang with red interior when I noticed a man parked out front. This man came up to me with paperwork for me to sign and explained that he was repossessing the car because the payments were six months behind. I was stunned and pissed at the same time. What else could happen to our marriage? This was not the marriage I dreamed of. But I could not tell anybody. I was too proud. For the next few weeks, I drove James to work until he got a company car.

The following week, I set up an appointment with my gynecologist because I felt crappy and was having female problems again. Oh no, another thing going wrong. I was throwing up in the mornings before going to work. I thought it was the machine at work giving out fumes, but my desk had been moved, and I was still feeling lousy.

The doctor examined me and when finished, made me get dressed and asked me to meet him in his office. That is when I got the news: I was pregnant.

"What?" I said, "I can't be pregnant. You told me a few years ago it was impossible for me to get pregnant. That is why you never prescribed birth control pills. You even told me I could adopt a baby." What was I going to tell James?

The doctor went on to explain that I needed to buy special vitamins because my iron was low. As he wrote the prescription, he asked me to set up another appointment in a month. Is this great news, or was it bad news?

I was in a state of shock, as I walked towards the front of the office. Oblivious to my surroundings, I wound up in a closet. It was dark and scary. The nurse, passing by, opened the door and began laughing as she walked me to the front door. She heard the doctor tell me earlier, I was pregnant and couldn't stop giggling.

After getting into my car, I began crying my eyes out. What was I going to tell my husband? He knew the doctor told me I could never have children.

Then something inside me changed. This is truly a miracle. Maybe this is what we need, a baby. Oh, my God, I was having a baby! I could not process it at the time. But I knew in my heart I would be a great mother.

I tried to rush home and make James' favorite dinner before he got home from work. I thought about how I would break the news to him.

When I got in the front door, I walked into the dining room and the table was all set. There was a beautiful flower arrangement in the middle of the table. Our good crystal, china, silverware along with candles on a lace tablecloth was set up for a romantic dinner. As I smelled the wonderful aromas from the kitchen, I walked in and James was cooking. Soft romantic music was playing in the background.

I knew exactly what he was doing. He was apologizing to me after I found out he was cheating on me AGAIN! The woman had the nerve to call our home number and I answered. I would not confront him now. We truly needed to celebrate my good news.

I went into the kitchen and thanked him for whatever he was cooking. Then I grabbed him and kissed him passionately. After he looked down at me in wonder, I socked it to him.

"Darling, we're going to have a baby!"

"What?" he said in disgust, "we can't have a child. The doctors told you, you could never conceive." Then he went into a rage and asked me if I slept with his buddy. During the past few months, when James was off with a new woman on the weekends, his best friend would stop by to make sure I was alright. One-night last month, when Beverly and Mama were over for supper, his friend stopped by and was drunk. I was so glad Mama and Beverly were with me. Nothing ever happened, I would never cheat on my husband. NEVER!

I said, "You know me James. I would never cheat on you. This baby is yours, OURS."

Several months later, on April 26, 1968, a beautiful pre-mature son was born. He was a little over three pounds and 21-inches long. Beverly and I were also born premature and we each weighed a little over three pounds, so this was not unusual.

The night before our son's birth, James came home drunk and raped me with such force, I began bleeding.

"I'm so sorry Barbara, I didn't mean to hurt you. I was taking my frustrations out on you. Let me help you get dressed because this is an emergency and we have to get you to the hospital—now."

After helping me into the car his entire face changed in the blink of an eye as he blurted out on the way to the hospital, "I hope you die, I don't love you anymore. In fact, I have a girlfriend and I'm leaving you after you have this baby."

James had a Dr. Jekyll and Mr. Hyde personality at this point in our marriage. Being in so much pain, I did not notice we had parked by the emergency room door as James went inside then yelled out, "Somebody get a wheelchair, my wife's pregnant and bleeding."

This was not happening to me. Damn it, he is leaving me. The pain was so bad, I doubled over as the nurse put me in a wheelchair and yelled out to the head nurse, "Hurry, get the doctor, I'm taking her into the operating room. Something is wrong!"

James gave them the insurance information after turning white. Did he really want us both to die?

The doctor from ER came in and gave me a shot. They were waiting for my gynecologist to arrive. The pain subsided and I fell into a deep sleep. I was startled awake by having to pee. I begged the nurse for a bedpan. She helped me on it while explaining not to strain, then left me.

A few minutes later when I finished, I looked into the bedpan and it was nothing but blood. The nurse saw what happened, found my doctor who had just arrived, and prepared me for an emergency caesarian section surgery. I was stunned and scared to death as my doctor leaned over and told me if I did not have this surgery, I would die. God was truly with me!

Our son was born but I was not allowed to see him right away. He had to stay in the hospital until he was five pounds due to complications from being so tiny.

After everything that happened it surprised me that James was there during the birth. Was he there out of guilt?

The next morning, I was in my room hooked up to IV's, bandaged from caesarian surgery, and looked like hell. James had the nerve to bring cigars, letting everybody know he was a proud dad. What a crock of crap.

I named our son, James Dale, Jr. because I could not think of another name since I was numb from everything. Did my husband really want us to die?

A few days later, I was feeling a little stronger. After the nurse checked my IV and vitals, I asked the nurse if I could see my son, Dale.

"No, not yet honey, perhaps tomorrow. I'll ask your doctor," she said as she left the room.

I looked down at my IV needle, stuck in my hand, yanked it out without thinking and let out a blood curdling scream. The pain was excruciating. What did I just do? A nurse came running in just as I was about to slip off the bed onto the floor. As she held me against the bed, she called for backup. Other nurses nearby along with a doctor, hooked me up to my IV after making sure I was not going to faint.

"We'd better let her see her son now. We don't want this to happen again," a nurse said to everyone.

The nurses put me in a wheelchair, with the IV trailing behind, then took me down the hall to see my son for the first time.

"Oh, my God, he's adorable. Look at those tiny fingers and feet. His hair is bright red. I thought babies had to be nine months to have fingernails." I babbled on and on, amazed at the most beautiful son in the world. I began sobbing. The nurses began crying. The doctor told them to give me a sedative when I got back to bed. The nurse explained that when Dale gained a few more pounds, I would learn how to feed him before bringing him home. He would have to be bottle fed because he was a preemie.

Beverly gave our older sister, Jackie, the telephone number to my room so she could get an update on my condition. I was on heavy duty drugs at the time and had asked the nurse for more because the pain was unbearable. The nurse was getting the doctors permission for more meds when I got the call from Jackie.

"Barbie, sweetie, how are you doing? I heard the great news that you had a baby boy," she said.

As we spoke, I kept rambling on and on about my son. Then the pain hit me again and I have no idea why I said what I said next. It flowed from my lips as I held my stomach with the huge pillow, they gave me to ease the pain. Where were the nurses with my drugs?

"Listen, Jackie, a man who is a wealthy dentist in town, came into my room this afternoon with his wife in a wheelchair. They had a baby girl, but also wanted a boy.

They explained they heard my story about my husband leaving me for another woman from the nurses. They offered me a lot of money for Dale. I'm so confused right now, Jackie, but if I were to give him up, it would be to you and your husband. I know you'd love him as much as I do."

It was a very strained conversation. She and her husband had not been able to have a child. I knew how much she wanted a child for herself. "Wait a minute Jackie, the nurse is giving me my pain medicine, don't hang up," I told her. After the nurse gave me a shot, I got back on the phone.

"Jackie, I don't think I can raise Dale by myself with no husband. Maybe I should give him to the two of you. I know you'd be great parents to any child."

"Barbie are you sure? You want us to take Dale and raise him as our son?" she asked.

The drugs were kicking in as I answered, "Yes, I think so." Then I hung up the phone and began crying, trying to remember who I spoke with what I said.

I had to stay in the hospital for two weeks or longer due to complications from the delivery. The day after Dale was born, I called my boss at WPTV. He was the General Manager. I explained my situation about having a caesarian and Dale being in the incubator. He came to visit both of us that evening.

"Barbara, your son is amazing. Only three pounds and a fighter, just like you," he said. Then my boss told me not to worry about my job and take as much time off as I needed to heal. I never mentioned my husband was cheating on me and wanted to leave me as soon as I healed. Even then, I was a good actress.

A few weeks later, I went home without Dale. My husband was not around to pick me up, so Muffin brought me home after seeing Dale. There was no car in the driveway, and it was after 6 PM. Where the hell was he? The next day after being alone in the house and making leftovers from the refrigerator, I called Muffin to see if she could pick me up that evening to see Dale. She agreed, but never asked about James's whereabouts. That is a true friend.

At the hospital, I learned how to hold and feed him properly. I was told I could bring him home in another week. He was almost five pounds and still adorable. James bumped into Muffin and me when I was visiting Dale at the hospital the next evening. It was very awkward because he handed me a present. It was from his new girlfriend.

James and his new girlfriend must have been having fun together while I laid alone in bed sobbing, knowing my marriage was over.

How dare James bring a baby outfit from his new girlfriend. Then he said, "She works at a baby clothing store." What balls he had. I wanted to throw the damn outfit in his face.

I smiled and said, "Oh, honey, tell your girlfriend it's beautiful." As my mind wondered at how I would break them up, I hoped I would never meet her in person. I had a strong desire to make her life miserable like she had made mine.

The following week I was able to bring Dale home. It was a glorious day. James agreed to pick me up and get our baby from the hospital. He had been staying at his girlfriend's house. I did not dare hope we would get back together… or did I?

The crib was set up in the bedroom. I was so happy since James wanted to stay with us that evening. Maybe he wanted to stay married after all. We had pizza and Cokes® delivered for supper. After putting things away in the kitchen, I went into the living room and saw James holding his baby boy for the first time since he was born. He was feeding him his bottle when I noticed tears in his eyes.

After putting Dale to bed, we watched a funny movie, then headed to bed. He told me he wanted to stay with me overnight. I shyly told him okay, then went into the bedroom to find my most beautiful negligee and put on my favorite perfume, Chanel No. 5®.

It was too soon for sex and he realized it as he got into bed beside me. Instead, he held me after kissing me goodnight. We snuggled and I was soon out like a light. It was the first time I had slept in weeks. There was hope in my heart as I prayed silently to God to let our marriage work.

The next day, Muffin picked us up to go to lunch and shop for a baby blanket. When she dropped me off and I entered the house I felt something was not right as I laid Dale in his playpen. James came out of the bedroom with clothes that he threw on the couch. MY CLOTHES!

"What are you doing?" I asked.

"I'm moving you back to your mother's house because our marriage is over," he said.

"What? You slept with me last night and now you're telling me it's over?"

Dale was over in his playpen making noises. I picked up my precious baby and watched while James took the folded crib and the rest of my belongings out to the car. My mind went blank. I could not believe this was happening.

When he came back in, I asked, "Where are you going to live?"

"I'm living with my girlfriend," he stated.

"What do you mean, the slut? You've already moved in with her? Oh, and by the way, I HATE YOU!"

We drove to Mama's home in silence, while hate bubbled up inside me, as I wished I could hurt my husband as badly as he hurt me. James parked the car in the driveway as I picked up Dale from the car seat and took him over to the neighbor's home across the street to get the house keys Mama always left with them. "Your baby son is beautiful. What's his name?" she asked, as she took Dale from my arms and invited us inside.

"Dale. Mrs. Thomas, do you have Mama's keys to the house? My husband, James, must leave immediately for Georgia to pick out a place for us to live next month. His job, at the insurance company, has given him a raise and we'll be moving to Georgia. I'll tell Mama and Beverly after they come home in the next few weeks," I lied.

"Oh, darling that's wonderful. Let me get the keys for you. Oh, here they are!" she said as she headed toward the front door with us tagging behind her. She kissed Dale and me goodbye, then handed me the keys along with her phone number if I needed anything.

We had one car, so I asked James, the idiot, how I was going to get to work in the next two weeks.

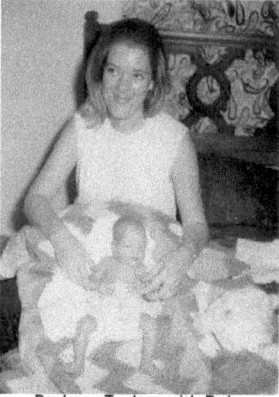

Barbara Tucker with Dale
at 5 weeks old - May 1968

"How the hell do I know? That's your problem," he said. After everything was brought into the house, he dropped my clothes on the chairs and sofa.

At least he was nice enough to set up the new crib with its crummy mattress in the bedroom. Yeah, that was really nice of him to set up the crib since he was about to abandon his son and wife. He even had the nerve to kiss me on the cheek, fold a $10 bill in my hand, shut the front door and leave.

We used to have two cars. My beautiful 1967 white Mustang with red interior got repossessed a few months before we had Dale. Why? Because he forgot to make the payments. He was taking his girlfriend out with my car payments. What a creep!

I was devastated, distraught, depressed, and could not believe he was doing this to us. He drove out of the driveway without a care in the world, anxious to get back to his new love. Little did I realize, God was toughening me up for what lay ahead in the future.

"GOD, I NEED YOU NOW, please help us!" I screamed inside to myself as I cradled my beautiful baby son in my arms. I wept uncontrollably letting the hatred I felt for James slowly leave my body. This was a beginning for me and my son. I could not let fear grip my soul. I had to trust the Lord. I would be okay.

Mama and Beverly were up in North Carolina for the month on vacation with my sister, Jackie. There was nothing for me to eat or drink, except water from the faucet. Mama's cupboards and refrigerator were bare. Thank heavens I was given a case of Similac milk and baby bottles from my soon-to-be ex-husband.

I could not believe there was nothing to eat or drink to gain back my strength. besides that, the house was a mess. And what was I going to eat with $10 and no car? That is when it hit me. I was married to a man I never really knew for six years. He was cheating on me from the very beginning. I did not see the signs; I was warned by the pastor about James, but I did not listen. I guess love is blinding, but not brain damaging. I finally learned you cannot change someone. They must want to change themselves. James was not only a womanizer, but an alcoholic and loved his pot. How naïve was I to believe his lies and deception?

The general manager at the TV station asked Linda, my co-worker, to find me because my phone at home was disconnected. Linda drove over to the address that work had on file. The landlord told her we moved. Linda remembered where my Mama lived and drove over to her home.

She rang the doorbell and was shocked to see me at the door. I invited her in to see my baby. She turned and looked at me in the light and was flabbergasted at how skinny I had become. Because of the caesarian birth, I still was not ready to go back to work. She took Dale in her

49

arms, went to sit on the couch and cried along with me. She was afraid I was sicker than I said because at 5'7", I was down to a little over 100 pounds due to not eating properly. I looked horrible. I could not eat after he left me because I had no appetite. Apparently, milk shakes were all I could keep down.

Unbeknownst to me, Linda called my best friend and neighbor, Muffin, to ask if she would help put together a baby shower the following night. Muffin was so excited she called Linda back after asking her boss to let her take the next day off. The next morning Muffin came over with her cleaning stuff along with her vacuum cleaner and said this was her baby gift to me. She brought take-out from Kentucky Fried Chicken™ along with a thick chocolate milkshake for our lunch. Since I could not eat much, I put the rest in the refrigerator I had cleaned the day before. It took us over four hours to clean the house. She had hung up my clothes and made space in a drawer for the few things I had for Dale.

It was around 3 PM when she left to go home. She kissed Dale and me goodbye. She was wonderful to help me, and I felt very grateful.

Dale was hungry. I picked him up from his crib and brought him out to the living room to feed him his bottle. After burping him, I laid him in my arms and sang my favorite lullaby. *"Hush, little baby don't say a word, papa's going to buy you a mockingbird…,"* as he fell asleep in my arms. This was what it was all about—LOVE. Dale was my life!

There was something going on. My intuition kicked in and I felt like something good was going to finally happen. While my baby slept, I took a hot shower, put on makeup, and wore my favorite sun dress. I even put on heels for the first time since Dale's birth. I looked and felt better than I had in days, even though the dress was loose.

Why did she take the day off during the week to clean this house? Around 6 PM, Muffin returned but drove into the carport to park. That was my first clue something was up because she lived next door. I knew I was having a small baby shower. Or was I?

"Wow Barbara you look great. I'm so glad you dressed up," she said.

Why would she say that? I thought to myself, as I was in the kitchen finishing cleaning the countertops.

As I turned to go into the living room to answer the doorbell, Muffin was already there.

"Hi George, everything is already set up," she said. Behind George, our station manager, was Linda, Phil a salesperson, Penelope the receptionist, Katie a copywriter, and Neal the engineer.

"Hey Muffin, what's happening?" I asked.

"Oh, we're giving you a baby shower to help you out." she said.

More cars started coming up the street. We had over 20 guests in our small two-bedroom house. Everyone brought gifts, food, a new baby mattress and money. Even the neighbors came and went. I was blown away and began to cry. All of a sudden, from the bedroom, a baby started screaming. I was absorbed in what was happening and too busy crying to hear my own son.

"Barbara, don't worry, I'm getting Dale changed, then I'll bring him out for everybody to see," said Muffin.

After everybody ate pizzas that George so kindly bought, they visited with me and the baby. It was around

10 PM, when they began leaving since they had to work early the next day.

That is what life is all about: love and support from friends who are like family. After everybody left, Muffin put Dale to bed, and we sat down to talk. I was so overwhelmed with joy, knowing how blessed we were to be Christians. Then she went home. What a beautiful friend.

The following week, Jackie and her husband, Jim, came from the Carolinas to bring Mama and Beverly home. They booked a hotel for the evening. I did not want to face them. I knew I had to be brutally honest with them because they were not only bringing Mama and Beverly home, but they also thought they would be picking up their new son, Dale. After everyone settled in and Jackie began feeding Dale over in the chair, I saw the love she had in her eyes, as she tried to hold back her tears.

"Jackie and Jim, I'm so sorry but I can't give up my son. I love him too much. I was on strong medicines in the hospital, the pain was horrible, when you called me. Plus, I was crazy because James was leaving me. I can't give up Dale, he's a part of me. You can visit whenever you want."

Mama and Beverly cried when they heard me talking to Jackie and Jim. We all cried and went to bed saddened by the evening's events. I knew I had just stunned them both, but I could never, ever give up my son. Jim and Jackie left that next morning because they were both devastated. It would take time for them to forgive me. After getting back to work and settling into a schedule, life went on. James visited his son a few months later, one time only. It was better that way. After that, he never paid his child support for Dale. I would manage, as I always did.

Mama and Beverly were happy to have us living with them. The house was always clean, I made dinners ahead of time, and we had wonderful times together. There were a few rough patches here and there, but God always took care of our family. Beverly had to have surgery once again on her knees. With so many surgeries during her lifetime, she was always my miracle twin sister.

God had me move in for a reason. Not only to help Mama and Beverly, but for them to help me cope. I always believed there was a reason or explanation for everything. Little did I realize Beverly and I would become even closer than we were as children.

Beverly and Mama were always there for Dale and me. My mother was still working at Burdines. Muffin and I took Mama out to nightclubs occasionally to have fun. Dale's second mother, Aunt Beverly, babysat because she was happy to do it when she did not have plans with her friends. Mama worked hard all her life but loved going out nightclubbing with Muffin and me every few months. She had plenty of friends to play cards or go to barbeques with, but really liked to go to the Palm Beach swinging nightclubs with us.

Going to a nightclub with Mama was an experience I would not do very often. Only because she liked to drink beer, and at times over did the drinking. Watching Mama dancing with the 30-year-olds was too much for me. I could never do it on a regular basis, but she made me laugh, which was good.

Two weeks before the divorce was final, James took me out to dinner to update me on the proceedings. After dinner he had the gall to drive me to a motel and invited me in for a drink. We had our drinks, then he came over and tried to undress me.

"You're a bastard. Take me home!" I ordered and he did.

The divorce was final in August 1968, yet I went through all the emotions of love and hate again. I felt I was no longer worthy of love. After the divorce, which devastated me, I found out he eloped two weeks later with supposedly the love of his life. This would be his third marriage. Good luck you stupid slut!

At the time, I still worked at the TV station over in Palm Beach doing logs for the DJ's and being in commercials for the salespersons. At the end of the day, I could not wait to get home to see Dale and my family.

Dale had become my life. He turned out to be the heart of our family. Everybody loved him.

I took one Friday off because I had a doctor's appointment with the pediatrician. As I washed Dale's head, his beautiful red hair fell into the water. I panicked and got Dale dressed, then drove to the doctor's office. I was early, but I did not care. I told the nurse what happened, and she laughed at me.

"This is part of the process. Babies lose their hair, but it grows back," she said.

I always worried about Dale because he had been in and out of the hospitals. Because he was born premature, he developed asthma when he was four months old.

I always took time to sit with Dale and rock him to sleep when he had a bout with asthma. I finally knew how other mothers felt with their own children who had health problems. I would often sing lullabies while holding him and praying to help him get stronger. I knew he would be okay, for now. We will survive.

FINDING NORMALCY

A few months later, Jackie and Jim came down for a short vacation. They brought baby clothes, blankets, along with other baby accessories, like talc powder. I realized they had bought the baby items thinking they would have Dale, my son, to raise as their own. I was feeling guilty having told them that I could not live without my son. I had a heart-felt talk with Jackie and Jim. I assured them they would ALWAYS be an integral part of Dale's life. Mama and Beverly were so happy they came to visit. We all were!

I hugged and kissed them both as I took the gifts into the bedroom and closed the door. After laying them on my bed, I looked at the gifts and sobbed. Jackie and Jim would have been great parents. We had a wonderful time that week, going to the park, the beach, and out to dinner. It was bitter-sweet saying goodbye to them at the end of their visit.

Working hard at the TV station during the following weeks were good for me. It helped me forget how tired I was after coming home nightly to make supper for Beverly, Mama, and myself. I wished they were better cooks! Dale smelled like Johnson & Johnson baby powder after his baths. I was blessed to hold him in my arms, while feeding him, and breathe in the beauty of his presence.

DECEMBER 1969

The following year in December, I finally gave in and went out with my single girlfriends.

Betty, a co-worker, and Muffin, my best friend, knew I needed to get out and have fun. We wound up in Palm Beach at the same nightclub where I met my ex-husband. I was not in the mood to meet anyone to date; I wanted to dance and have fun.

We ordered our favorite drinks. Mine was Southern Comfort® on the rocks with a twist of lemon, Betty and Muffin drank beer. I never danced more in my life, than I did that night. The evening sped by and I knew I needed to get home. "I'm getting tired girls; we need to leave soon," I said. All of a sudden three men showed up to our table and asked us to dance. Muffin and Betty took off for the dance floor leaving me there to look up and see a tall, dark, handsome man who took my breath away.

"Hello, my name is Jack, would you like another drink or do you want to dance?" he asked.

He was around 6'4", with coal black hair, brown eyes, and a tan that made me think he came back from the Caribbean. He was gorgeous. I had to stop to collect my thoughts before I could open my mouth.

Why did he ask me to dance? "No thank you, I was getting ready to leave. I have a big day at work on Monday and haven't even cleaned my house yet," I explained. Why did I say that? I thought.

"What's your name?" he asked.

"Barbara," I stammered.

He took my hand and led me out to the dance floor and an electric shock went up my arm. Damn, that happened with my first husband. I needed to think about this. Was I so lonely, I wanted to feel this way again? What was he doing to me?

Nights in White Satin was playing as I sunk into his massive arms, feeling tingly and warm all over. I needed someone but was scared and did not want to get involved. It was too soon!

After dancing a few more dances and finishing up my drink, he walked me to the car where my friends were waiting. "I had a wonderful time, Barbara. Would you give me your phone number so we can go out for dinner or a movie?" he asked.

"Yes, that sounds like fun," I said as I wrote down my phone number. He leaned down and kissed me on the forehead and said goodbye as I got in the car to go home.

"Barbara, how did you manage that? He's really handsome. Our two guys left us without even asking for our phone numbers. We're jealous," they said.

"I can't believe I gave him my number," I said.

After a few weeks passed, I gave up on Jack calling me. Then out of the blue, he called. "Hi Barbara, I'm so sorry I didn't call earlier. I had an emergency up in New York. I'd love to see you if you still want to go out," he said.

"That sounds great," I said. We made plans for the weekend.

After meeting Mama, Beverly, and Dale, Jack quickly became part of our family. They thought he was terrific and could see how happy we were together. When we first began dating, he told me that he was not the marrying kind. I agreed, because at that time, I felt the same way. Being young, pretty, and vulnerable, I knew I could change him, like my ex-husband. HA, HA.

After a month of dating, we could not stand another minute of not having sex together. He was being polite. I had been stubborn because he told me he was not the marrying kind. But he will change. Right? After going to a movie together, then stopping by the local bar for a drink—or was it four drinks? We went to his home and made mad, passionate love. It was as if I were floating on air. I never knew another man could be so passionate. I never looked back on sex and never asked about marrying me in the future, because I did not want to ruin a good thing. A few weeks later, Jack and our family went on a trip to Disney World in Orlando. He did everything right to make me fall in love with him. Jack was an aeronautical engineer, who made good money, and explained that he traveled to northern Florida several times during the year with his job.

In 1973, Jack had to travel with his job for three weeks. He was kind enough to give me money to take a week's vacation to see Jackie in North Carolina. Jack kissed Dale and me goodbye at the bus station and said to have a great time. The bus trip was so much fun. We went through cities I had never seen. Everyone loved Dale, as they pinched his cheeks or told me how cute he was at the tender age of five.

As we arrived in Fayetteville, NC, Jackie and her girlfriend, Barbara picked us up at the bus station. Jackie did not know how to drive so Barbara drove us back to Jackie's house. Jackie could not stop hugging me and kissing Dale. Her home was more than I could imagine. It was lovely. The rose bushes were in full bloom and made the front garden look beautiful. After settling in, Jackie gave Dale a plate of cookies to go with his milk as a treat before supper.

Her friend, Barbara, asked Jackie if she could take me out to the NCO club the next evening. This would give me a break and Jackie could have her special time with Dale. Jackie agreed and I thanked her for giving her a chance to bond with her nephew.

The next day Jackie, Dale, and I went for a walk in the neighborhood before stopping off to meet Jackie's friend Cheryl. She invited us in for a cool drink and then decided to show Dale and me a boar's head in her freezer.

"Oh, cool, Mom can we have it?" he asked.

"Dale, no. Close the freezer, it's making me sick." Is this what they did in the Carolinas, buy the entire hog? I thought to myself.

Jackie, Cheryl, and I decided to play Scrabble™ while Dale went into the other room and watched cartoons with Cheryl's younger children. I could not concentrate on Scrabble™ because all I could think about was going to the club tonight with Barbara and Marvin, her boyfriend.

Around 4 PM, we arrived back at my sister's home. There was plenty of time to get my outfit ready for the evening while Jackie made dinner and entertained Dale. After we ate, Dale played with Jackie while I got dressed. I picked out my favorite black and white polka dot sundress with off the shoulder ruffles. I slipped into my black high heels and added jewelry to match the outfit. After applying makeup, I chose a hot pink lipstick. I walked into the living room to show off in front of Jackie and Dale.

"Mommy, you look pretty," he said.

"Aren't you still going with Jack, Barbie? What's he going to think about you going out tonight?" my sister asked.

I thought to myself, why is she asking this now? "Jackie, I'm not going out to meet anyone. I want to have fun and dance," I said.

Barbara and Marvin picked me up and told me how nice I looked. Jackie and Dale kissed me goodbye and said, "Have a great time."

At the NCO (non-commissioned officers) club, Marvin dropped us off at the front door then went to park the car. He told us to go in and find a table. After adjusting our eyesight to the dim light, I noticed a band in the front of the room. They were playing *Diamond Girl* by Seals and Croft.

"Barbara, since we both have the same first names, call me Barbie." I said. Jackie gave me that nickname when I was younger."

A short Filipina girl was shouting out to Barbara, "Hey, come over and sit with me," she said. Barbara introduced me to her friend, Toy, who was darling and about 4'8".

Marvin found us and came over to join us. Everybody ordered drinks and continued to listen to the band. Barbara and Marvin left us to dance. Toy and I spoke for a few minutes then two servicemen came up and asked Toy and me to dance. Rusty was short and looking at my boobs when we hit the dance floor; the taller one asked Toy. They were playing a favorite song of mine, *Long Train Running* by the Doobie Brothers. When we got back to our table, Toy suggested we switch partners if they both asked us to slow dance, stating, "He just too DAMN tall!"

They ordered drinks and sat down to talk. The tall guy was really good looking. He had light blue eyes and a long face, which exuded rugged masculinity. I was wondering how tall he was. I had to calm down because I was still going with Jack.

We've Only Just Begun was being sung by the band when Rusty came up to me and asked me to dance again, I politely agreed as he helped me from my chair onto the dance floor.

I turned around as Toy switched partners then walked into Rusty's arms.

Jim was flustered. His hands started sweating as he rubbed them on his jeans. He was not moving. Then it dawned on me, he was shy and a little drunk! I looked up at him and asked, "Jim, how tall are you?"

"Six foot six inches tall, why?" he said.

"Because I like tall men." I told him. He took me in his arms and we danced the night away.

Later, when the band finished, Jim walked me out to Marvin's car. "Barbie, tomorrow's my day off. I know I just met you, but I'd love to take you out for pizza and a movie. That's if you'd like to go," he said shyly.

My heart was beating when I took a pen and card out of my purse and wrote Jackie's home phone number on it. "I'd love to go out with you tomorrow night," I answered back. Then I did the stupidest thing I had done in a long time. I whispered something in his ear and out of the blue I kissed him on the cheek. It was the booze; I know it was the booze!

Then I heard Barbara saying, "Come on Barbie, it's time to go see your son."

I could not pinpoint what was happening to me because I really liked Big Jim. He was fun to be with. Or was it the drinks talking? Jim was so drunk he wanted to ask me out the next day to make sure I was pretty. Or was it me that was tipsy, and hoped he was good looking? I would find out tomorrow night and promised myself I would stay sober.

Jim called that morning and I told him to pick me up around 5 PM. I already told Jackie about Jim. She now thought it was great he asked me out, because Jack was never going to marry me. Jim arrived a few minutes early and came inside to meet Jackie and play with Dale for a few minutes before leaving on our date.

He took me to his favorite pizza place and ordered a large pizza with everything but anchovies and a pitcher of beer. I saw just how good-looking Jim really was when I was sober.

We talked about everything. I told him about Jack, he told me about his ex-wife and daughter. Then we headed for the movie. *Live and Let Die*, with Roger Moore, was playing. After being seated, Jim put his arm around my shoulders. I could not think straight. Being with Jim, alone in the movie theatre, was scaring me. Without warning, he took me in his arms and kissed me. My mind went numb. He is not supposed to kiss me in the theatre. Why did his lips feel so good? Then we both shook it off, smiled at one another, and continued to try to watch the movie. I did not want to feel this warm tingly feeling that made me feel safe. Feeling safe in his arms? What could that mean? I thought to myself.

What a wonderful evening we had. Jim parked out front of Jackie's home and said, "Barbara, remember last night when we were dancing? I was so drunk, I really asked you out to make sure you weren't coyote ugly. Don't get mad at me because you're gorgeous. Everything about you is great. The truth is, a long time ago, I woke up in the morning after being out getting plastered and wound up in bed with a coyote ugly woman. She was so ugly I would rather have chewed my arm off than wake her up because she was not only ugly, but she was also fat. I rolled myself off of her and tiptoed out of the motel door."

I laughed so hard at Jim's story. I decided at that moment to keep in touch with him. He was handsome and funny. That is when I handed him my home address and phone number in Florida. Dale and I had a few more days to spend with my sister.

She approved of Jim and told me to get rid of Jack. "You've gone with him long enough; he's never going to marry you. He told you that himself," she said.

Jim became my friend. He would call and write, when possible, with his busy schedule in the service. Jack and I still dated, but it was not the same anymore. Jack was never going to marry me and my love for him was almost gone after finding him cheating with another woman when I returned home from our vacation in North Carolina. Jack began traveling to Pensacola with his engineering job and I knew we were drifting apart. It was a matter of time before we both realized it and let each other go. Hopefully, we could remain friends. I was not ready to lose Jack's friendship.

GUARDIAN ANGELS

FEBRUARY 1974

Big Jim called to tell me he had to leave for Germany for a few years and wanted to fly down to Florida to meet Beverly and see Dale again. Mama had been in a nursing home for over six months and was dying. She had Alzheimer's disease and did not know us any longer. It was heartbreaking. Six months before, Beverly caught Mama walking up the street. She was disorientated and did not know where she lived. The neighbor brought Mama back home and I had to have her committed to a nursing home close by. It was devastating to Gary, Jackie, Beverly, Dale, and me. Jim knew about Mama, but we decided it was best if he did not meet her.

Two days later, I picked Big Jim up at the entrance to Delta Airlines. He was standing there looking around for me and did not realize I was checking him out before parking behind another car. What a hunk. I forgot he was so tall. He actually looks better today than when I met him months ago at the NCO club in North Carolina.

I got out of the car and walked up to him, noticing the big grin on his face. That is one of the things I admired about Jim, his smile. Then in an instant I was in his arms and we were both kissing each other passionately as if we had not seen each other in years. What happened? My knees felt like rubber and my heart was racing a mile a minute when I finally got myself under control. People passing by smiled, wishing that were happening to them. I was embarrassed for a second, then got myself together as Jim opened the back door of the car and threw in his duffle bag.

We only had four days to visit before his flight back to Ohio, so we made our time count. Beverly adored Jim when she met him for the first time. "Jim, are you really serious about Barbara? I need to know because I see how happy she is with you," she said.

"Barbara means the world to me Beverly. I have to convince her to drop Jack. She told me he never wants to get married and settle down. I do want to marry and settle down. I realize it will take time to convenience your sister," he said.

We had a great time while he was here and promised to write each other. Even though I would have preferred making love with Jim, I could not. I had a hysterectomy due to female complications and was on the mend. Jim understood and would not do anything to hurt me, even though that kiss at the airport almost did me in.

Jim and I wrote each other while he was stationed in Germany. I knew I would never get close enough to marry any serviceman because I never wanted to be alone. Servicemen were called to serve this great United States of America and could leave at a moment's notice for a few months or several years. That was not for me. I decided at that moment, I would never marry again.

Working at WJNO was good for me because I loved being creative and writing commercials for the salespersons. Mary, a co-worker was a different story. Ever since I was hired a few months back, it felt like she could not stand me. My intuitions were usually right. Mary put together the radio logs with commercials for the DJ's. Sometimes she joined with others in recording commercials. The animosity that exuded from her towards me from the first day we met, overwhelmed me to the point I had to stay out of her way. I would be typing commercials and see her walking in the hallway, I was surprised to see her jump in the air and there was nothing there! This happened several times.

Barbara Mabee Tucker - January 1974

A few weeks ago, she screamed bloody murder from the lunch area after almost getting electrocuted from the coffee pot. I learned from one of the DJ's that she and her husband belonged to a commune. I left work this particular day feeling on edge.

When I arrived to pick up Dale at the Christian school, Pastor Miller was there to talk to me. "Barbara can you and Dale join my wife and young daughter Chelsea for dinner tomorrow night after work if you're not busy? It's important we talk, or I wouldn't give you such short notice."

"Sure, we'll make it. I have to check with Beverly first. Dale, would you like to go to the pastor's house tomorrow for dinner?" I asked.

"Mommy that would be so cool," he squealed with joy. "I can play with Chelsea."

"I guess that's a yes," I said with a smile. "See you tomorrow after work."

The next evening at the pastor's home, we had spaghetti with meatballs, salad, garlic bread, chocolate chip cookies and sodas for supper. It was delicious. Chelsea took Dale into the den to play games. The pastor and his wife took me into the living room to sit and talk.

"Barbara, you have an aura around you. It's keeping you safe now, but I want you to know that something or someone is trying to get you. I know it sounds crazy," he added. Then he stood up and took a cross out of the box and made me stand up, as he put it around by neck.

The next half hour, Pastor Miller explained what he felt was happening. In between, I told him about Mary at work. How she hated me because she thought I wanted her husband, whom I worked with at a different radio station a few years back. He actually got me my job at WJNO. I even told Mary, I never wanted her husband, I had a boyfriend. After we finished and it was time to go home, I thanked the pastor and his family for having us over and giving me the gift.

"Don't forget to wear this cross at work and let it show, don't tuck it under your blouse," the pastor added. Everyone hugged each other as we headed for the car. I was so glad it was Friday and I did not have to face Mary until Monday.

That Monday, after dropping Dale off at school, I headed to work. After getting settled in to begin typing commercials the salesmen left on my desk, Mary walked in the door.

"Hi Barbara, what did you do this weekend? Are you still going steady with that rich guy?" she asked. Then she looked like something was going to grab her by the neck and strangle her. Her face turned a pasty white and she appeared to be going into shock.

Damn, she is glaring at the cross. It is the cross! What is the matter with her? I thought. She stumbled up the steps from my office and headed toward the lunchroom. Was the pastor right? Was she the evil one after me? I decided to stay out of her way because I did not want to know.

Mama passed away in May 1974, of a massive heart attack. Our entire family was devastated. She was cremated and my older sister, Jackie, told the pastor to have her ashes thrown out to sea in the great Atlantic Ocean because she always wanted to go to Tahiti. The pastor relayed the message to the funeral director. They promised to take care of her ashes.

I overhead the conversation and went up to her and said, "Jackie, Mama doesn't know how to swim!"

"It's only ashes. Mama's up in Heaven," she told me as we began to laugh.

The love we had for one another, we still have today. When our dear mother passed away, we thought

71

this was the worst possible thing that could happen to our family. It was such a shock to all of us. She was only sixty-seven years of age.

Jackie and her husband left for Pope Air Force Base in North Carolina a few days later.

That evening, I moved Mama's favorite chair out to the Florida room where Dale slept on the couch that opened into a single bed. Dale was already asleep when Beverly and I finished watching TV and headed off to bed.

In the middle of the night, I was awakened when I heard, "Mommy, Mommy help!"

As I stumbled out of bed, I reached for my robe and met my son on the porch.

"Look mommy, its Grandma sitting in her chair!"

I looked over at the chair and saw Mama sitting there in a ghostly form. It was Mama alright. I held Dale in my arms and we sat on the couch bed starring at Mama.

When I said to her, "Mama, it's alright. We're going to be okay. We know you're watching over us and know God will take care of our family. Go and be with Him now!"

"Mommy, Grandma's not there anymore. I want my Grandma!" Dale cried out.

"No, honey she's gone up to Heaven. But don't worry. She will always be watching down on us."

I opened the carport door and scooted the chair outside to have someone pick it up in the next few days. Dale walked into the living room with me and sat on the couch. I got up and fixed myself a stiff drink before taking him back to my bed. We were both shook up.

In the morning, our next-door neighbor, Muffin, whose family believed in the afterlife, came over and asked, "Barbara, did you see your mother last night? She was lost and I sent her to you."

"Yes, she was here. Dale saw her first, I told Mama to 'Let go and let God take her to Heaven.' We will be okay. We will survive."

Thank God we were Christians and went to church regularly. I decided to tell our pastor this story after church on Sunday. I knew most people would never believe me. It would not be the last time I would see a ghost.

DID THIS REALLY HAPPEN?

THURSDAY, NOVEMBER 14, 1974

I love Palm Beach, Florida, I thought, as I drove on Flagler Drive heading north to WJNO radio. I loved my job and most of my co-workers. The tall, majestic palm trees swaying in the cool breeze with gorgeous mansions spanning the waterfront, helped calm my soul as I thought back to this morning. This impressed upon me to want more for myself, my twin sister, and son. We were still grieving the loss of our mother several months back.

Earlier this morning, as I raced to get Dale ready for school, I fixed the three of us cereal with orange juice. Rich aromas from the coffee pot made me remember to get myself a cup. The warm dark liquid eased down my throat to my stomach and helped me wake up. The outside temperature was in the low 60s but would probably be in the 70s around noon.

"Barbara, what are you fixing for dinner when you get home?" Beverly asked.

"I made spaghetti sauce last night, remember? It's in the refrigerator. I'll cook pasta and make a salad later," I answered. I grabbed my purse, put a couple of diet pills in my pocket and left the bottle on the kitchen counter. I kissed my sister on the cheek after telling her I loved her, then headed for the front door to put our coats on.

"Mommy wait, I have to kiss Aunt Beverly too," he said as he ran to her chair and, jumped in her lap. He threw his small arms around her neck to give her hugs and kisses. "I love you Aunt Beverly."

"I love you both more," Beverly answered as we left for the day.

On the way to school, I got chills as I was walking Dale to his classroom. Something was off today, and I did not know what it was.

The day began like most days, rushing to meet deadlines writing commercials. In addition, I had to train another new young girl to answer phones and do clerical work. Even though my new position came with better pay, I was doubting myself. I tried to call Beverly around lunch time and felt sheer terror for an instant. I let the phone ring over 20 times. Maybe she was doing dishes. She will call me back later, I thought to myself, as I hung up the phone.

One of the salesmen came in and asked, "Good morning Barbara. Would you please type a couple of 60-second commercials for this local seafood restaurant? I need to take them with me in the next half hour," he said as he handed me his notes.

"Sure, no problem I'll type them now," I answered.

Sitting by my typewriter, my mind was boggled with worry about Beverly. I called again and again there was no answer. This was not normal. Maybe my girlfriend next door called Beverly to babysit for her son if he was home sick. But I knew Beverly would have called me if that happened. We always kept in touch during the day. As I began typing the commercials for the seafood restaurant, I could not wrap my mind around being creative. I finished them as best I could, then put them down for a minute before I read them for the last time. It is a good thing I did, because the second commercial had a glaring error on the page. It read blah, blah, blah... "wonderful lobster tails for the whore family—the '*WHORE*' family." Barbara, get yourself together. I corrected my mistake and took them over to Marty. He thanked me and headed for the front door.

Damn, that could have gotten me in trouble, I thought to myself as I went back to my office to finish more commercials. This time as I eased myself into my chair and gazed at the typewriter, I prayed silently, to let Beverly be okay. I was getting edgy. Something eerie was happening that I could not pinpoint. Why was I so nervous? After trying to call Beverly from after lunch until almost 5 PM with no answer, my nerves were on edge. It had to be a twin thing.

When I was finally able to leave work at 5, I told the other secretary that I was glad today was over, because this had been the day from hell.

After arriving at the school and going inside to pick up my son I asked him, "Hi Darling, how was your day?"

"Mommy, my teacher drew a chalk line in front of my chair so I wouldn't move. That was so cool. When she drew the line in front of my chair, all the other kids were laughing at her," he said.

I said, "Okay," as we both hugged and kissed each other before heading out the door.

Dale jumped into the back seat. Then I buckled him into his car seat and started driving home.

HOME SWEET HOME?

I think it was near six that evening when Dale and I pulled into the driveway of our home. I noticed the kitchen and back porch lights were on. I was relieved to think Beverly was next-door babysitting and forgot to call me.

As I unlocked the front door, I shouted out for Beverly but there was no answer. The silence seemed strange to me at first because not only did she not answer, but the TV set was on and not the living room lights. I asked my son to go look for her in her bedroom while I headed to the kitchen for some water.

Dale yelled out, "Mommy she isn't in her bedroom. I'll look in the other one."

If Beverly was not in the kitchen, and she was not on the back porch, where could she be? I had a terrible feeling. The kind of strange feeling you get when you feel that something is not exactly right.

"Mommy, Bev's sleeping in your bedroom."

"Thanks Dale, let her sleep. She must be tired. I'll be there in a minute. Let me get some water first," I answered Dale. Then my mind came into focus and I thought Damn, Mama died a few months ago and I sleep there now.

Then I felt a strange overwhelming shadowy presence lurking behind me. The fuzzy little hairs on my arms immediately stood up. All I wanted to do was get a cold glass of water from the kitchen faucet. Little did I know, that would never happen. A man's booming voice startled me back to my present reality when he uttered the most chilling words I have ever heard in my life.

The man said, "Don't turn around I have a gun. I'm not going to hurt anyone. I need your car and money."

I did not hear him say, "Don't turn around I have a gun." I heard him say, "Don't turn around, or I'll kill you!"

What is happening? What did he really say? My mind went numb. It was as if the words already had the power to take life from me. The glass of water I so desperately craved fell crashing to the floor shattering along with my hopes and desires to escape this dreadful ordeal I would never wish on my worst enemy.

Trying to keep my cool I replied, "You've got to be kidding." I looked around and there was a man standing behind me.

He was about six feet tall with reddish blonde hair, blue eyes, thin, and desperately in need of a shave. He was not bad looking. For a moment, I thought it was my ex-husband, but it was not him. He moved slowly and grabbed my arm. My eyes fell to his knees, when I noticed he was wearing dark slacks and had a gun. My God, he had a gun! To say my throat was tightening is an understatement. I felt like I needed to say something, felt like I needed to do something. But I did not know what to say, and fear kept me from doing anything.

"Please don't hurt any of us. Please don't hurt us! I will get the car keys for you; I have some money you can take." I turned around thinking to myself that if I looked up, I was going to be a goner, and I kept wondering—how did this person get into my house? What have we done to deserve this? How in the world are we going to get out of this? It is amazing how many things go through your mind at a time like that.

Recalling a police-story I had seen on TV; things began popping into my mind. Do not panic, and do not scare him, panic makes a killer. But a split second later, I forgot everything I had seen on that TV program, and turned around, then looked up at his face. He was livid!

He got very defensive, "Why did you look at me? I told you not to look, now you are going to have to be tied up. Oh shit, here comes your boy."

"Mommy, who is that man?"

"Mommy, Bevy's tied up in your bedroom, she's bleeding. Mommy help!" Then Dale grabbed my hand and pulled me towards the bedroom Beverly was in.

The intruder hid the gun and said, "Remember, you'd better stay calm. Tell your son to go into the other bedroom, not the one your sister's in, and make him stay there until I can tie him up. I'll tie all three of you up and then I'll get going."

"Dale, honey come with me and keep calm. You have to mind me now, it's very important. We don't want Beverly hurt. Do you understand me, Dale?"

Where in the world was my calm voice coming from? My heart was thumping a mile a minute, I thought I was going to faint from sheer terror or drop dead on the spot.

"But Mommy, she's bleeding from her mouth. She's got something in her mouth Mommy. Help her," he said.

My son's main concern was to untie Beverly. He kept repeating over and over, "She's hurt, she's hurt."

Dale Tucker, 5- Jan. 1974

My God, he is only six years old and he wants to help his aunt.

I did not have time to respond. The man said, "Come on, come on, both of you. Get that kid into the front bedroom. Do it quick and get your keys and money. Hurry, I don't have time to waste."

I reassured my son, as best I could, not to go into mama's old bedroom where Beverly laid. Then opened the door to Beverly's bedroom and said, "Dale be a good boy and stay here and play until I come back to get you."

Again, I tried to stay calm and reassure him. This time a little more sternly, I told him that we could not fool around. "This isn't a game Dale. Go and go now." Finally, my son went into the other bedroom begrudgingly, as I shut the door.

"Where are you going?" asked the man.

"I'm going to see Beverly and tell her Dale and I are okay for now."

A feeling came over me and I knew I had to take control. I prayed silently to myself, Dear Lord, give me the strength to help Beverly and Dale. Then I said, "You'd better not have hurt her, she's handicapped, you know."

"Okay, okay. I didn't hurt her. You can see her."

As I walked across the hallway to my bedroom where the door was partially opened. I was afraid to go into the room. I knew Beverly would never go willingly into Mama's room this soon after her death. It was too painful.

I noticed this man was a nervous wreck. He was getting agitated and fidgety. Moving the wrong way could trigger him to use the sawed-off shotgun by his side. I was not about to aggravate him.

Before I opened the door to the bedroom I thought, why did he pick our house? How did he get in? I need to talk with my sister. I need to find answers.

I went into my bedroom feeling sheer panic, when I noticed Beverly lying on her right side facing the east wall by the window. She was lying there so still with a sheet and pink and white bedspread over her body. Is she dead?

Beverly being tied up all day must have been very uncomfortable. I remembered calling her the first time around lunchtime and she did not answer. I walked around the bed and sat down by her side. Her head was bound, she was gagged, and tied to the bed. My bedroom was a total mess. Things were strung from dresser to floor, but my sister was alive!

Getting impatient, the intruder spoke, "Listen, she's okay. I promise I didn't hurt your sister; now let's get going."

I burst out in tears when I saw the blood dripping from the gag in her mouth. It was too tight. Her eyes got bigger as she focused to see me and was relieved to see me alive.

That is when I turned around and said, "You hurt her, she's bleeding from the gag. Please make it looser!" He did. I was shocked. I did not think he had a heart. When will I talk with Beverly?

What is going on in her mind right now? I know she must be relieved to see Dale and me still alive. Where am I getting this courage from? GOD? God must be with me now. I need you God. This is not going well at all.

"Come on. The police are after me for a robbery. You need to give me your car keys and any money you have. You need to hurry up. I have to get out of here," the man said, his voice shaking. He tried to grab my wrist and push me out of the bedroom. That was when I lost it.

Totally out of what could have been described as sheer stupidity, I yelled at him. "You wait a minute! I need to talk to Beverly to make sure she's alright."

Surprisingly enough he said, Okay, but hurry up."

"Beverly, I know he has a gun. Try not to panic. Dale is in your bedroom and we all have to stay calm." I was trying to reassure her the best I could. I told her I was going to try to get rid of him. I was not calm. My stomach was in knots as I bent down and said softly to Beverly, "Don't worry honey, God will get us all through this. God will give me strength and the right words to say."

I have no idea why I decided to take him out onto the back porch. As luck would have it, Dale came back out of the other bedroom and started to cry. He had to go to the bathroom. After he finished, I led him back to the front bedroom. Then the man took Dale and led him back into the bedroom Beverly was in, as I followed in shock.

The only way that I could think to keep things together was to tell Dale that we were going to play a game. It is called *Save the Family* game. This man will not hurt you if we do exactly what he tells us to do. Now, you know he has a gun."

"Yes, Mommy, why does he have a gun? Is he going to shoot us? I'll give him my karate kick!"

I explained to Dale to please be quiet or he would hurt all of us. "You don't want that to happen, do you?"

"No, I'll be quiet, but why did he tie Beverly up?"

"Dale, you're asking too many questions. Please do exactly what he tells you."

Then the man turned to my son and said, "Okay son, I'm not going to hurt anyone. I want you to play like a cowboy, and I'm going to tie you up with your mom's pantyhose. You stand still while I tie you up. It's a game, don't try to get loose, either, because I'm not going to hurt anyone. I need your mom's car and some money."

He started tying Dale up next to Beverly with my pantyhose and lifting him on top of the covers. My brain was having a hard time registering what was happening. I wanted to wash it away from my mind. I couldn't imagine what thoughts were going through Dale's and Beverly's minds. At least Beverly was under the covers. Did I really believe this maniac was not going to hurt us?

A million thoughts were rambling through my mind. This is a dream. This is a nightmare. This is not really me. This is a fantasy. After tying his little hands and feet up with two pair of my pantyhose, he finished by putting a ripped sheet around my son's face. He is only six years old for God's sake. It was real, alright, and it was happening to us. The man said, "Okay, he's tied up. Now you're next." Then I lost it. I really lost it!

"Dale, stay here on the bed honey. Don't you or Beverly move."

"I'll get the money, come with me," I said to the man.

Next, I gently grabbed his hand and began walking towards the back porch. I did not have a clue what I was doing. Something drastic had to be done and right now. I did what I had to do to hopefully save our lives.

"Where are you taking me?" asked this stranger.

All I could think of was to get him away from my sister and my child. While leading him through the living room onto the back porch, I could sense he was waiting for me to do something foolish. He reluctantly followed me onto the back porch over near the couch. I sat on the couch, took his hand, and guided him to sit down so we could talk. "What's your name and why are you running from the law?" I asked.

"My name is John. I was in jail before and don't want to go back," he said. He explained to me he was running from the law for something he had not done and had to leave.

I made small talk for a few minutes so he could calm down, then I would give him the money and keys to the car. I talked slowly and what came out of my mouth was from the dear Lord. I watched this panicked man calm down to the sound of my voice. I did not even know what I was saying, but it was working. "I want to see Beverly and Dale again," I said as we got off the couch and headed towards the bedroom.

That is when all hell broke loose. A knock came at the front door. Who the hell was at the door? I was pushed out into the living room to answer it. "Get her out of here." John whispered in my ear.

I walked into the living room, opened the front door, and saw Muffin, my neighbor standing before me wanting to come in. As I gazed outside towards the street, I tried to get my wits about me and say something, anything. "Get out!" I said softly, hoping to myself that she knew me so well, she would figure out something was wrong. I motioned with my hand for her to get out of the house. She did, and I quickly shut and locked the front door behind her.

I prayed that Muffin would not be suspicious and call the cops right away. If she called the cops now, we would all be killed. Oh, my God, how are we going to get out of this? I know he saw her. He is the one that told me to get rid of her. Damn, now she is in danger too.

I was whipped back into reality once again when he yelled out, "Hey Barbara, that's your name, isn't it?" He heard Beverly talk about a Barbara and Dale all day.

"Yes," I said.

Then he yelled, "Come on. Get your keys and the money *now*!"

I handed him my car keys then headed to my room. "Beverly, Dale, we will be okay I'm getting my cashed paycheck from the drawer to give to John, and then he'll leave," I said, making sure he knew I was not getting a gun. I pulled a white envelope out of the drawer and handed him the envelope with the money. I could not really say how much it was at that time, but afterward I remembered there was enough to pay the house payment that was due.

"Listen, your son is causing a lot of trouble; he's crying too loud, he won't cooperate. I've had enough. I'm taking him with me."

"No, you told me that you would tie him up. No!" I was pleading, "Take me instead, he has asthma and needs his medicine daily. No, don't take me either, I have to stay with Beverly and Dale, they both need me!"

"I mean business! Hurry up and get what you have to get. I'll leave the kid, but I'll have to take you. Now get what you have to get."

"Wait a minute, wait a minute. Let me see my son and my sister first."

"Alright, alright, but make it snappy and I mean snappy."

After kissing Dale on the cheek and telling them both I would be okay. I went over to Beverly and pulled down the covers. She was bleeding. There was blood all over the place. She was stark naked. I thought I was going to faint, but I managed to keep control. I retained my composure for her.

Then in an instant, I lost control! "Did you rape my sister? If you raped my sister, I swear I'll kill you!" I must have startled him for a moment, for he turned white. Perhaps no one had ever spoken to him like that before, perhaps now, he was afraid.

"I didn't touch her; I didn't hurt her. I didn't do anything, nothing. I promise, I didn't rape your sister."

At this point, I could not get my thoughts together. I knew I did not have control. I did not know what I was going to do from this point on. I had to say something, but what could I say? What could I do? It had to be the dumbest thing that a person could say in a situation like this. "I need a cigarette, really bad." Amazingly enough, he told me it was alright. I got a cigarette from the dresser, lit it, and took a big, long drag to steady my nerves. Thoughts kept running through my head. Thoughts like, what am I going to do? God, help me, please help me! I begged him, "Let me stay. Please let me stay here with my son and help my sister. We won't call the police, we promise. Please let me stay!"

Dale got loose and I waited in the living room by the front door while John tied Dale up in the bedroom with Beverly for the last time. I could not watch him tying my son up this time, knowing I was being kidnapped and most likely would never see Dale or Beverly again. My heart was silently breaking as I thanked God for being able to hug and kiss Beverly and Dale earlier.

It was obvious by this time, however, that he would have no part of going alone. He was taking a hostage and that hostage was me.

My only hope at this point was that the neighbor would get an idea that something was wrong and check back at our house after we had gone. I never would have believed that anything could be worse than being terrorized with my family, in my own home, by this man. Little did I realize HELL had just begun.

He took me outside by my arm and guided me towards my old beige Volkswagen Beetle that kept on going, like the energizer bunny. I did not want this used Volkswagen; I wanted a new Mustang. Who cares about what I was thinking now? Thoughts burst into my brain, thoughts that made no sense whatever. I headed towards the passenger side and got in noticing Muffin watering her lawn. Muffin never watered her lawn.

"She saw me, Barbara," John said as he got in the driver's seat and put his window down as he pointed the sawed-off shotgun at Muffin.

Then I put my hand on his arm and said, "You don't need any more attention, so lets' just go," I calmly said to him as my heart was about to burst. He started the engine, threw the sawed-off shotgun into the backseat, and we drove down the street to go who knew where. I prayed to God this maniac would drop me off up the street but knew that was not going to happen.

As John maneuvered the car up to Dixie Highway and headed north, a lightning bolt struck my subconscious. Muffin *never* waters her lawn! She was suspicious and would check on Dale and Beverly after we drove off. I could only pray that she had put it together and would call the police. All I could think about was my chances of survival.

BEVERLY AND DALE HAD THEIR OWN HELL TO FACE

Years later, I was given Beverly's police report to look over before agreeing to do a *Movie of the Week* by New Dominion Pictures that would air on the Discovery Channel. Dale and Beverly had told me bits and pieces right after I got home from being kidnapped. I shuttered thinking about the torture Beverly went through being with Paul John Knowles for over five hours before Dale and I got home. The panic and sheer horror of it all made me sick to my stomach. Poor Dale was only six years old when it happened.

Part of Beverly's police report stated from her own lips:

```
...and then he came into my bedroom
and he tied Dale up with you know,
the stocking. He didn't tie him up
very well because after they left
the house Dale just shook his hand
like this and got himself undone.
I told Dale to get the scissors—
he had pulled the gag down by then
and I took the cloth out—it was
all bloody—and I said, 'Dale go
```

get the scissors.' Go in the hamper and get the scissors. He got the scissors then he started to cut the stocking, but it came off. He must have tied it very loose. I heard Barbara leave with him and Dale came around and got me and I said, Dale go into the bathroom and get me my robe off the floor, I'm going to have to go in the bedroom and get dressed. So anyway, Dale got the gag off me. He pulled it around my neck because it was still on my neck when the ambulance came up, you know, then it was cut off. And Dale came and got me, and I put the robe on and got out of bed and he walked me to the bedroom because I couldn't walk because I was paralyzed. And he just took me and walked me to the bedroom and then I got my clothes out of the drawer and got dressed and he said, 'I will run over to Muffins and get Muffin.' And I said, 'No, don't you dare—you stay with me and I will go with you. So, after he helped me get dressed, because I couldn't even move this shoulder, I fastened my bra the best I could and then he put the straps up on my bra and then he put the shirt on and the shorts, cause I couldn't even hardly move I was in so much pain. And then I said, 'Don't leave me Dale.' And so, he stayed right there with me and he untied me. He untied me—he went, and he got the scissors again—this guy had doubled the sheet, doubled it three times over, you know, and Dale couldn't get the scissors through—he tried. So, I said, 'Dale go get the knife in the kitchen and see if you can do it.' So, then he put the knife through the wrist and he started sawing it and he got it to the point where it was real thin and then I took over and I sawed it and then I took it off. But Dale stayed with me and then we went over to Muffin's and I said, 'Call the police.' I got to the middle of Muffin's grass over there and I almost collapsed. I couldn't even stand up I was hurting so much.

What did I just read? This could not be true. But of course, it was true, Dale and Beverly were my heroes!

As I read the report, I was beside myself weeping, as if it were that same day when I was taken from my home. Beverly was naked and the murderer tied my son up to her ankles and wrists. What horrible lifetime memories this created for Dale, to be bound by this strange madman, to be strapped to his disabled aunt's naked body that he considered as his second mother. My only solace is that my brave little boy acted like a grown man—a hero quickly, freeing himself and Bev, getting her dressed and aiding her to get the neighbor's help.

Shortly, after I was kidnapped, I wondered what lay ahead or if I would ever see my loved ones again. How would Beverly and Dale survive without me? I could not imagine anyone else taking care of them. They needed me and I needed them.

Thursday, November 14, 1974

Now I am faced with my ordeal of being kidnapped. I could not believe I was in a car, driving with this man who had forced me from my home. It was something I could not get straight in my mind. What was I doing in this car? Why do not I open the door latch and jump out? Because he will stop and shoot me, that is why!

He kept asking me, "How do we get to I-95? We have to get to I-95 and later go up to Georgia. I have killed someone, and everyone will be after us. We have to get out of Florida by tomorrow." What is he mumbling about going to Georgia, tomorrow? I thought to myself.

I still could not grasp what he was saying, but it did not take long to realize that this was all planned. It had to be a plan. He wants to drop me off somewhere remote and kill me. I cannot let that happen. I know he is going to kill me. I have this feeling, this mighty eerie feeling. I had a feeling he had done this before. There is no way I will survive; he definitely is going to kill me. I know that I must try to be one step ahead of him. I have to use my reverse psychology because he is starting to show that he is two different people, I thought to myself. I think it was at this point, I realized there was only one way to save myself. I needed to put on an Academy Award winning performance by acting brave. I cannot let him know that I am scared to death. I tried to take deep breaths to relax.

I asked, "Honey, do you want a cigarette?"

"What, you're calling me honey?" he asked.

"Yes, what's wrong with that, you're not so bad."

"Listen, keep talking. I do not want any silence. I have had silence all day. Talk about anything, anything at all." John said.

There were probably a million things that I could talk about but all I wanted to know was what he was going to do with me, and I could not ask about that. We talked trivia, me talking more than him. I tried very hard to make jokes. How in the world can you make a joke at a time like this? I told him about my boyfriend. Damn, why did I mention him?

He kept fiddling with the radio, sometimes it worked. Since the Volkswagen was a stick shift, he tried to tune in a station as we drove on. He was getting agitated when he got the news station, and nothing was on it. "Keep talking Barbara."

What was he trying to hear on the radio? Something was not right.

The only thing I could think to do was keep things light. Keep things light and maybe he would see that he could let me go. God, please let him see that he can let me go. The radio was working again, and I blurted out. "I love this song; *The Way We Were* with Barbra Streisand. I saw the movie with her and Robert Redford a few months ago. Wait a minute, you remind me of Robert Redford, a little. I knew you reminded me of a movie star."

"What? I remind you of Redford? Somebody I met from Georgia told me the same thing not long ago," he said smiling.

After the song was over, he asked me to try to find a news station. He wanted to hear the news. I jiggled the knob on the radio. I finally found a station. The newscaster was talking about local events happening in St. Lucie County, Florida. Nothing was happening that interested John. He got agitated and told me to turn the radio off so we could talk. However, I did wonder what he wanted to hear on the news.

Trying to get control of myself, I realized that there must be a way that I could keep him calm. But the only thing I could think of was to try to charm him. Yes, that was it. I would try to charm him. Is it possible, to have a game plan when you are literally falling apart? That would be mine. I would try to charm him. I was in desperate need of time!

I needed to keep him on U.S. 1 and away from I-95. I-95 is an expressway, and U.S. 1 is a surface road with many stoplights and slower traffic that may provide a chance for escape or be seen. Maybe someone would find my family and would be out looking for my car.

I had to keep him on U.S. 1. At various intervals up the road, I kept suggesting that he could let me off.

But he would have no part of it. He kept saying, "You're staying with me." It seemed that I had charmed him into thinking he needed me. Sure, he needed me, and I needed him like a hole in the head!

It was true at this point that I wanted to get out, but I wanted to get out in a place where I could get help, not out in the middle of nowhere. It seemed that we had been driving for hours and hours and hours, but I could not guess what time it was. He talked a bit about his life and his hard knocks. As he was talking, I realized he had no intention of letting me out.

Whatever came out of our mouths while driving was nothing but small talk. He asked me "What do you do for a living?"

"I work in radio," I answered.

"What did you do in radio? I heard from your sister you were a writer or something," he continued.

"I'm a copywriter. I write commercials for a living and love it."

"This is good. Yes, this is good. So, you can write a book?" he asked.

"Why not!" I told him as I wondered why he asked in the first place. Then he dropped the subject, which made me wonder why.

As we drove on, he had the nerve to ask me if I was afraid of him.

Can you imagine that? Am I afraid of him? You bet your life I am, but I told him that I was not. I told him that there was really no reason to be afraid of him because he seemed like he was very kind. I did not want to be raped or killed by a maniac, so I kept dishing out the compliments. I was hoping, hoping that someway, somehow, I could get myself out of this mess.

FORT PIERCE, SO THIS IS HELL

When we reached Ft. Pierce, he pulled into a parking space out front of The Skyway Motel. It looked like most small motels I had seen driving up U.S. 1.

When we got out of the car, I noticed this motel was on a hill overlooking the highway. How could anyone looking for me ever find me here? I thought.

Looking around I wanted to get out and run, run away, because I knew he was going to rape me.

I felt terror once again in my gut as we got out of the car. He put his jacket on to bring along his sawed-off shotgun as we walked together to the motel office. I put my arm around his waist, feeling the gun inside his jacket. I told him not to worry. I would play it cool. I am not sure why or how I said that, but I knew that I would try not to act nervous. Never for a second, did I forget about the gun he carried.

Once inside the motel office, I wanted desperately to say something to the woman behind the desk. She told us she was Mrs. Johnson, the motel manager. My throat was too dry for words to leap from my lips. Being in a state of shock was not helping. This cannot be me. I do not know what I am doing.

After making small talk with the manager of the motel, he signed ourselves in as Mr. and Mrs. Joe Smith.

Mr. & Mrs. Joe Smith? Quite clever, I thought trying to make myself laugh instead of cry.

After he paid with cash, the proprietor took us down to room No. 10 and handed him the key. As he opened the door to the room we walked in and I was overwhelmed with odd smells. John was standing next to me and he smelled like a sewer, which I never noticed when driving because the windows were open.

He told me, before kidnapping me that he was running from the cops when he found our house and jumped over the fence. He went to our backdoor and knocked. Beverly opened the door. He barged in and was with her from noon until I got home. I wondered what he really did to Beverly but had to come back to reality. I gazed at the ceiling, then around the entire room trying to think how to escape from this madman. How could this good-looking man be a madman? He did not look like a bad guy. His shoulder length reddish blonde hair was not combed, and he had to be over six feet tall.

Damn, I am kidnapped. It hit me between the eyes again, but I refused to let myself panic now.

I looked over at the twin beds covered with white chenille bedspreads. The dark dresser and nightstands matched. There were scratches on the one nightstand. I noticed they had glass tops with a lamp on one. This was not The Breakers Hotel in Palm Beach. He was not happy with the room because it had twin beds. What in the world am I doing here? This is insane, I thought.

"Come here, Barbara. Come and sit down beside me."

"Okay."

"I want to kiss you."

He wants to kiss me? This smelly, crazy man wants to kiss me? Great. What choice do I have? It seems like we are playing some kind of bizarre game. Now, it is his game and not mine. I have lost the upper hand if I ever had one in the first place.

As we sat on the bed together, he gathered me into his arms and turned my face towards his and kissed me gently on the lips while telling me, "Barbara, I wish this never happened. I didn't want this to happen to you. I promise not the hurt you."

After kissing me, I was thinking to myself, he is not horrible after all. Or is he?

He then startled me by asking me if I were thirsty and I said, "Yes." I am thinking, maybe this is where I can make a break for it. Maybe he will not take the gun. Maybe there will be someone there to help me. Maybe, maybe, maybe, there are a million maybes. What am I going to do now? As we walked together, hand in hand to the drink machine near our room, he bought one soda.

It was when we got back to the room that he very nonchalantly told me to get undressed. I acted like I did not understand what he was saying, but he seemed to get agitated and demanded I get undressed. Trying to stall for time, I told him I had to go to the bathroom first. He told me that was alright to go to the bathroom, but I had to get undressed first. I asked to keep my underwear on—I was embarrassed about the scar I had from my C-section birth to deliver my son.

"No, take off everything!" he demanded.

As I undressed ever so slowly, I kept eyeing things around the room, nightstands, ugly white bedspreads, and dust in the corners.

In a calmer voice he said, "Go ahead, get undressed, I'm not going to rape you." He is telling me he is not going to rape me. What would he call it? I could not believe this was happening to me. I had to snap back into reality and answer him.

"I know you're not going to rape me; I'll cooperate, then you'll have no reason to hurt me." When I was totally undressed, I was about to freeze to death. He was drooling as he looked me up and down with sinister eyes. He was looking at me as if he could see into my soul. He was scaring me; I did not want to be hurt. I did not want to be raped! I realized that he thought this was part of his game.

Well, I suppose I will have to play his game. I was angry, but I tried to be calm. Then, of course, the obvious happened. I knew there was no way to get out of it. No way at all.

He laid me down onto the bed, on my back, as he tried to have intercourse. He was kissing me like I was his girlfriend. He mentioned how much he liked me. The stench from his body waifed through my nostrils. His body next to mine repulsed me. I wanted to throw up. I closed my eyes; I did not want to see him. He quit talking and raped me once again.

What was going on in my mind as the room seemed to spin around in circles? Something was not normal about any of this. He was being gentle with me this time as if he cared for the moment. Why was he so frustrated? He came and had his fun with me.

In a blink of an eye he turned on me. I thought he was going to beat me to death. The rage in his eyes was horrible. He turned from Dr. Jekyll to Mr. Hyde in an instant. I feared for my life at this moment. First, he was gentle, then afterwards he was evil, plain evil, as he tried to break my wrist.

"What are you doing John? You promised you would never hurt me. You're hurting me!"

Then he let my hand go after hearing my calm voice. Everything stopped, as I glanced over at the clock on the wall, realizing an hour had passed as we laid on the bed exhausted. Was he a maniac, or was I dreaming?

I was thinking too much. No, I was in denial. Maybe he was hitting me, maybe he was raping me, and I zoned out into a different day, time, and place. Then I noticed the bruises on my wrist and finger. He was starting all over again. The heavy breathing, trying to enter me, going from nice to being enraged. I could not handle much more. "God, I could not handle much more, where are you?" I whispered to myself. Perhaps this was not happening at all. But it was, and it was taking too long. Why was he taking so long, is there something wrong with him? This is not normal, I thought to myself. As he continued to rape me, all I could think about was Beverly and Dale being safe. Did the neighbor call the Police? Please, dear Lord, do not let anything happen to my family. They are the love of my life.

Wait a minute. He held my poor twin sister hostage all day until Dale and I got home. What the hell had Beverly gone through? She was handicapped. I wanted to kill him. His shotgun was under the bed and the knife was on the nightstand. If I had reached for the knife, he would overpower me with his rage and stab me to death. Think Barbara, think!

A minute later he grabbed me with such force and raped me again, scaring me to death. Then he turned me over, put his legs around me and told me to take a nap with him as he dozed off.

I could not pinpoint what was wrong with his lovemaking, screwing, whatever he called it. It was not right. Something was nagging at me. I did not want to look down at his penis. I do not even know if he had one. I was too terrified and exhausted to continue much longer with this charade. I wanted to see my loved ones.

He woke again and started repeatedly raping me. Afterwards he finally fell into a deep sleep. I could not keep up with how many times he tried to rape me. It seemed as if he would go from being cool and thoughtful, to having murder in his eyes. That was not sex, but I would keep pretending it was.

I finally dosed off and then I was startled awake by John's voice. "Barbara, honey I have to go out and make a few telephone calls. I'll be back soon." He was fully dressed and grabbed the keys then laid them down for a moment on the nightstand and told me to get dressed. He took a sheet from the other bed and ripped it into pieces. I was told to lay down on the bed because he had to tie me up and put a gag in my mouth so I would not scream for help.

"What are you doing to me? Don't you trust me John?" I said as he began tying my wrists to the headboard. Next, he tied my ankles. Last he put a small wad of sheet in my mouth so I could not scream. He bent over and kissed me on the cheek before leaving to make his phone calls.

I was staring up at the ceiling and looking around the room as best I could being bound and gagged. The television set was on and I tried to watch *Ironside,* a wheelchair-bound detective starring Raymond Burr as Robert T. Ironside who battles the bad guys on the streets of San Francisco. I was trying desperately to make myself forget for a few minutes. I needed to try and forget what was happening to me because I finally realized this man may have killed somebody. I could not concentrate and began crying.

As I lay there, through my tears, I saw the most beautiful image. It was Mama who had died a few months before. I blinked through my tear-filled eyes and she was still there. "Mama, help me, I pleaded." This could not be happening; Mama was dead, and I was hallucinating.

All of a sudden, I got chills throughout my entire body. Then a warm glow began creeping from the top of my head to the bottom of my feet. It was real. The warmth remained constant.

Mama was holding her arms up to the Heavens, then with her hands, pushing me away from her. Everything else in the room was in a haze. That is when I realized I would be alright. My Mother was there, and so was God!

It had to have been about 20 minutes later when John was back from his phone calls. As he entered the room, he came over to the bed and told me we would be leaving the next day to go to Georgia. He said, he had friends up there that I would love to meet. Then he untied me from the bedsheets wrapped around my wrists and ankles. After taking the gag out of my mouth, he noticed me fidgeting. This time he did not come with me to the bathroom. Was he beginning to trust me, or was it my imagination?

"Hurry up Barbara, the news is starting," he yelled. Why was the news so important to him? I came in and sat on the chair near the television, while he sat on the edge of the bed, to watch the news. He did not ask me to sit with him on the bed, which surprised me.

This was the first time we were able to watch the news. "And now from NBC News Tonight we have the top story. Paul John Knowles is wanted for murder and kidnapping." A picture of John and myself flashed on the screen and I about lost it. "...Barbara Tucker was taken from her home tonight and ...," the newscasters said.

"What did I hear John? You're wanted for a murder and kidnapping?" Did I really hear John tell me he killed up to 35 people earlier? In my mental state, I thought maybe he only killed one person.

"I didn't kill anyone, honest, it's all a misunderstanding!" he said.

The people they were talking about on the news were us. He told me that we were going to stay the night and I got livid!

"Damn it, John, you said that you were going to leave. You said after the news that you were going to leave. You have to get going; it's 11 o'clock. You can make it to Georgia by three in the morning if you get going now. You need to get going."

"No! We're staying overnight."

I begged him to tie me up and leave, after reminding him, of his promise to let me go. After the news, we watched some program that did not interest me. All I kept thinking was he really killed somebody...maybe many people..., and I was next. About a half hour later, he turned off the television. "Go lay on the bed Barbara, I'm getting a towel from the bathroom to tie our ankles together, so I can get some sleep," he said.

While he laid there snoring, I noticed the lamp on the nightstand. It was not that heavy. I could grab it and slam it into his brain while he was sleeping and kill him before he killed me! I then reached over for the small lamp to crash his skull in. He woke up with a jolt and, noticing the small lamp in my hand, asked me what in the hell was I trying to do.

I quickly told him I wanted to turn the light out. Then I said that I had to go to the bathroom really, really bad. Would he please untie my ankle so I could go to the bathroom?

He refused and said that we would have to go together. I could not believe that he would not let me go to the bathroom by myself. He would not even untie our ankles. Why did he trust me before, but not now?

We both tried to not fall off the bed with our ankles tied together. It was crazy. We managed to walk like two idiots to the bathroom for me to go. It was not easy sitting on the toilet seat, but we managed. Only a maniac, a lunatic, would do this to a person. The whole thing was so ridiculous that after managing to get back into bed with this strange man, we laughed hysterically. Being mentally and physically exhausted could have played a part in the hysterical laughter. Finally, we went to sleep.

HOW AM I STILL ALIVE?

FRIDAY, NOVEMBER 15, 1974

I woke up startled to see John in the bathroom washing up. Thank God, I thought to myself. I would do the same. Those tiny soaps will help a little.

I could not believe I actually went to sleep. I was still groggy, but not enough to have forgotten the news broadcast last night. He was not a murderer; it was all a mistake.

I realized it was daylight, and he could not get away safely. He raped me again, only this time he was not nice. He threw me on the bed and slammed his body into mine and began pumping up and down with blood thirsty evil in his eyes. Why was he so mean? Why did he almost hit me? Was it just frustration or was he crazy? My God, what was wrong with him? I wasn't sure I wanted to know. Now, his face changed into the face of a monster. I thought he was going to kill me. All of a sudden, while looking at him with tears in my eyes, he changed. I saw regret and sorrow as he began to cry. He grabbed me and held me in his arms. "I didn't mean to hurt you," he said, "I'm so sorry!"

We discussed checkout time and I tried to make him think that it was 12 noon. I wanted him to leave me there, leave me safe. I suppose my subconscious knew that this was going to go on and on and on. I could not understand the conflict I was feeling nor understand what was happening to me. I questioned, *where was God?* I decided, I needed to pray.

We had intercourse again, but this time I kissed him, and held him because I wanted him to think I actually liked him. For me, it was not like making love with one you cared for. It felt like air, it felt like he could not make love at all. I had to keep pretending, to him, how great he made me feel. I wanted him to feel like we had been friends forever, dear old friends that wanted a more intimate connection. We dressed, exchanged pleasantries, and went down to the office together to find out about a restaurant and see if a room was ready with a queen-sized bed. The manager would let us know about the larger room after we got back from the restaurant. I knew I was losing my mind. I had either brainwashed myself or had I been brainwashed by this man.

It is unbelievable what transpired next. We went out for breakfast at a nearby restaurant, which had a bakery. The aroma of freshly baked goodies, donuts, baked breads, rolls, and cakes filled the room. It made my stomach rumble inside, I was starving. Those candy bars, sodas, and crackers the night before did not satisfy my hunger.

The booths were full of people having breakfast, while others shopped at the bakery. A motherly-type waitress seated us in a nearby booth, handing each of us the menus, while asking if we would both wanted coffee. "Yes, please and make it high test!" John answered.

She came back a few minutes later to fill our cups with steaming hot coffee, then asked if we were ready to order.

"We'll have the breakfast special: ham, eggs, hash brown potatoes and orange juice." John told her as she wrote it down. When she left to get our order, I began thinking to myself. We spoke to a man in the bakery coming in the front door, and nobody, literally nobody, knew or had any idea who this man was or what he had done. Does not anybody read the newspapers or watch TV anymore?

Am I in fear for my life? Well, maybe at this point not so much fear for my life, but acceptance of what I had been through, and of what was going to be. I was mentally trapped. I realized that these good people did not have a clue who we were.

His sawed-off shotgun was wrapped in his jacket on the seat of the booth. The knife was in his pocket. I could have told him I had to go to the bathroom and quietly tell somebody nearby in the other booth to call the police. That would not work because John never let me go anywhere by myself. Then it dawned on me. I would never, ever put another person's life in danger. I realized that he had murdered someone. I had to keep up my game face and continue being the great actress that I pretended to be.

I believed I was doing exactly what was needed of me. I was staying with this man, so others would not get killed. The breakfast was delicious, and I really needed it for strength. The waitress came back and handed John the bill then asked, "Are you newlyweds?"

"Yes, we're on our honeymoon and headed up north to meet her family," he told her.

"Have a great day and be safe driving," she added.

Newlyweds? Is he crazy? I thought to myself as we went to pay the bill.

While he was paying the bill, I looked around at people nearby, wishing I could make a run for it and escape this insanity. It was impossible! We left and bought a newspaper on the way back to the motel. Again, I mentioned I wanted him to tie me up and leave me.

"There are too many people on my tail now that I'm on TV and in the newspaper. I have to think," he said as he opened the car door.

When we got back to the motel, Mrs. Johnson, the motel manager came out to give us a key to Room 5, which was bigger and had a queen-size bed. That is all I needed, a bigger bed.

As we entered the bigger room, I looked around and noticed it was not much different than the other room. Everything was the same except the bed was bigger and the bedspread was a different color.

Looking back things seemed like a comedy of errors. The morning progressed like any normal day that you would spend with your husband or significant other. We watched TV, he raped me again, as I screamed to myself—this is not happening—it is not real. Pretending it was perfectly normal. It was not! He was two different people, once again.

I had to think, really think. "Honey, let's go out front and watch the cars go by, I need the fresh air!" So, we went outside, walked down to the soda machine, and got sodas we each liked.

The only difference between this day and a normal day with a friend was that I was not allowed to go to the bathroom alone or walk outside alone. I was a prisoner, a hostage, and a play toy for this madman.

We sat down in the two chairs by the room, then watched the State Troopers drive by. First one way, then the other way. They were out looking for us and could not see us.

"Damn, what idiots!" he said. He changed subjects and asked, "Barbara, you said you worked at a radio station. Do you know how to write books?" John asked.

"I write commercials for a living but writing a book couldn't be that difficult. Yes, I could write a good novel. Why are you asking?" I said, thinking this was a strange question to ask.

"Just curious, that's all. Do you like sports?" he said, avoiding the question. He stood up. "It's time to get back inside," he said as he held the door to the room open.

I guessed the time to be about noon. I could not be sure as my watch had stopped working and there was not a clock in the room. I went over to the chair while John turned on the TV. He motioned for me to come over and sit on the bed with him. Suddenly there was my picture on the screen, as big as day. The incredible thing about it was that the police and news media knew I was a hostage. I could not understand why all the people that had seen me with this man at the bakery, at the store, and in the motel did not recognize us. Our pictures were on TV and in the newspaper! How could they not know?

My abductor, John asked, "What's the matter? You don't trust me. You're looking so sad; please don't be sad. I promise I won't hurt you. I'm going to wait until its dark and then we're getting out of here tonight. I'm taking you with me." In the next breath he said, "Maybe I'll leave you, but you have to promise not to get loose until morning. I'll have to tie you up. I promise I won't hurt you. You think I'm going to kill you, don't you?"

I thought to myself—yes, you are going to kill me. You must kill me; I am a witness and a hostage. You are going to do it anyway. What are you waiting for?

He asked me to come and lay down on the bed next to him. I wondered if his intention was to talk me into going with him to Georgia, or was he ready to kill me?

I finally had enough! All the lies, all the back and forth of rage, then unsettled calm. The terror in my soul was getting to me. I knew it would happen eventually. In my frustrated state, I could not stand another minute of this insanity. He was making me go mad! I yelled out in frustration, "Okay, I know you're going to kill me! How are you going to do it? Are you going to stab me with the knife, blow a hole through my head with the sawed-off shotgun or cut a sheet and strangle me? KILL ME, DAMMIT, AND GET IT OVER WITH!"

In an instant, rage pulsed from his eyes as he grabbed his sawed-off shotgun from under the bed and put it to my head saying, "BANG! BANG!" I fell to the floor, hiding my face, knowing my life was over.

In a blink of an eye, he changed back to being nice. "I will never hurt you, Barbara, I'm too emotionally involved with you," he said as he lowered the shotgun to the floor.

I had to go to the bathroom and wash my face. He finally let me go by myself but made sure the door was open. When I got myself composed enough, I walked over to the bed and sat on the edge. That is when he told me how sorry he was for putting the gun to my head.

"No, you're not."

"Yes, I am. I think I'm in love with you," he said. "I know I'm falling in love with you because you make me laugh and will help me write my story."

"I think I'm falling for you too." God was putting these words into my mouth. God does not want me to die. I must do and say ANYTHING to get back to my precious son and my twin sister. I even worried Jack, my boyfriend, would never want to touch me again, since I had been violated by a murderer. I have to do ANYTHING to make John let me go. I was NOT in love with him. I felt sorry for him and I would make sure he thought I loved him to save my life. Please God stay with me, I am so tired, and I do not want to die, I said to myself.

I told him I believed what he said about loving me and not hurting me. I laid there on the bed, knowing in my heart, I was only safe for this moment. My fate was cast. I was at his beckon call. The next conversation was one I was not thrilled to hear.

"Come closer, I want you to satisfy me."

I could not believe my ears. "No, no, not that! I don't like that," I cried as he unzipped his pants and pushed my head into his groin area. Oh my God, the rash was all over his bottom area. What the hell does he have? I thought to myself as I carried out his wishes as best I could.

I snapped back into reality as he pulled me away and zipped up his slacks. He was smiling.

Wait a minute, is he gay? Something was wrong. I realized he was not normal and thought he might be gay because what happened was NOT normal sexual activity. He thought he was satisfied, and I had let him believe it.

We were both playing mind games. Who would be the winner? Him, of course. What was I supposed to do? There was a sawed-off shotgun under the bed and his knife was on the nightstand. My guts began to rumble, as the fear ripped through my soul and I thought my head would explode. I put my calm face on and let him have his way so I could survive. I needed not only my strength, but my belief in God to get me through this day and night. I could not worry about tomorrow or if there would even be a tomorrow.

I tried hard to put what happened out of my mind, but it came back to haunt me. I was so tired. I wanted to be home in my own bathtub soaking in fragrant hot bubbles to wash away the smell of horror and terror I was facing each minute being with this killer.

There was nothing else I could do except to satisfy him and lie once again—And the Academy Award goes to....

I kept saying repeatedly, "You're not a bad person, John."

"Oh, yes I am. I'm a very bad person, I've killed over 30 people."

Wait a minute. He said something about killing people yesterday. My mind shut down for that instant and I would not believe what he said. It was impossible. HE WOULD HAVE TO KILL ME! I snapped back to reality and continued to talk to him in a soft, calm voice.

"Listen, you're really not a bad person. I think, maybe you had bad things happen in your life and need to resolve them with help."

He kept saying, "Yes, I'm really a bad person."

He then turned on the TV to watch the news. This time the news station had the entire story. Oh my God, I am so glad the FBI was now involved. Being in radio myself, I knew the FBI did not go after anyone unless they are true killers.

"Well, did you hear my name? Did you hear my name, Paul John Knowles? Honey, you can still call me John. Now, you know the truth, they've really got me now," he said boasting but I could see the terror in his eyes. I had to calm him down from the news—but how?

His name was Paul John Knowles and was sought after in connection to multiple homicides across the country. I was thankful for the news because it gave me a chance to be silent. He is a killer. The news said so, multiple homicides, and now I knew he would have to kill me. But when? All I could think to say was, "It really doesn't look like you."

I realized now, all the times I could have run or screamed out for help. There was a chance at the bakery, also with the motel operator. Thinking about this now, I realized I would never put other people in danger.

Am I that great a person that I cared for other people more than myself?

No, it was not me. It was God who knew I was his precious child and I needed His help.

I told John, "It's dark now. Please leave me now, tie me up, and just go. PLEASE, JUST GO!"

He said, "I can't do that, we have to go out and buy another newspaper. Maybe after the 11 o'clock news, I can do what you asked. I'll think about it when we're out."

We got into the car, the three of us, the man, me, and his sawed-off shotgun. We drove to the Ft. Pierce Food Mart. He got his paper and then he went into get sandwiches for us to eat. When he came back to the car he asked, "I saw a bottle of diet pills in your kitchen. Do you have any on you?"

I told him I did. He said to hold onto it because he would need it later. In the '70s, prescription diet pills were like a speed drug, methamphetamine, which were later taken off the market. I really was not that hungry, but I did not want to anger him, so I told him I would eat the ham sandwich.

While driving back to the motel, we both noticed State Troopers driving ahead of us. He made sure we got to the motel safely.

We got back to our room and I went inside to eat while he went out front to find a different tag to put on the car. There were a lot of Florida tags around, but those did not satisfy him. Finally, he came across a California tag and said that he could get away with that.

When he came back, he had strange look on his face, and I knew that he was again toying with the idea of taking me with him. I had to think of something. I had to think of something to get his mind off the primary concern, his getting away. I told him, "Lay down on the bed, and try to relax. I want to try to satisfy you again."

He seemed surprised and said, "Really?"

"Yes. You're getting too nervous and that will calm you down before you leave. Then you won't hurt anyone."

He asked, "Do you want to have sex again?"

"Yes, if that will satisfy you," I said.

After it was over, I asked him again to tie me up and go. Just go. He was not ready to leave and wanted to listen to the news again. He told me after the news, he would leave. I began to feel sorry for him again. I wanted him to get away safely and not get caught. In his mind, he had not really hurt me. I am not sure why I felt this way— the compassion. Where did it come from? It was a very strange feeling and it did not make sense.

"Now when you leave tonight after the news, please be careful. I don't want them to catch you. I want you to be safe. I know you won't hurt me." As I said this to him, I was not sure if I truly meant it or was still acting. Either way, I wanted to leave the idea in his mind that he was going to leave me here.

"Let's go down and see if the motel people have their TV set on. They weren't watching television earlier when we checked." John wanted to keep checking to see if they became suspicious.

He could not believe how dumb people were. After all, we had been sitting out front most of the day. We had been out to breakfast. We had been to the food store. We had been out for papers and no one had even spotted the VW with the strip missing down the front. I noticed that the office did not have the TV on and told him that everything was okay. We went back and sat outside for a few minutes. A black man from next door to our room peeked outside, saw us, and went back in, shutting his door.

"John, was that the man on the news this morning from Miami being hunted down for killing somebody?" I asked, looking pale.

"You may be right. We'll check when the news comes on. Besides if he is a murderer, I'll protect you. Nobody's going to hurt you, I promise," he said. "Come on inside, I want to talk to you. I don't want to tie you up; I want you to come with me to Georgia. Please, I know I'm falling in love with you. Please, please come with me."

This is what I had been afraid of all along. It was the only thing my conscious mind could be afraid of. "No John! I don't want to be in your way. I don't want to get other people involved. It's not fair to me. You promised you'd leave me here! Please, please keep your promise," I said.

Here I am talking to this madman about promises. Who is kidding whom? I was beginning to believe that he never had any intention of keeping his promise—his only intention was to murder me. Oh no, here comes his two personalities again, which will it be this time, Dr. Jekyll or Mr. Hyde?

What is happening to me? I am not thinking clearly. I think I am going nuts. Have I become delusional or what?

Finally, he said, "Let's lay here and talk and then I will tie you up and leave. But I really want to take you with me." Then out of the clear blue sky he said, "Okay, I'm going to tie you up now."

I asked him to please leave my clothes on. I did not want to be found the next morning naked. As he tied me up, he left the sheet parts loose enough so they would not cut my wrists or ankles. Then he asked if I was alright.

"No, it's not too tight. Please leave, you have to get away."

The entire time that he was cutting the sheets with his knife and doing it like he had done it many times before, he kept telling me that he wanted to take me with him.

When he finished tying me up, I asked him to make the gag smaller because I had a problem with a cleft palate—not really—and it could gag or choke me to death. Amazingly, he believed me.

Being tied, I managed to take my diamond ring off and give it to him. I told him he could pawn it. He declined, put it back on my finger then put the small gag in my mouth and tied a sheet piece around my face. He asked if I was okay. I nodded yes.

I watched him put his things into his pockets, the key to the motel room, his sunglasses, and the blank post card from a hotel in Miami, Florida. Why is he taking the motel key? Why? I wondered.

He leaned over and kissed my cheek. As he walked out the door, he said he would come back and check up on me.

I prayed that he would go and not come back, but about 20 minutes later he opened the door and said, "Hi Honey, I came back for you." He threw the motel key, postcard, and change on the nightstand, "I am going to untie you and take you with me. I need you; I need you *real* bad. They will not hurt either of us, don't you see? Everyone is after me now."

Why does he need me so bad? Is it because he wants me to write his life's story? Is it because I accepted him the way he was, and he fell in love with me for the moment? What truly happened in his childhood, he never wanted to tell me when I asked earlier. Something bad must have happened to John. Perhaps I would find out later if this nightmare ever ended.

He was extremely nervous. He removed the gag from my mouth then leaned over to talk to me. His voice was trembling. As he leaned over the bed, blood started dripping on my arm. "What's happening, honey, you're bleeding! How did you hurt yourself?" he asked.

"It's not my blood John, you're bleeding from your chest. Take your shirt off and I'll tell you how to get the blood out." I told him to go into the bathroom and put the shirt in cold water, but not to rub the blood in. "Don't forget to get a washcloth and wash the blood off my arm and the bed sheet when you're finished."

When he finished, he tore a huge piece of sheet and wrapped it around his chest so the wound would stop bleeding. I thought he needed stitches. But somehow, I knew he could not go to a doctor, not if he actually killed a person.

By this time, I knew for sure he had murdered at least one person. What a great actress I had become. He is insane and needs help—if it is not too late, I thought to myself.

"Please let me take you with me," he said.

"No, you'd have to buy clothes for both of us because I'd freeze up in Georgia. You have to promise not to hurt anyone else," I said, as he left to go out again.

"Okay, I am coming back to check on you after I make a phone call. I will never let anybody hurt you. Now, I'm going to put the gag back on and tie you up."

As he put the gag in my mouth and tied the cloth around my head, I looked up in his face. He was quietly crying; the tears were flowing down his cheek as he tied me up for the last time. Then he kissed me again and said, "If only we would have met before all this started. I know you're the best thing that ever happened to me. I'm coming back later; you can bet on that. Goodbye, I love you," then he left.

It seemed like an eternity had passed when I heard the car being parked. He knocked on the door but could not come in. That is when I looked over at the nightstand and saw the motel key.

Through the door, John said that he would turn himself in. I hoped he would. He has two different personalities. I did not want him to be killed; I want him to be helped! Or did I?

There were a thousand thoughts going through my mind and the most prevalent of them all was that I was safe at last.

"Barbara, Barbara, let me in, please let me in! I need you!"

I could not believe it. I was still bound and gagged.

A few minutes later he must have realized I could not answer the door, nor could he bust into get me.

"Barbara, I love you. I'm leaving now darling. Take care of yourself. I never meant to hurt you—I never really hurt you!" Then he left me alone with my thoughts in the dead of night.

The NBC TV logo was on for a while, then plain static came on the TV. I had no idea what time it was. Back in the 70s, we did not have 24-hour TV. Somewhere around 12:30 AM, the *Star Spangle Banner* played and then it went to static until around 6 AM.

Suddenly, he was back at the door! Please God, please, do not let him in. Make him go away. Should I have gone with him? Could I have helped him? I have got to stop these thoughts—make them go away!

Soon I heard the car driving off again, but for how long? Didn't he leave an hour ago? Things were getting to me now; I feared that my mind was playing tricks again?

I began to hear sounds that were not there. I heard sawing and tugging at the door. Someone was going to break it down. But the sounds are all in my mind. My mind kept reliving my nightmare over and over again. How can you blank out something that you do not understand? What can you possibly think about at a time like this? The waiting—the waiting is driving me crazy. I tried to sleep. How can you sleep at a time like this? Oh God, please ease my pain.

I began to think about my ex-husband, James, our life together, the good times and the bad. What a life we could have had together; why was I such a fool? My terrible past. My wonderful past. I began to think about my father who died when I was only six; I began to think about my loving mother.

I remembered the day my father died; I thought about my sisters and brother. My entire life flashed before me. Am I going to die from a massive heart attack like my mother and father did? I thought. Is that going to happen to me? Why do not any of these thoughts make sense? God, please help me!

The more I tried to move my arms, the tighter the sheets on my wrists got, but I could move my head. The glass on the nightstand where John left the keys and postcard came back into sight. I can get loose and set myself free in the morning, I thought to myself, as my eyes became heavy and I drifted into a deep sleep. Thank you, God! A smile crossed my lips as I envisioned vivid colors of the rainbow with small baby angels flying over my head letting me know I would be alright.

WILL I SURVIVE?

SATURDAY, NOVEMBER 16, 1974

I was awakened awake by the TV. The news was on again. It was the same story as the night before. Nothing new meant they had not caught him. Did I really want him to get away? If it is true that he murdered people, I would want him caught and punished. Wouldn't I? I silently talked with God at that moment. "God, please do not let him kill any more people. PLEASE!"

I spit the gag out of my mouth, pushed the sheet tied across my face down with the pillow, then reached for the nightstand that had the glass top. My hands were tied together so I moved my fingers to pick up the drinking glass. I carefully grabbed the glass and tried to hit it against the wall. I tried over and over to break, hoping it would splinter when it hit the floor.

My breathing became unsteady. I was feeling sick and the room began to swim. I turned my head and was about to give up when I heard a voice in my head— Barbara, don't you dare give up now, you've come this far dammit.

I was startled back into reality and turned toward the nightstand when I noticed the glass top on the nightstand had a jagged edge on the corner nearest me. I grabbed the corner of the jagged glass top, as best I could with my fingertips, then cut my wrists apart. My wrists still had sheets tied around them, but they were no longer together. I wiggled to get my body up, then managed to grab the glass top with the jagged corner and cut my feet free from one another. I paused, trying to catch my breath and figure out what to do next. I promised John that I would not call anyone until around 8:30 AM.

The bloody sheet from where he had his chest wound was on the floor. I picked up his sunglasses and washed the prints off with water then put them, along with the postcard, in my purse. What did I just do? Was I crazy? I am helping a murderer! Get a grip before you call the front office. You are falling apart. God, help me, I must be having a nervous breakdown, as I stumbled into the bathroom shaking. I looked in the mirror. That was not me, my makeup was gone from crying and having the sheet tied around my face to hold the gag. My long, beautiful hair was tangled. I needed a shower. I needed to hug my sister and son. I went into the bathroom to wash my face, grabbed my comb from my purse, and tried to look presentable before calling the office.

I peeked out the blinds to make sure he was not out front. My heart was thumping so hard I thought I was having a heart attack.

When I noticed no Volkswagen out there, I opened the door and looked all around and down the street. He was not there. Thank God, he really left.

I finally got my composure and called the front desk.

"Good morning, this is Mrs. Johnson. How may I help you?"

"What time is it please?" I asked.

"It's 7:30 AM," she answered.

"Okay, Mrs. Johnson, wait a second." How did I remember her name? "This is Barbara Tucker, I'm in Room No. 5 or No. 10, I don't know, the one with the queen-sized bed, and I'VE BEEN KIDNAPPED! Please call the Sheriff. I've checked outside, there's no Volkswagen outside my door. The man has a gun." Why was I rambling on and on? I did not think she believed me. Then I began to cry.

A16—Palm Beach Post-Times, Sunday, November 17, 1974

Staff Photo by Wayne Herdlicka

Motel Operator Betty Johnson Saw Nothing Unusual

Mrs. Johnson came in the room about five minutes later and was horrified seeing me on the bed with stripped sheets around my neck, wrists, and ankles. "Oh, my God, it really happened? Here let me help you up," she said.

I could not get the rest of the sheets off because they were tied too tight with triple knots. I apologized for messing up the glass top on the nightstand. She made me tell her what happened so she would have something to make the Sheriff's department believe her. You could see her loving face, wanting to hug me, but not wanting to harm me. After talking for a few minutes and getting me a glass of water from the bathroom she told me she had to go to the office to make phone calls.

While sitting on the bed, I lit a cigarette as she left the room to call the Sheriff and any other law enforcement officials. "I'll be back in about ten minutes; I have to call the Sheriff from my office. Don't move, watch TV, I'll be back as soon as I can," she told me as she headed out the door.

When she was gone, I went berserk and lost complete control of myself. I grabbed the bloody sheet John had wiped his chest with and hid it behind the dresser… or was it under the bed? I was driven to hide everything. I went around the room to find hiding places. I even went into the bathroom, washed the prints off the glass and took the washcloth with soap and water and wiped everything I could think of he touched, that would incriminate him. I wiped his fingerprints away. My thinking was not clear. I wanted to wipe the time we were forced together, AWAY! IT DID NOT REALLY HAPPEN.

About fifteen minutes later, several men stormed in the door wearing different uniforms. One man came over to the bed and asked me if I was alright. Another looked at me in shock. Were there four men? Were there 20? My mind was whirling. My head was pounding. Then more men came, and they all tried to fit into the small motel room. Their chief or supervisor made them go outside. They were waiting on the paramedics to arrive to check me out. They all wanted to see the freak, the woman who was kidnapped by a serial killer and survived! They could not believe I was still alive.

I asked about my sister and son and they told me they were alive and well. The detective that was in the room with me was so kind. I got up from the bed after they cut the sheets loose from my neck, wrists, and ankles. Tears began to fall from my eyes as I sat back on the bed. I felt an arm around my shoulder which startled me at first, making me feel uncomfortable. Then I looked up and saw an officer smiling back at me. He was only trying to ease my fears. What was happening to me? Another officer handed me a tissue to dry my blurry eyes. I thanked everyone for coming to my rescue.

Afterwards, I was taken to the motel's front office where Mrs. Johnson had a cup of coffee waiting for me. You could see she was clearly shaken by finding me in the state I was in.

They let me call my sister. "Hi Beverly, are you okay honey?" I started to cry because she began to sob into the phone.

"Barbara, I prayed he didn't hurt you; I'll see you soon." Then she handed the phone to Jack and he told me to please get home safely, they would meet me soon. His voice faded. He gave the phone to my precious son.

"Dale, hi darling, are you alright?"

"Mommy, Mommy, did the bad man hurt you cause if he did, I'll give him my karate chop!"

"No sweetie, I'm okay now. You take care of Beverly and Jack and I'll see you soon." I got off the phone and everyone let me cry for a few minutes. The damn burst opened again. That would not be the last time either.

The officer took my hand and helped me from the chair. We were to go back to the first room John and I stayed in, to be questioned.

"I want to go home. Please take me home," I whispered to the officer that was holding my hand, as we entered the first room. "No, I don't want to go in there, I don't want to see that room again. Take me home. Please take me home!" I screamed out.

They tried to reassure me, but insisted they had to question me. I was questioned over and over by different law officers.

"Are you alright?"

"Did he hurt you?"

"Where is he going?"

"What was he wearing when he left you?"

I was so tired and frightened. I just wanted to go home to my family.

Then an agent with the Ft. Pierce FBI approached me to tell me we had to go downtown.

"Aren't you having someone take me back to West Palm Beach? I want to go home," I asked.

"We found the blood-stained sheet hidden under the bed; we also found a glass with possible fingerprints on it," said one of the officers.

I heard the sheriff's deputy and FBI guys talking. They are talking about Paul John Knowles murdering more than one person. He murdered children, too! I did not want to hear this. It cannot be true; this is a dream. This is a nightmare! Why didn't John get help before he murdered anyone? I asked myself. I lost my composure again and began to sob uncontrollably. The officer sat me in a chair and let me cry until I got under control.

One of the officers led me outside after telling me we had to go to the police department for processing. I did not even know who the officer was, but he was good to me. So, I let him take my hand and walk me to the waiting police car.

The entire motel was surrounded by news media and police. A reporter managed to jump in front of me with his microphone and ask, "How does it feel to be alive?" I would not answer.

I thought to myself, I am a survivor!

We arrived downtown in Ft. Pierce and I was led into the FBI office to be debriefed. They gave me something else to wear so they could take my clothes for evidence. I heard them discussing that it was unusual for anybody to have survived anything this horrific. They attributed it to the fact that Knowles did not need to kill me at that particular time in his life and he left me tied to the bed.

Are they all nuts? I thought. Knowles loved me. I made him fall in love with me for the moment. I did not love him; I played his game to survive. My thoughts were all scrambled. But I played Knowles' game and won. I was the only one that survived.

I would be home soon to see my beautiful son, twin sister, and boyfriend. I hoped he was driving up with the

Chief of Police from West Palm Beach. That was my prayer; I needed my family.

The police had Beverly call my brother and sister to tell them they found me at the motel in Ft. Pierce and I would be coming home soon. What were Jackie and Gary thinking about what happened to me? They must have seen me on television these past few days. After all, John and I were on the national news. Then, I realized that I talked in great detail about my entire family with Knowles. He knew I came from a loving, Christian family and said he wished he'd had one. John was most impressed by my being a copywriter for radio and television. Oh no, what if he goes after my family? Please God keep them safe.

The clerk for the FBI took me to a room where people were waiting for me. I was to be fingerprinted first. Fingerprinted? Are they kidding me? I am not the criminal here. What in the hell do they want to fingerprint me for? Are they sending me to prison? Then the nice man reassured me that everything was going to be okay. I was introduced to James Franklin along with William Gentry, both with the Ft. Pierce FBI team.

I will be seeing them again, I thought to myself. The questioning was the same as at the motel.

"Did he hurt you?"

"What was he wearing last?" It went on and on and on.

I think it was Mr. Gentry that told me, Chief Barnes from West Palm Beach Police, called to tell him they had a flat tire on the road and would be there as soon as possible.

It was over an hour later, when Chief William Barnes, Lt. James Griffin, and Sgt. James Gabbard from

West Palm Beach Police Department came to take me home. Chief Barnes was an older gentleman, stocky build, dark hair, very nice looking, and was very understanding. His looks reminded me of our father who had died when I was younger.

I remembered seeing Chief Barnes on TV a few times on the local news. I was escorted to the police vehicle after Chief Barnes hugged me like a daughter and said, "I didn't think you'd come out alive." They each asked a few questions before heading out the door.

The same newsman from the Skyway Motel was waiting for me. He was the only one I noticed out front among the others waiting like vultures. The cameras flashing made me see dots before my eyes. Now, I knew how real celebrities felt when the paparazzi were after them, like caged animals trying to escape. I did not want to talk to anyone, even though I was in the radio business. I was led around back after telling reporters, "I have no comment."

Chief William Barnes, Det. Sgt. James Gabbard, and Lt. James Griffin helped me into the back seat of a police vehicle. Where was Jack, my boyfriend? I asked. They explained as we drove off towards West Palm Beach that Jack would meet me later. I got a whiff of one of the men's cologne and it was hypnotizing. It smelled wonderful because I smelled so bad. I had not taken a bath or shower for over 37 hours. I never realized, at the time, I would be questioned so often, by so many different people. This would not be the end of my nightmare. I would be a hostage in my own mind for who knew how long?

I remembered at the Ft. Pierce FBI office, one of the officers whispered, "I believe she has Stockholm syndrome because she's not telling the truth on part of her answers."

I had no idea at the time what he was talking about and really paid little attention to his comment at the time. Patients with Stockholm syndrome experience symptoms similar to Post Traumatic Stress Disorder patients. They may have flashbacks, nightmares, distrust of others, and the inability to enjoy previous pleasurable activities. Stockholm syndrome has been defined as a condition in which hostages develop a psychological alliance with their captors during captivity. Emotional bonds may be formed between captor and captives, during intimate time together, but these are generally considered irrational in light of the danger or risk endured by the victims. A victim believes, unconsciously, that forming a relationship with their captor maximizes their chances of survival.

Chief Barnes asked me if I had already talked to Beverly and Dale.

I told him, "Yes. Why?"

"Barbara, we have more questions to ask you when we get back to the police station," he said.

What else can I possibly say that they have not heard before at the motel or the FBI office? I was so confused; I began to get nervous. I wanted to go home and see my sister and my son.

I wanted to grab my son, pick him up, and hold him to my chest while smelling the fragrance of Johnson & Johnson's Baby Powder® on him. I also wanted to cradle poor Beverly in my arms on our couch and let her cry in my arms because we all survived an unspeakable ordeal.

Beverly and Dale were both so brave. She was with this maniac from early Thursday until I got home.

Dear Lord, Beverly was bound, gagged, and bleeding because he tied the gag too tight. At least he had a heart and made it loose before he took me from our home. She could have died by choking to death. I had to get these thoughts out of my head. It was too much. I do not want to go to any police station, take me home! I thought to myself.

I found out later that Knowles' first victim was Alice Henrietta Curtis, 65, of Jacksonville, Florida. He gagged her on July 26, 1974, while stealing her belongings. She choked to death on her gag.

After driving for miles and miles, trying to answer more questions, the Sergeant, in the back seat with me, noticed I was dozing off and asked the Chief to play some soft music. He did and they allowed me to go into a deep sleep in the back seat of the police vehicle. I was startled awake by nightmares. I can't believe I said out loud, "No, he didn't hurt me, he was in love with me. He needs help. Please get him help."

As we entered the West Palm Beach Police Station, Chief Barnes let me know that Lt. James Griffin and FBI investigator for Palm Beach County, James Cavanaugh, were working this case along with Det. Sgt. James Gabbard and others. They led me down a hall and opened the door into the room where I would be questioned.

It was not any different than the other rooms I had been in. Large dark tables with chairs, telephones nearby, and stark, non-descript walls. I smelled coffee brewing. They asked me what I would like to eat. They had a lot of food for all of us. I was not hungry, but knew I had to eat something to survive. The only thing I can remember drinking was the coffee. I think I had a sandwich back in Ft. Pierce. Too many hours had passed. I was exhausted and forgetting what day it was and how to answer the stupid questions.

They finally finished questioning me. I was ready to go home when Lt. Griffin asked me if I wanted to go to the hospital. I had told the FBI agent in Ft. Pierce that Knowles had a bad rash on his chest and thighs and at times would scratch frantically.

For all I knew, he could have a horrible contagious disease. I thought it was poison ivy, but I'm not a doctor, so I agreed to go to the hospital that evening.

After making a call to Good Samaritan Hospital and finding out who my gynecologist was, it was all set up. Dr. Carter agreed to meet us at the hospital. We drove from the police station to the hospital to be greeted by the staff who heard the story and treated me kindly. They could see my clothes the officer had given me, were a mess. I was a mess! I was taken into a small room and then in came Dr. Carter, looking at me with concern. He was my best friend at that moment. He delivered Dale at this very hospital. He came over and hugged me. Neither one of us wanted to let go. I felt safe for the first time since being kidnapped from my home. He asked the police officers to go outside.

He pulled the curtains, after calling the nurse in, to help supervise the GYN exam. The doctors and nurses were so wonderful. One of the nurses came up to me after the exam and hugged me, while she cried. "You are so brave!" she said.

The exam seemed to take forever. I watched the large clock on the wall. Why was I having bloodwork done? Why did they have the x-ray done? A tetanus shot? A complete examination? It took over two hours. Then he gave me a prescription to take to my pharmacy the following day. What was going on? Did I have some sort of disease? I have to stop thinking, I want to go home! I thought.

The following day was Sunday. Pharmacy's were not opened on Sunday. I still didn't understand why I needed a prescription. When Dr. Carter finished the exam, he called in the police officer to tell him I was ready to go home. I handed the prescription to the officer. I didn't know what I was going to do with it. I hugged Dr. Carter goodbye and told him thank you.

We went back to the police station. The officer called Beverly and Jack. That was when they found out the press was in front of our house waiting for me to arrive. Jack spoke with the officer and told them to take me over to my friend Jane's home. Jack already called Jane and worked the details out. They would keep me over there and I would be safe until the press would leave us alone. It was arranged that Jack, Beverly, and Dale would meet us over there later. I assumed that the police would escort them.

I knew I would be safer staying with my friends out west of town for a week before I would return to work at WJNO.

When we got to my friend's home, the officer met privately with Jane. He explained what would be happening the next morning and told her not to tell me anything because he wanted me to relax. This was the beginning of what had to be done to capture the maniac. They were told not to turn the news on, not even the radio.

Jane and Perry welcomed me with open arms. I needed a shower and clean clothes.

Jack called Jane and Perry earlier and told them the news media were up the street and he would bring my clothes in a small suitcase for the week as soon as the police escorted them out to their home, about twenty miles away.

"Barbara, darling I've put clean underwear and a colorful muumuu on the bed for you to wear when Beverly, Dale, and Jack get here. Enjoy your shower!" Jane said as she shut the bedroom door and left me with my thoughts.

The water was as hot as I could stand it, as I stood in the shower scrubbing and scrubbing the dirt from my hair and body. Scrubbing with too much soap, too much shampoo in order to cleanse the hurt and pain from my soul. I had to survive this. I had to survive for Beverly and Dale. What about Jack? I was not thinking of him at the time. My thoughts were focused on Beverly and Dale.

I was so happy to be clean; I did not want my family seeing me dirty and smelly. While getting dressed I noticed Jane's bottle of perfume on the dresser for me to put on. Ahh, Chanel No. 5. I was in Heaven!

It took the police over an hour to get Beverly, Dale, and Jack to Jane's house. They had to dodge the press. When they finally arrived at the front door, I was standing there waiting. Jack dropped my suitcase on the floor and grabbed me. He gave me the most passionate kiss and told me he loved me and would never leave me. Then Beverly and Dale hugged and kissed me as I did the same to them. It was madness. It was Heaven.

Beverly, Dale, and I all survived!

THE MANHUNT

SUNDAY, NOVEMBER 17, 1974

Jane woke me up early and told me Detective Wald called and was on his way to take me to the West Palm Beach Police Department in an hour. I was to be dressed and have eaten by that time. The manhunt for Paul John Knowles was on. At this point, I could not remember what happened the night before being rescued. My entire mind had been fried. I slept like a rock and did not have nightmares, though I feared I would in the future. This was mind-numbing. Who was who and why was I going to the police station again?

I got up, took a fast shower, and while the water was drizzling down my body, I tried to shut this nightmare out of my mind. So, why were they picking me up? I have had enough questioning; I have told them everything I know at the Ft. Pierce FBI office. Enough was enough.

After picking at my breakfast of eggs, bacon, toast, jam, coffee, and orange juice, the doorbell rang startling me. Detective Wald was here already to pick me up. What did he do, speed from West Palm Beach out here to the boondocks, an area called the Acreage? I hugged Jane goodbye, as she looked at me with tears in her eyes sensing the hell I would be put through this day.

As we drove to the police station, I made small talk once again. Small talk, as if we were friends forever. What an actress. I will show them later if they try to make me say stuff I do not want to say. I will show them all.

We got to the police station and I followed the detective to the third floor for questioning. My hands were shaking, I did not want to be here. Wait! This is the same conference room I was in last night, or was it? It looked different. There were charts on easels, a large map of Florida and Georgia, I think. Glasses of water sat on the large conference table along with coffee and donuts, lots and lots of donuts, just like in all the cops shows. I was asked to be seated by one of the officers. He motioned to a chair. He started setting up a tape recorder.

"Good morning, Mrs. Tucker. May I call you Barbara?" he said kindly after he finished fiddling with his equipment.

"Good morning, and yes, you may call me Barbara."

"Would you like something to drink?" Another man asked.

I told him "No thank you," and then looked about at the stark dullness of the room. It needed something bright to cheer it up. Oh, of course, this is not about brightness. Why are there so many chairs at this conference table, I thought?

In the side door came the cavalry. Who were these men and women? Damn! I was introduced and several handed me their cards, a State Investigator from the Courthouse in Andalusia, Alabama; Sgt. J. Marion Brewer; Assistant Chief Charles Newton-Osbourne from Milledgeville Police, Milledgeville, Georgia; Brewton, Alabama's Chief of Police; next our men, Glen Holt, Chief Barnes, and Lt. James Griffin of West Palm Beach and FBI Agent James Cavanaugh, West Palm Beach office.

I did not know why they wanted me here. The TV was playing in the background. The news broadcast was all about the hunt for Paul John Knowles. The officers told me he was in the woods somewhere in Georgia. They needed my help.

"What color clothes was he wearing?"

"Any distinguishing marks on his body?" and on and on.

Fifteen minutes later, I finally blurted out, "Why are you asking me all of these questions, he never hurt anybody. Besides, I answered all these questions last night. You're confusing me."

They all gasped at my statement.

"He never hurt anybody?" one of them said.

Then one big man came up to me in a fit of anger and said something like, "What do you mean, he never hurt anyone?"

By this time, another man came around the table and laid down a few files. Files of murdered victims, some in glorious color and others in black and white.

"Here's one case," he side, "Carswell Carr and his daughter. The father died of a heart attack; the daughter was strangled to death by this monster Knowles. Now, how do you feel? You think he never hurt anybody?"

Another man approached me with pictures of people who were murdered in cold blood. One by one, files were dropped on the table in front of me. It was all too much for me to digest. It looked like more than 10. Women, men, and children murdered, right there on all the pages blurring together in front of my eyes.

I put my head down on the table and began sobbing out loud. He really and truly killed children, too? This is a nightmare. This is not happening to me. I am exhausted and want to go home. Oh, yeah, I thought to myself. I do not have a home right now. I took a sip of the water then tried to breathe in and out to relax and get my composure back.

We were all watching the TV while everything was unfolding in Perry, Florida and Milledgeville, Georgia. These officers were just as tired as I was. They wanted this man captured so they could stop the killing. Throughout the day, the local TV station broke into broadcasting, bring yet another news bulletin.

I heard the state troopers. I heard the commotion. I heard the fear in these police law officers' voices that still another might be shot and killed by this maniac.

Another officer, around the table, mentioned Knowles had an attorney down in Miami, Florida. His name was Sheldon Yavitz.

Yavitz was holding tapes that Knowles had handed to him on his murderous spree. What? Tapes of people he murdered. Why were they telling me all of this? I did not want to hear anymore. I already knew he was a murderer, a cold-blooded murderer.

The final straw was when the officers told me that he viciously murdered two more men in Georgia after he left me tied up in that motel. Paul John, the murderer, promised me he would not hurt anyone else. What a liar! God, why am still alive? Why?

Photo Credit: FHP

Trooper Charles Campbell

I was told that Florida Highway Patrol Trooper Charles Campbell was abducted while on patrol in Perry, Florida and shot by Knowles in Pulaski County, Georgia along with James Meyer, businessman who Knowles abducted a short time after taking Campbell. They were looking for their bodies. I turned white as a ghost, after viewing the horror. I remembered the past three days. I remembered him putting the sawed-off shot gun to my head and going, "BANG, BANG," and then laughing hysterically like a madman.

Paul John Knowles tried to break my finger and wrist the first night he kidnapped me. Was that the first night or second day? I was getting mixed up in my mind. What were these law enforcement officers doing to me? Why can't I think clearly? Am I dreaming this? Where am I? At the police station in West Palm Beach? In Ft. Pierce? In a lawyer's office? This is not happening to me. I felt like I had been abducted again! I did not know the answers to the questions they were asking me. They seemed like they were mean and hateful towards me at the time. I'M NOT THE CRIMINAL!

After not answering their stupid questions, one of the men threw a folder on the table in front of me. Another opened it and I saw a murder victim. The officers were acting sort of like Dr. Jekyll and Mr. Hyde, just like Knowles. Why where they victimizing me?

It was all a horrible mistake. Suddenly reality became clear. I then believed it all, Paul John Knowles was a murderer. He even murdered children! The police and FBI were talking about eight known murder victims that had been found previously, along with two new ones in northern Florida. This made 10 people murdered by this lunatic.

Why was the number 35 popping up in my mind? Had I had a nervous breakdown? Most people would have, wouldn't they? I was sure Knowles told me he murdered over 30 people. I knew he did because he told me more than once and I tried to block it out of my conscious mind. I AM NOT CRAZY!

My mind cleared and I told them everything I had said, in Ft. Pierce at the FBI's office, when questioned: the bloodstained polyester yellow shirt and the black slacks Knowles was wearing, the color of his hair, strawberry blonde, the color of his eyes blue, not green, or were they brown? I opened-up, I rambled on and on. He was a murderer who killed innocent people.

God, thank you for letting our family live, I thought to myself. I prayed to God that he would be found and killed, just like the animal he was.

It was dark now and he was still on the run. At least I finally told the FBI and Police everything I knew. Why was I remembering everything now? It was too much for me to bear. All those folders with murdered people in color and black and white being thrown on the table. My subconscious mind was finally opened, and I was finished. The officers were finally satisfied and knew I needed to rest so they drove me back to Jane's home.

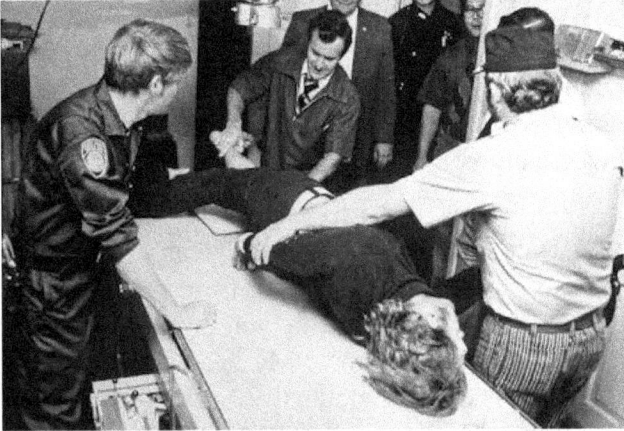

John P. Knowles captured & given a medical exam.

For several days, I remained at Jane's house. Beverly, Jack, and Dale came to visit but I yearned to go home and get back to a normal routine. I was having terrible dreams every night, as I sobbed quietly into the pillow.

The same thoughts kept running through my head. How can a person return to a normal life? Why were we still alive? Only God knew what would happen next. When you have had an experience like this you look at yourself differently. You wonder if you could have done something heroic, like bash his head in while he was sleeping back at the motel, so he could not kill that State Trooper and the poor businessman—family men.

I was riddled with guilt. I hated myself. Those poor families lost loved ones. Their lives are shattered from a senseless killing spree and perhaps I could have done something to prevent it. I was shattered and ashamed.

What should Beverly and I say to our other family members when they call? Have I already spoken with everybody? My brother? My older sister? I could not remember. My thoughts were all clouded. I felt so alone. God, where are you now? I pleaded.

My life was not my own, I knew how scared Beverly, Dale and I were. Beyond fear, what did my precious son feel when I was torn from his life for that moment in time? I believed in our Lord, Jesus Christ, before. Where was God now? My heart was heavy, and my soul was racked with doubts.

I was eventually able to go back home. The press was no longer outside our front door waiting to pounce on me. Thankfully, I was finally old news to the media. I was happy to be with Beverly and Dale, but I was still heavy-hearted and numb.

A few days later, Jack picked me up and took me out to dinner in Palm Beach at the famous Taboo Restaurant. Jack ordered two Chateaubriand steak dinners with asparagus tips, stuffed mushrooms, with chocolate layered cake and coffee for dessert.

Later, the band began playing as he guided me to the dancefloor. The wonderful meal, along with two Brandy Manhattans helped eased my nerves. Why was I nervous? I thought to myself as Jack held me in his arms and his new cologne flowed through me. I envisioned making love later. Does he really love me? Was I afraid to make love with Jack after being kidnapped? I had to quit thinking so much and just enjoy the moment.

When we arrived at Jack's house, he kissed me tenderly on my lips. Then sparks burned us both into beautiful, wonderful madness as we stumbled into the bedroom with wild ideas of making love. I needed a real man!

The clothes were thrown onto the floor, as I stood there in my new aqua lace panties and bra. We were both turned on and it did not take long for the drinks to take affect. We flung ourselves onto the king-sized bed, Jack began undoing my bra, then ripped off my panties, as we made mad, passionate love. It was magical, exciting, demanding, and wonderful. I would be alright in the sex department from now on. Jack made me feel special and loved. I would cherish this day forever.

GETTING BACK TO MY LIFE

I was trying to get my life back and go to work. After getting Dale ready to go back to school, I kissed Beverly goodbye. Dale and I headed toward the Cadillac convertible Jack gave me to replace the stolen Volkswagen. I helped buckle Dale into his booster chair in the back seat.

My hand started shaking as I got the keys from my purse. I plopped myself into the front seat and placed my hands on the steering wheel as my mind wandered back to the kidnapping. I began sweating and was terrorized by my own thoughts. How was I going to go to work today? I dropped Dale off first, then had to figure out what I needed to do about my job. I decided to drive on the scenic route to work on Flagler Drive, by the waterfront, to see the beautiful mansions across the way in Palm Beach. I had to get my mind ready for what was to happen.

It was over a week and a half after the kidnapping that I returned to work. My co-workers were not able to talk to me or even look me in the eye. What could anyone say to help me feel better about myself? God was the only one who would help me sort everything out, but not now, not yet.

Our General Manager, brought me into his office, made me sit down, and handed me a cup of coffee. Everyone had already hugged and kissed me and told me how they had prayed for me. One even whispered that Walter-Weeks Broadcasting Company, who owned WJNO and other Florida radio stations, raised over $25,000 ransom to find me alive. I was glad Knowles did not know it at the time of the kidnapping, even though it made me feel good. The General Manager told me I did not have to come to work this early and he would still pay me. I thanked him and told him I needed to work. I left his office to do just that—work.

After sitting down at my desk and pulling off the cover to my typewriter, I noticed a note which read, "Dear Barbara, Well I see you've done it once again haven't you! Only you can come out alive from anything so horrific. Only you!" Signed with a big fat "M!"

I was so upset, I marched back into Mr. Hanson's office to show him the note. He kind of fluffed it off stating he would have a talk with Mary. So, I went back to work to begin my first day—upset and shook up.

An hour later, my favorite DJ, Bill came into my office explaining that when I was kidnapped, Mary and her husband went over to his house for a get together on the weekend. While there, she said to Bill and his wife, "I hope Barbara gets run over by a truck after the kidnapper throws her out of the car and gets killed." He then explained that she had been drinking, but he did not think this was right and wanted me to know so I could watch out for her.

My memory shot back to a few months before being kidnapped when I received the cross I was now wearing. It was given to me by the Pastor of the church school Dale attended. Something evil was trying to get me back then. Was it to ward off Mary, the serial killer, or both? Something happened to me after listening to Bill, the DJ. After work that day, I called home and Beverly answered.

"Hi Bev, I'm going to be about 20 minutes late because I have an errand to run." I packed up my stuff, closed the door to my office, and I left for my car in the parking lot. The drive from WJNO radio station to Southern Boulevard was not that far. As I turned the corner onto Southern Boulevard heading east toward Palm Beach, I knew where I wanted to park. I drove over the bridge then noticed on the left-hand side, by the waterway, nobody was there. After all the traffic passed, I drove into a parking space overlooking the water.

What a beautiful site. You could see the famous Mar a Lago and other mansions on the Palm Beach side. While the other side were condominiums and buildings in West Palm Beach. This was where I used to park and make out with Jack.

This time was different. All my windows were closed, and I had the radio on full blast for noise. That is when I lost it. I began screaming at the top of my lungs, then broke down and sobbed as my hands gripped the steering wheel. This was not happening to me; nobody could live through something like this. Then I asked God, "Why am I still alive? Why?" As if I would get an answer right away. In reality, I knew God was watching over me and it was all in His time, not mine.

I remembered part of a saying from the Bible that went something like "be anxious for nothing." Still, I wanted to believe that none of this really happened to me. Would I get on with my life and pretend to be okay? I decided I would try to better myself, make more money, perhaps write a book, and leave West Palm Beach, Florida, with Dale and Beverly to start over. What did I have to stay for? All the looks, pity, and pain would not go away. Did I still love Jack? I wanted to live a better life. Time would tell.

The following day the West Palm Beach Police called to warn Beverly, Dale, and me that Sheldon Yavitz, Knowles attorney from Miami, was at the Georgia jail with Knowles giving him advice. His attorney was meeting with his client daily in the jail. We were told to be careful because someone overheard him asking his client, why he left Beverly, Dale, and me alive. The police and FBI knew of this and would keep watch on our family's behalf. But we did not have round-the-clock protection. Frankly, I am not sure if we had any protection at all.

Now, I was beginning to have a different type of nightmare. In my sleep, I envisioned Beverly and Dale shot in cold blood before he came at me with the rope to strangle me. Stop this insanity! How much more could I take? I had to work; I had to pay the mortgage.

I had to be an actress once again for my sister, son, and boyfriend. I did not let them know the terror and fear I was going through. Beverly and Dale had already been through enough. It was not important for my young son to know about the alarming phone call. God was with him, as I watched Dale and his friend, Edward, play and have fun.

My dear friend Muffin had married and moved away a few years after the kidnapping and we both drifted apart.

When I got home from work a few days later, I was flabbergasted to see Eleanor and her husband Bob waiting in their car as I drove up with Dale.

I invited them inside to see Beverly. Eleanor said, "Hi" to Beverly and then came up and hugged me. "Barbara, I'm never going to be away from you again, ever! You scared the beejeebees out of us. Thank God you three are alive!" Then we all started crying. We visited for about an hour and I knew she would keep her word and never be far from me from now on.

Jane and Perry, my saviors from the news media after the kidnapping, invited Jack, Beverly, Dale, and me over for Thanksgiving dinner. We gladly accepted since I could not think about cooking. The day went by with me pretending I was having a great time. Laughing and having fun was nothing more than a figment from my imagination. I tried to convince myself nothing bad happened to Beverly, Dale, or myself. I tried to be the great actress once again as my turn came around the table to tell what I was thankful for this year. "I'm thankful to be with beautiful friends and family. I am thankful for Beverly, Dale, and Jack being there for me. But mostly I'm thankful, I survived!" Where did that come from? God.

Wednesday, December 18, 1974

I was home with a migraine headache and needed something to eat. As I walked into the kitchen for a bite to eat, the phone rang.

"Hello."

The voice on the other end exclaimed, "Barbara, Knowles is dead. He's dead! He was shot to death trying to escape from the Georgia Sheriff and GBI agent earlier! Turn the TV on."

"Okay, I'll turn the TV on and tell Beverly." I told Lt. Griffin, or was it Det. Gabbard? As I hung up the phone, I called out, "Beverly that was the police. Knowles is dead, I'm turning the news on now!" I hurried into the living room.

Channel Five, NBC news stated, "Knowles, 28 was in a car with Douglas County Sheriff Earl D. Lee and Georgia Bureau of Investigation Agent Ronnie Angel, when he was shot while trying to snatch Lee's revolver," authorities said. "Knowles picked the lock to his handcuffs with a paperclip, getting off a single shot before he was killed."

I then switched to another station, "John Paul Knowles, a serial killer, is killed trying to escape from deputies in Georgia. He was supposed to take the officers to the woods in Georgia to find the gun that killed his last two victims."

I turned the TV off to go hug Beverly. We both began to sob with relief. Knowles could murder no more. He could not come after me or my family. It took a while to grasp what this news meant to me and my family.

The door opened. Our across the street neighbor, Marion brought Dale home from school. "Hi Darling!" I said after hugging and kissing my son. "Go wash up before we eat, Honey."

"Mommy, I love you," he told me. He walked over to Beverly's chair to give her a hug and kiss before heading towards the bathroom to wash his hands.

"Barbara, here's your Kentucky Fried Chicken dinner with the works. Enjoy! Don't pay me. It's my treat. Got to get home to my family," Marion said as she headed out the door.

Marion had brought a bucket of Kentucky Fried Chicken with French fries, coleslaw, and fried mushrooms. Yum, another one of my favorites. We were now in the mood to celebrate and eat a scrumptious dinner. I even made myself a drink. Good ole Southern Comfort® on the rocks with a twist of lemon. Beverly got sodas for Dale and herself. After eating supper, we talked about the relief we were feeling as a result of the news story.

"Mommy, the bad man can't come back to kill us!" Dale said, as we all looked at him in awe. This beautiful child of mine understood the meaning of survival.

That evening, a reporter knocked on the front door. As I opened the door to tell him to go away, he showed his press credentials. He wanted a few lines for tomorrow's paper from us. I would not let him in and I would not go all the way outside. He continued with his tape recorder on. "How do you feel, now that Paul John Knowles is dead?"

"How do you think we all feel? Relieved," I said as I shut the door. The next morning, when Dale and I left for school and work, more press was there again along with a truck from WPTV TV station. I yelled out "No comment," as I raced Dale to the car and buckled him in the back seat. I waved goodbye to the reporters as I drove off. Over and done with, I thought to myself.

It seemed as if Christmas day was the same as Thanksgiving. Being invited over to Jane's again along with Jack, Beverly, Dale, and myself. Jack had gotten us a Christmas tree and we put up all the beautiful ornaments, but it just was not the same. At least Beverly and Dale got the presents they asked for. I just did not care, but pretended once again, that I did.

January 1975

After being back at work for a while, Burt Reynolds was having a grand opening at his ranch in Jupiter, Florida. As the copywriter for WJNO, I had the privilege of writing commercials and being invited to the grand opening with all the celebrities. The big event was a few weeks out.

Meanwhile, one of our best salesmen, Harry, came in and asked if I would be willing to write a book about the kidnapping.

"Why should I write a book?" I asked.

"Well, after all you and your family's been through, wouldn't it make sense to write a book and get some money for yourself and your future? Besides, I know a really nice guy who'll help you," he said.

"I'll think about it and get back with you tomorrow," I told him.

I went home and discussed it with Jack and Beverly. They agreed that I should write a book to help other victims of crime. In the process, I might even make some money. The next day, I told Harry, "Yes, I would love to write my story.

A few days later, while I was typing a commercial, Harry came in and surprised me by saying, "Barbara, this is Mr. Walter Colbath, attorney at law. He's the one that will help you get your book started with professionals."

"Hello, Mr. Colbath, it's so nice to meet you," I said. "Please sit down and explain what we need to do." I may have seemed calm and confident on the outside, but inside I was scared to death thinking about what I would have to go through remembering the horror again. In my gut, I did not know if I could handle it.

Mr. Colbath brought me back to reality by explaining everything and putting me at ease. Marilyn, his secretary, would help me with my story.

A few days before the grand opening of Burt Reynolds' Ranch, Mrs. Peri Winkler from International Literacy Agents, Beverly Hills, California, called me and introduced herself. She would be my Literary Agent. She explained that her husband was Burt Reynolds' agent and that we would meet in a few days at the grand opening. After hanging up from the call, it hit me: I would be writing a book, not just a story. It was exciting and yet why was I petrified? God would get me through it if it were meant to be.

why was I petrified? God would get me through it if it were meant to be.

Marilyn, Mr. Colbath's secretary, picked me up at my house and met Beverly and Dale before heading out to Burt Reynolds ranch for the grand opening. Marilyn was happy to meet them and gave Beverly and Dale each a hug before leaving.

When we got into her car, I was nervous and began my story. "I met Burt Reynolds for the first time, earlier last year. Burt brought his press people along to WJNO radio station and was guided into the recording studio to do Public Service Commercials or PSA's. I was sitting at my typewriter, typing away as usual, and in he comes. He came over, took my hand to help me from my chair, then sat down, put his feet on my desk while placing his hands behind his neck. Then he said to me, 'Hi, why didn't you come out front to meet me along with all the others. Don't you want my autograph?'"

I looked at him and said, "Okay, make it out to Beverly."

He yelled for his assistant to bring one of his glorious black and white pictures, then signed the picture beginning with "To Beverly...." I laughed to myself, at the time, because he thought he was so wonderful. I heard Burt Reynolds never signed autographs. I still was not impressed, but TV-Radio personalities never impressed me before, anyway. I remember meeting Sonny and Cher when they were cool. They were just the same as you and me.

I needed funny memories like that to survive what was about to happen in my life. I was supposed to write a book and bring back all my fears.

I mentioned to Marilyn how nervous I was as I took a deep breath.

"Barbara, this is for you also. You've been through so much. Let's just have fun today, okay?" she said.

"I'll try Marilyn," I said as we walked to the front door and rang the doorbell.

Burt's mother, Fern, greeted us and led us into the den where everyone was visiting. Some turned their heads and began whispering. I heard one lady whisper to another, "That's the woman who was kidnapped. I can't believe she's here; I can't believe she's alive."

I had chills go up and down my spine as Burt Reynolds came up and gave me a hug whispering in my ear, "I'm so glad you're alive. You are amazing Barbara." He then walked Marilyn and me into the family room to meet a few of the stars that were there. As he said their names, my mind went blank. More would stop by later. Burt mentioned something about the horse races in the afternoon because this would be an all-day event. I thought differently about Burt now. He was not the egotistical person I had met earlier last year. He was genuinely happy for me to be there.

While I was seated, others arrived at the grand opening of the ranch. John D. MacArthur shook my hand and remembered me. My first husband worked for John at Banker's Life & Casualty Insurance Company in West Palm Beach and later in Savannah, Georgia. I had met Mr. MacArthur several times in the past few years before my divorce. He told me he was so glad that I was alive after that traumatic experience and bent down to give me a kiss on my cheek.

As I gazed around the room, I saw Burt's father. He was an older version of his son and very good looking. Stars were there from his television shows and movies. We were all introduced, and I immediately forgot everybody's names, just like before. There were just too many people to keep track of.

From the kitchen, I heard this southern drawl, "Barbara, do you like swamp cabbage?" You have got to be kidding! It was Dinah Shore making her way over to ask me in person. She made me feel so comfortable as she helped me out of my chair and led me into the kitchen to try her famous swamp cabbage after letting me stir it first. It is a dish made from the Cabbage Palm also known as the Sabal Palm tree. The Cabbage Palm's heart was used by the Seminole Indians as a food source, but it kills the tree. Since the swamp cabbage had to cook another hour, she asked me in a whisper if I would like to see Burt's bedroom.

"Of course, I'd love to!" I exclaimed. No wonder Burt fell in love with Dinah, what a beautiful woman. She was short, probably a little over 5 feet tall. I towered over her because I was 5'7".

I looked down into her beautiful brown eyes as she took my hand and walked me out of the kitchen. "Come on, Barbara, let's see Burt's bedroom!" Her sparkling brown eyes showed compassion for me, which let me know she really cared deep down about my feelings. When I met her earlier, she hugged me, and I think I saw tears in her eyes.

Barbara, get a grip, you are going to see Burt Reynolds bedroom! I thought. The bedroom was Hollywood flashy with a spectacular color scheme. It was decorated in red and black velvet. There were mirrors everywhere, even the ceiling. I wanted to reach out and touch the wallpaper but did not because Dinah would think I was nuts.

I was not prepared for all the attention I received. Everybody was so nice. I knew they did not have a clue what to say to me. After all, I was kidnapped by a mass murderer. Or was he a serial killer? I did not understand what he was at that time. He was a murderer. That would have intimidated even me, had I been in their shoes.

I was still acting, but I was enjoying myself and my short-lived fame. Then Burt came in to get me from Dinah and walked me into the family room to meet his agent's wife, Peri Winkler, Literary Agent. We had already spoken on the phone. She was very attractive and shorter than me with blond hair and a beautiful smile. I noticed her beautiful California tan and wished I could have a tan like hers.

We sat down with Marilyn and talked for a while about what I needed to do to write a book. I was to begin writing and give everything to Walter's office. He would get the pages back to California and we would go from there.

We were offered food and drinks before the afternoon races. Dinah's swamp cabbage was delicious. I would have asked for the recipe but knew I would never make it.

Dinah came over to get Marilyn and me for the horse races. I tried to see as much of the ranch as possible. It was huge. I saw the important parts of it along with the store, home, and stables on the way to the races.

After being seated with Dinah, we looked around and watched the first race. The horse I picked lost.

After the first race Dinah said to me, "Barbara which horse do you want to bet on honey?"

"I didn't bring any money and I don't know which one I'd bet on anyway," I answered.

"Here, take this and bet on any horse," she said as she handed me money. I took her up on it and bet on a few races. My horses all lost.

Dinah leaned over during the race and gave me her binoculars. "Are you two having fun?" she asked.

"Yes, these horses are beautiful and amazing."

Even though my horses did not win, the thrill of the races made me forget my fears for a short time. Meeting the stars that were dear friends of Burt's was so much fun. When Marilyn and I had to leave, we told everyone how much we enjoyed the day. Everybody nearby gave me a big hug. Burt walked Marilyn and me to the door then whispered in my ear, "Barbara, you made it this far darling. You know you had an angel watching over you."

I then said, "It wasn't an angel, it was God!"

When Marilyn dropped me off at home, I burst in the door to tell Beverly and Dale all about my awesome adventures. After mentioning all the stars, especially Dinah, who were there, she asked if I got any autographs. "No, I never thought to ask." I said.

Beverly said, "Barbie, you need to go out more and have more fun. You know we love you and you deserve to be happy." I got my sister back for the moment.

That night, I fell into a wonderful deep sleep dreaming in vivid colors. It was not the usual kidnapping nightmare I had most nights. In my dream, I was on the Johnny Carson show. I talked about being kidnapped and how God was with me every moment. I saw my mother in the dream. She had wings this time and was wearing a flowing white chiffon dress. Her arms were outstretched, but her hands were pushing me away.

"Mama!" I screamed in my deep sleep, as she faded away on a billowy cloud with an angel guiding her into the sunset. Mama had wings; she was my angel watching over me.

She died six months before I was kidnapped. My dream continued. After the T.V. show, a movie was made. I was rich, famous, and helped other victims of crime through my best-selling book. Beverly, Dale, and I moved to another city in another state. My wonderful dream was interrupted when I heard Dale screaming. I let him sleep with me when he got frightened and could not sleep in his own bed on the back porch. So, I went to get him.

"Mommy, Mommy, they're coming after me." I reached over to pick him up, held him in my arms and began singing another favorite lullaby, since birth. *"Rock-a-bye Baby, on a tree-top, when the wind blows the cradle will rock...."* As I continued to sing, I looked down at my precious son and he was fast asleep. This hideous occurrence had deeply affected all three of us.

THE NIGHTMARE CONTINUES

Working five days a week helped me ease the pain and kept me from feeling sorry for myself. Unfortunately, the nightmares were still there. It would be a long, long time before they would end.

Jackie's husband left for overseas to serve our country, in the Air Force. She could not go overseas with him, because it was on a top-secret mission. She decided to come stay with us for a while.

We welcomed her into our home, with open arms, for the months he would be gone. Even though our house was small with two bedrooms, one bath and a Florida room, it was home. It was easy to see the love she had for Dale, Beverly, and myself. We were family.

My brother, Gary, worked at the Weston Hotel and was Director of Marketing in Seattle, Washington. Gary and Ylwa kept in touch by phone. Their young children, Sean and April, were bundles of joy from heaven.

The writing of the book was underway with Peri Winkler and Walter Colbath overseeing the rough draft manuscript pages. Grief overtook me, as I forced myself to continue writing. It took all of my strength to type my inner feelings onto the stark white blank pages facing me at my typewriter. I prayed about typing the right words for this book, while keeping my sanity.

As I began typing, my mind kept drifting off. Did I really want to move away from Florida? Yes, no, maybe? If Mama could move four children down to West Palm Beach, Florida from Detroit, Michigan and raise us to be good Christian children, so could I, I told myself. Mama had more courage than anyone we knew, because she kept us together and loved all of us equally. Jackie, Gary, and I were the ones who truly spoiled Beverly, not Mama! I never knew what a dysfunctional family was until I heard about Paul John Knowles' story, when I started to write my own book.

I finished typing the first draft up to Sunday, November 17, 1974, the day of the manhunt for Knowles. Then I put the book away so I could enjoy my family. I would re-evaluate my life later and decide whether or not to move. God was guiding me. Life would go on, whether the book was finished, or not.

When you see your picture in the newspapers and watch all three-networks CBS, NBC, and ABC nightly news, with your face along with the serial killer plastered for all to see, it intimidates and changes you.

I continued to write my story after work when Beverly, Jackie, and Dale went to bed. I could not sleep much, for some reason. I needed to continue writing my story. As the days went by in a flurry, I still tried to keep my wits and humor.

Peri called me one Sunday night with news on the book. "Barbara, first edition was impaired. You need to re-write more of the story. Otto Preminger, the famous film producer, did a similar story three years ago in fiction. The industry believes this is not really a unique story. Perhaps when the book becomes a hit, a movie could be made. You'd make around $20,000 after they got their cut from the profits. Think about it, Barbara. Go ahead and write more. Good night," she said, as we ended the call.

How could she say this to me at a time like this? I have typed from my heart and it was God who stayed by me every time I sat down to type and re-type. Now, I am told the industry believes it is not a unique story. If they think the story is not unique, how would she sell it or even have a movie made later? It did not make sense to me. Something was not quite right, but I still had to hope.

It would be nice if Beverly, Dale, and I got some money for all the suffering, pain, and heartache we had been put through. It was God's plan, not mine, I thought to myself as I let the subject go, for now.

In the weeks that followed, all I did was work and come home to type and re-type new pages for the book. I was exhausted. I prayed to God nightly because the nightmares would not go away. It worked most of the time, until someone or something triggered the horror in my mind all over again.

From August 1975 to January 1976, I kept the letters Peri wrote. Thank heavens for that because I needed them for my book.

Peri wanted Walter's secretary to re-type the rough draft of the book, with correct punctuation, etc. She liked my style of writing and wrote, "it's very unique, very smooth, flashbacks are fantastic!"

My mind wandered back to re-live bits and pieces of being kidnapped: John and I sitting down in the two chairs by the room, and watching the State Troopers drive by, first one way, then the other. They were out looking for us and could not see us.

"Damn, what idiots!" he said. "Barbara, you said you worked at a radio station. Do you know how to write books?" John asked.

"I write commercials for a living but writing a book couldn't be that difficult. Yes, I could write a good novel. Why are you asking?" I said, thinking this was a strange question to ask—Why does he need me so bad? Is it because he wants me to write his life's story? What truly happened in his childhood, he never wanted to tell me when I asked earlier. Something bad must have happened to John. Perhaps I would find out later, when this nightmare was over.

I was forced back into reality and became frustrated, again, on the book delays. If I had known how hard it was to write a book, I never would have begun. I typed how many pages of what? I could not even remember my name. Going to work all week, taking care of Dale and Beverly, cleaning the house on Saturday, and trying once in a while to see Jack when he was available, was wearing me out. Thank God Jackie was here to help because I wound up with bronchitis and was so sick, I did not care about anything. I wanted it all to go away. That is when I remembered all the money, fame, and moving. It kept me going. Someday I would be a star, just like Knowles told me, "I'd be a star!"

A few days later I felt better and wrote Peri.

Hi Peri,

I'm writing today to fill you in on the facts. Marilyn has stopped in mid-stream of typing due to her vacation. She did not inform me until this morning that she had to start from the very beginning, since single spacing was not correct. She's at the end of my book and having a difficult time since some parts are a dream and others reality. ~Barbara

I was beginning to feel better about writing, until I received the following letter from Peri, a few days later.

Dear Barbara,

I've received your letter, along with one from Walter, your attorney. It seems that everything is progressing at a steady pace, so please be patient. I certainly am! Barbara, of course I'm going to read it before going to another publisher. You must understand that since this is a total rewrite, I must consider it as a new submission and if I'm not happy with it, I certainly can't take it to the publishers. But I'm thinking positively and hoping I'd love it a lot.

Warmest regards, Peri

cc: Walter

A total re-write? I have to re-write certain chapters all over again. This was making me feel as if I had just lost my marbles.

THE FCC REPORT

NOVEMBER 6, 1975

Eleanor, my friend, met me for lunch. I brought along more pages of my book with a copy of the FCC report from Walter's office. I called Marilyn around noon to tell her we would be bringing them by.

WJNO is not a fun place to work anymore. I wish I did not have to work; I would quit today if I could. The atmosphere is thick with prejudice, hate, and fear. Everyone including one of the salesmen who had been here for years, is worried about their jobs. I overheard that the FCC is involved in investigating the station. They have logs from 1974 through part of 1975 and four months are totally missing. At least 20 accounts are not there. The copy is missing also. Bookkeeping is a mess. Damn, I had heard of payola, persons paying radio stations to air their record(s) with top radio stations, but not this!

The new bookkeeper wants me to tell her what is going on. I will not go to lunch with her. I know everybody thinks I am so sharp, that I know the truth behind the scandal. But I do not. I can only guess, and I have a good idea who is behind it: a woman so vile, she wrote a note when I got back from being kidnapped and left it on my typewriter. She was the devil, I thought back then. I must get out of this office.

I took my FCC report to Mr. Colbath's secretary, Marilyn, along with the extra insert pages of my book to send to Peri. I have this fear now that WJNO is trying to pressure me into quitting. They cannot fire me; the FCC is hot on their tails. So, I just have to grin and bear it.

There was a tremendous amount of tension at work for those of us who still had our jobs. The FCC was relentless.

One Saturday morning, in the midst of cleaning house with my sisters, I told them I was going to clean the bathroom. That is when I had a strange feeling as if I were about to faint.

I vaguely remember stepping into the bathtub, fully clothed, turning on the shower, and letting the water bead down my face and body as I began screaming bloody murder at the top of my lungs. I could not stop. Neighbors rushed from across the street and next door. Everyone was asking my sisters to call an ambulance.

"Mommy, Mommy, what's wrong? Please stop crying Mommy!" Dale shrieked.

I was startled back to reality at that moment, saw my son and others in shock, then grabbed Dale, my baby, into my arms as I said, "I love you Dale, I love you Jackie and Beverly. I'm so sorry. I'll be okay!" I headed toward the bedroom to change into dry clothes. I did not need an ambulance. I knew I was having a nervous breakdown, but I never thought it would take this long.

The following week, after work at WJNO I decided to go to the Mental Health Clinic off 45th Street. Jackie was still living with us. I called and told her I would be late and would heat up my supper when I got home. She asked me where I was going, and I told her I had to finish up a few more commercials.

I left work early and arrived at the Mental Health Center around 4:45 PM. When I got in the front door, I almost backed out. Instead, I buckled up my nerves and stepped in.

I went up to the receptionist and quietly said, "I think I'm having a nervous breakdown."

She walked me over to a chair and had me take a seat while giving me paperwork to fill out. Then said, "It's okay, take a few deep breaths, it will help you." She told me the therapist would see me within the next 10 minutes.

Five minutes went by and a large black woman with a beautiful smile, held out her hand to help me from the chair. "Hello, Ms. Tucker, you may follow me. Please come this way." We walked up to a door and stopped. She opened it with a key. We walked down the hallway to her office. It was like any other office: nice, dark mahogany desk with chairs, files, and lots of pictures of her family. She mentioned her name, but I was not listening. I forced myself to focus and face her when she spoke. "Mrs.

Tucker why do you think you need to be here? And why do you think you're having a nervous breakdown?"

"I was kidnapped by serial killer, Paul John Knowles on Thursday evening, November 14, 1974, from my home. My sister, Beverly, who has Cerebral Palsy, had been in the house with him from noon that day until I got home around 5:30 PM. He tied my son up, who was only six years old, took my money, car, and me."

It took about 20 minutes to finish my story. She handed me a tissue because I began crying. That is when she told me I was not having a nervous breakdown.

Anyone who could survive such a horrific ordeal like being kidnapped by a murderer is not having a nervous breakdown. Barbara, you're a very strong, courageous person. I will tell you right now what has happened to you is just called stress. You are not, nor ever will be nuts with your perseverance and determination to survive. You even mentioned during this conversation that you believed in God. That's wonderful because you have faith. Get your purse and come with me, I'm going to show you nuts, as you would call them.

She took me down the corridor, opened another door with her keys and let me view what she so comically referred to as nuts. It was horrible, just horrible for me to watch these poor lost souls roaming about in the big room, some shuffling, some singing out loud, some swearing; then I knew once again that God was with me in this moment, just like He had always been and always would be. The woman gave me her card after giving me a hug, as she led me out the front door.

I was not nuts. I was going to be okay.

After getting home, I ate dinner and told Jackie and Beverly where I had really gone. They were both relieved to hear that I had seen a professional.

Eleanor came back into my life after the kidnapping and vowed never to be out of touch with me again. She and Bob, her beautiful husband, listened to me ramble on when I had bad days. They were beautiful Christian people who proved to be a true blessing by reminding me how God was always near to guide me, even when I doubted myself. I had to get back to church and get the fun Barbara back again. But it would take time. I just needed to be reassured I was not going crazy.

Poor Eleanor, I called her almost every night to hear my woes. I cannot believe her husband did not tell her to hang up on me.

At work, following the visit to the Mental Health facility, I learned to do my job and leave it there.

Marilyn and I talked; Peri wants more pages rushed to her. I really didn't want to type more pages!

Nothing at WJNO was the same. You could cut the tension in the air with a knife when you entered the front door. One of the DJs, Robby, was in the kitchen getting his coffee when I arrived.

Robby took me to the side and looked around before telling me that our favorite salesperson, Mr. Harrison, was fired. He continued by mentioning the General Manager, Mr. Hanson, was still here doing his job. "Barbara, Mr. Hanson is a nice guy and owns 5% in the Walter-Weeks Corporation with radio stations throughout Florida. They are all under investigation by the Federal Communication Commission (FCC). I heard that the FCC has radio logs for 1974 and 1975 from January to now. Four months of logs are missing, totally missing. It is a mess, I know little about it, but hearsay," he went on to tell me. Robby was really nervous and had to get on the air in the next few minutes, so left me by saying, "Barbara, please be careful." The misplacement of radio logs was a federal offense and he knew when it happened. I had nothing to do with it.

The next evening around 8:00 PM, I received a call from my favorite salesperson, Mr. Harrison, which took me by surprise.

Barbara, I want to warn you now that I'm no longer associated with the company," he said. "Please be careful who you talk to. Since you're so proud of the book you may be writing, don't let Harry, the other salesperson, know anything about it. He'll probably try to get a kickback from it since he referred you to Mr. Colbath as your attorney. Harry's a liar and they knew this five years ago when they hired him, but he's a moneymaker, in spite of his faults. Set up an appointment with your attorney and make sure he doesn't let Harry know any more about the book, or you'll drop him like a hot potato. Now, I'm going to read you a letter from 1973, that Mary wrote on accounts that never actually ran on the air.

"Wait a minute, I don't want to hear all of this. Why are you telling me this Bob?"

"Barbara, you have to hear this. She has a running radio log of everything. I have the original. The other salespersons have copies. You have to know this because the FCC needs you and the bookkeeper, since you two will be involved in a trial."

I was in shock from hearing what I thought was not true. The following month proved that it was true. The FCC did come into question the bookkeeper and me.

"Good morning Barbara, I'm Mr. Gadsby with the Federal Communications Commission," the man in the navy suit sitting across from me said. "I want to thank you for seeing me. Now, we'll get down to business and don't be nervous because this is just a preliminary meeting. Did you realize, during the years 1974 and 1975 radio logs were misplaced, stolen or destroyed?"

"No, I did not," I answered, as my mind went elsewhere realizing I was being questioned by the FCC and could go to prison for lying. As I came back to the questioning, it appeared that Mr. Gadsby was satisfied with my answers. He thanked me as he got out of his chair to shake my hand and let me know, that he knew, I was not part of this charade.

I left the room and went back to my office to finish the day off writing commercials, eating lunch at my desk, and being annoyed that I had been questioned.

Being questioned was frightening to me. I was having nightmares about being kidnapped back in November of last year. I certainly did not need this.

The following week, Mr. Hanson, General Manager, came in to give me my paperwork and let me go, stating that the radio station was getting a smaller staff due to losing advertisers over the FCC fiasco. What he told me was a lie. I was given severance pay and went to my office not in shock, but relief that it was finally over.

The box under my desk had already been packed up a week before. I knew this day would come. When I reached my car, turned the key, and locked my doors, I began to cry. It was as if I was going to drown in my own tears. First being kidnapped, now this. It was too much to think about, but I realized that I was a survivor and God would not let me down.

Barbara, Beverly & Dale - 1974

I went downtown the next day and applied for unemployment compensation. That weekend, the three of us took a much-deserved mini vacation to Disney World in Orlando, Florida, thanks to my sister, Jackie. We all had so much fun, I do not know who giggled the most, whether it was Dale, Beverly, or Jackie. It was a miracle that we could all have fun and forget the horrors of the year before. I survived.

ANOTHER GREAT JOB

Being a survivor, I had to work to keep Dale in school and put food on the table. I stayed home for a month before I had to look for another job. When I got back from vacation my girlfriend, Betsy, told me to try *The National Enquirer* newspaper. I was already wallowing in self-pity when I was let go from WJNO. After being at Disney World for a weekend, we were all recharged and felt terrific. A few weeks later, I got dressed in a pretty aqua-flowered dress with matching heels and drove to of all places, *The National Enquirer*. I was going to apply for an opening for a secretarial position.

As I walked in the front glass doors, the receptionist asked what I needed. Then she walked me over to Human Resources. Mary Jane Smith introduced herself. She was the manager and asked if I would like a cup of coffee.

I said, "Thank you, but I've already had breakfast."

She explained that I needed to take a typing test. My resume was perfect due to all those years in radio and television.

"What made you come here?" she asked.

"I wanted to change careers and try this out," I said.

She could not know how frightened I was to take a typing test. I had been typing for years, but never had to take a typing test.

She walked me into another room and had me sit down at the desk. She told me I could take a sample test first. I put the paper in the typewriter, and she said, "Go." I typed my heart out, pushing the keys faster and faster until it was finally over. I failed the first test, due to being a nervous wreck, thinking someone knew my true story of being kidnapped.

The woman knew I could type and brought me a cup of decaf coffee so I could relax for a few minutes before taking it again. The second time I passed. Thank you, God, I said to myself. I was hired on the spot and was told to begin work on Monday.

I was happy working at *The National Enquirer* but intimidated by the fast-paced work. When a story came in, you typed what was dictated on your machine to be sent to the editors. Joan Kennedy's DUI story was one of the most sensational front-page headliners that month. I was impressed and proud when the story was completed and made the front page.

Nobody knew about me and my being kidnapped last year. I finally had a job that I liked again. When a blockbuster story was being developed, everybody involved was scrambling to get the news out by deadline. That was nerve racking and exciting at the same time. If your team was not busy, we were told to look occupied when the big boss, Mr. Pope came around.

When I met Mr. Generosa Pope the first time, he introduced himself and made me feel at home. Everybody admired him for his work ethic. At the end of each week, we took home a complimentary paper. One week they had an article on a Miracle Gel for osteoarthritis. My Aunt Nadine lived over in St. Petersburg, Florida, at the time and I sent her the article. She actually took it to her doctor and got a prescription for the miracle gel and it worked.

After working for a few more weeks, four of the staff took me to lunch at The Fish Market Restaurant nearby. I ordered fish and chips from the menu. Then noticed a Martini with an olive sitting in front of me. Oh, I really should not be drinking at lunch, I thought to myself.

"That's not mine, is it?" I asked.

"Yes. We're celebrating, Barbara. You've made it over three weeks. Drink up," they said.

I kept telling them I should not drink, but they insisted it was okay. Little did I know they were trying to pump me for information.

"Barbara, where did you work before you got this job?" one girl asked.

A few minutes later, another chimed in, "Did you ever work for a magazine or newspaper like ours?"

They thought I was a spy working for another newspaper, like *The Globe* or *The Star*? Laughing to myself, I finished lunch along with two drinks after babbling about my radio and television career as a copywriter. They will learn my true story soon enough, when I become famous, I thought to myself.

CHRISTMAS TIME–1975

DECEMBER 23, 1975

As the year went on with work and just living, I sat down at my typewriter and wrote Jim, a quick letter in Germany, about being kidnapped. He was stationed at Wiesbaden Air Force Base. This time, I finally had the guts to tell him I had been kidnapped by serial killer, Paul John Knowles. It took Jim over a week to process my letter. He had read and re-read the letter not believing it. Around 6 PM, Jim called me long distance from Germany. He was stunned.

"Barbara, I just finished reading your letter again. You're telling me that you were kidnapped by a serial killer?" he asked.

"Yes, I was."

"My God, Barbara why didn't you get a hold of me back then? I could have told my superiors that we were engaged, and I needed to get to West Palm Beach to be near you," he shouted into the phone.

"Jim, there was nothing you could have done. Jack couldn't even help me!" I said. The operator came back on and told Jim to put more money in the public phone.

"I don't care about Jack. Damn it, he's never going to marry you. You need me!" he stammered.

"I don't need anybody but God at this moment, Jim. I'm not over this yet. But we'll still write and remain friends for now."

"Okay, if that's what you want. I'll leave you alone to process it all. But when I get back to the States, I'm coming down to Florida. So, tell Jack to get lost! Barbara, I lov…." Then the phone was disconnected.

I sat on my bed, with the phone still in my hand. The buzzing sound reminded me to hang up the phone and go on with my life. Something had happened during that call. Something wonderful. I was happy to hear his voice. Jim's voice!

I called Eleanor and cried my heart out after telling her I told Jim about my being kidnapped. "Eleanor, he was mad at me for not telling him sooner. I think he said he loved me, but he hung up. What am I going to do?"

Jim would never be out of my life from that day on. But would he wait for me forever?

Jack brought the most beautiful Christmas tree on Christmas Eve morning. Our family got together that evening and we all had fun decorating the tree. Jackie and I made Mama's famous hot chocolate with marshmallows and a sprinkle of cinnamon on top, to make it look festive. The stockings were hung over the mantle with candy and small toys inside. Last year, we only had a few toys for Dale, because none of us cared. Dale was overly excited to go to bed early this night because he wrote Santa asking for a Red Ryder wagon. Dale never asked for much. His wish would come true this year because Aunt Jackie and her husband had bought a Red Ryder wagon for him. It was the best Christmas ever, for Dale.

ANOTHER GOOD JOB GONE

Before Christmas, I received a letter that almost took me over the edge. It was short, sweet and to the point,

Dear Barbara,

Thank you so much for your Christmas card. I was so happy to hear about your new job and it certainly sounds like an interesting enough place for you to be working. I have decided to send "Abduction" to Charles Heckelman who is the book editor for *The National Enquirer*. Does his name sound familiar to you? Best wishes for a beautiful holiday season. Warmest regards,

Peri Winkler.

Are you kidding me? Mr. Charles Heckelman? Does his name sound familiar? Yes! He is one of the bosses!

Yes, he works at *The National Enquirer* and will be showing Mr. Pope the book. Well, I had fun while it lasted. Here I go again; it would not be long before I would be losing this job.

Nobody knew I was kidnapped because I never told anyone. That was one secret I wanted to keep to myself. At the time, I realized nobody knew the truth about me. I hid my story all this time from the people I worked with at *The National Enquirer*. How many days would it take before they would get rid of me? How would I find another job to support my family? I thought to myself. Wow, it has been over a week, and nothing, I am still working. Praise the Lord.

I should never assume anything because a month later, Mary Jane, Human Resources Director, brought me into her office to let me know I was laid off. She explained that my position was no longer needed.   I thought I had 90 days to prove I could keep up with the work, but it was not meant to be. She handed me my paycheck that would last for the rest of the month, which I did not expect. We both got up, hugged each other, and said our goodbyes.

I would never become a famous writer. With little money and no job, I went home to have a few drinks. Once I got up the nerve, I would tell Jackie, Beverly, and Dale that I lost another job. What more could happen? In my heart, I knew the real reason I lost this job. Most people who learned of my being kidnapped could not wrap their heads around it—neither could I.

I would miss getting my free *National Enquirer* each week. I had to laugh and make jokes. That is how I coped since the day I was kidnapped. Gee, now I get to look for another job. Wait till the gossipers tell others I was let go because I did not work for another newspaper as a spy, I was actually kidnapped by a serial killer and the literary agent mailed my book to *The National Enquirer's* editor, one of my bosses. He would probably think, damn, we had the actual woman who was kidnapped by that serial killer and they laid her off. That is cold! What a front-page story we could have had. I said to myself, in the car driving home.

After I was laid off from *The National Enquirer,* I waited several weeks before finding my next job. For now, I had Jackie to help with the money situation. Jackie's husband, Jimmy, called from overseas and told her he would be back to the States the following month and could not wait to see her. Beverly, Dale, and I would miss her, but life would go on.

Dale, Jackie, Dennis & Beverly - 1981

Within a few years, Jackie and Jimmy divorced. Around 1977 or so, Jackie married Dennis.

I realized I needed to face another problem: Jack. I knew it was over between us and it was mostly my fault. He tried to make it work. The last straw was never being able to sell my book. I was drinking more than usual. Southern Comfort® with a twist of lemon was no longer comforting.

STATE VS. SHELDON YAVITZ

DECEMBER 20, 1976

Around two in the afternoon I was given my first subpoena from The State of Florida Third Judicial Circuit Court. Taylor County subpoenaed nine people and me. We were to personally appear before the Judge at the Court House in Perry, Florida on Thursday, February 17th, 1977 at 8:00 AM to testify on behalf of the State of Florida, Plaintiff, versus Sheldon Yavitz, Defendant.

I thought everything was over. I never wanted to have anything to do with this Sheldon Yavitz character. He was a sordid attorney, who allowed a serial killer to keep on killing at the expense of innocent victims, by accepting detailed tapes from each documented killing Knowles committed on his murderous cross-country rampage. Knowles told Yavitz that he was a serial killer and wanted to become as famous as Bonnie and Clyde approximately one to two months before I was kidnapped.

In my opinion, he needed to be locked up forever. How could Yavitz allow a person to keep on killing? Did Paul John Knowles threaten him or his family when they faced each other at the Georgia jail?

Yavitz, in my own mind, was just as bad as any serial killer by representing those types of people while posing as an upstanding attorney. Yavitz had the responsibility to the public at large to protect them from this vile and prolific killer. You cannot even imagine how one feels after having as traumatic an experience as I did. It not only affected me, but family and close friends too. And here I was, handed a subpoena to be a Witness for the State of Florida. The only saving grace was, hopefully, Florida would win against this living monster called an attorney. I believe in God, but I also believe in justice for all.

What else could happen in my life?

"Are they nuts!" I said to Beverly. "I just got this subpoena and I'm supposed to appear over in Perry, Florida. I'm calling Mr. Colbath. This is insane. I don't need to answer any more questions. I'm done!" "How much more can we all go through?"

After speaking with Marilyn, Mr. Colbath's secretary, she reassured me that if it were necessary to go, I would not be there by myself. So, I gave up. The judicial system was confusing to me, and once again I turned it over to God.

On January 24th, 1977, I received a letter from George R. Dekle, Sr., Chief Assistant State Attorney. In the letter, I was advised that "....the case of State vs. Sheldon Yavitz, Taylor County, for the crime of False Imprisonment, Robbery; Resisting Arrest with Violence, for which you should have received a subpoena to appear for trial on Thursday, February 17th, 1977, has been postponed from that day. You are, therefore, excused from having to appear on that day, and you will be subpoenaed again should your attendance be required on a future day."

I turned a copy of my letter over to my attorney, to let him figure it out. Why was I being subpoenaed in the first place? Let the State of Florida and Georgia do their own dirty work and put Paul John Knowles' scumbag attorney in prison. What could I offer? Enough was enough! The first subpoena was to be in Perry, Florida, where the State Trooper and businessman had been taken to Georgia and murdered in cold blood, in the woods, by Knowles. That was a day after I had gotten loose from the motel in Ft. Pierce back in November. It was all flooding back. I would never forget my horrifying experience. Neither would Beverly or Dale.

Everything was postponed for now, but I realized it was not over. Why would I want to face Sheldon Yavitz or Knowles' other attorney, Ellis Rubin? I think I heard that Ellis Rubin was representing Sheldon Yavitz. Why did I care? Again, I was thinking too much. I prayed that I would never have to face Yavitz. In my mind, he was highly corrupt and a criminal!

I became paranoid and frightened all over again. I could not let my guard down for a moment. I had to protect Beverly, Dale, and myself.

Could my life get any harder? I was writing my book about being kidnapped when I received the bad news. Mr. Walter Colbath, Marilyn, and Peri had done everything humanly possible to get my book published, but after receiving the last letter from Peri, it made it impossible to continue being represented by Walter. I thanked all of them for their great effort throughout the years. I never knew it would take so long to write, re-write, and re-write again, a book.

It was exhausting. I knew I was not a famous author, and this was my first book. It was over and we all gave it our best. I knew in my heart I had a compelling true story to tell. But it appeared now was not the time. I had to let go and let God do it in His time.

By now Jack was my ex-boyfriend, and we had gone our separate ways. His attorney would represent me, since I now had been subpoenaed to go to trial as a witness for the State of Florida again.

Jack moved out of town a few months before the trial. He was working as an aeronautical engineer in Pensacola, Florida. Our relationship was over even before learning the book would never sell. Jack was a good man, but marriage was never in the picture for him. Being kidnapped did not help either. At least he was nice enough to get his attorney, Mr. Martin Haines III, to represent me.

Beverly and I received subpoenas in May 1977. We were both to appear downtown at the Associated Court Reporters office to testify at different times on the afternoon of June 2, 1977. Mr. Haines' secretary called me that morning to tell me he had received the subpoena and would call me later. Beverly and I had a week to stress over it, but we both chose to turn it over to God.

COURT REPORTER'S OFFICE

JUNE 2, 1977

Eleanor took the day off from work and drove Beverly and me over to the court reporter's office since we were nervous wrecks. She was our support team and knew how stressed and upset we were the night before.

Beverly and I went downtown in West Palm Beach to the Associated Court Reporter's office to meet with the Assistant State Attorney Gabriel S. Dean, Sr. from Live Oak, Florida. Beverly and I were there for our dispositions. We arrived around 1:30 PM; Beverly appeared way calmer than me though she was not happy having to do a deposition for the State of Florida against attorney Sheldon Yavitz. We really did not understand the legal process. The State Attorney was a good guy, just doing his job. Beverly and I did not trust Yavitz.

We did not know how long it would take for the depositions. Beverly went first. When she got in the room to give her statements it was exactly 2:00 PM. She went into the room alone. That made me so upset I went down the hall to see if Mr. Dekle could make sure that she was not left alone with that crooked attorney!

Mr. Dekle got out of his chair and came with me to check on Beverly.

"Thank you so much. Nobody should be by themselves with anybody being questioned, not even me," I said.

We got to the door and he went in to check on Beverly. They had already finished. As Beverly was wheeled out the door, her face was pasty white, like she had just spoken with a ghost. I was worried about her. She had just been interrogated by Sheldon Yavitz who was representing himself for the deposition.

Beverly could hardly speak. "Beverly, honey what did he say to you?" I asked.

"He wanted to know everything that happened when I met Knowles. He made me so nervous. Barbara please be careful," she said.

"Eleanor, do you want to drive Beverly home and come back for me?" I asked.

"No, I'm staying here with Eleanor!" Beverly said. And she meant it. We were in this mess together.

Mr. Dekle reassured me that I would have someone in the room when I was questioned. Now, it was my turn to face the unknown. All the nightmares I had during the past month could not compare to seeing this person in real life. Was I dreaming this or was I just going mad?

I told Beverly and Eleanor I would try to keep my composure. Beverly reassured me that if I could come out alive from being kidnapped by a serial killer, I could handle meeting with this crooked attorney.

A few minutes later, I was escorted down the hall to the very room that Beverly was interrogated in. The door opened and there he was, the monster I had seen on television many, many times. He was very short and chubby with lots of dark hair and wore glasses over malevolent eyes. I was so upset I told him something like, "I don't know what the hell you made my sister tell you, but we should not be here with you."

He smiled a sheepish grin and went on to say he was so sorry if my sister, Beverly, was upset, but he needed to ask her questions.

I was so focused on Yavitz, I never saw the court reporter and Assistant State Attorney Dekle in the room. All I could do was stare at this criminal of an attorney that should be charged with accessory to first degree murder on several counts. Knowing he was just as guilty as Knowles, scared me to death.

Did he just ask me if Knowles actually raped me? I certainly would not answer that question. I would not answer personal questions at all. He already had the police reports; he knew all the answers Knowles wanted him to know. I felt like I was alone. Why was I with this idiot answering questions as if I were the murderer? I wanted to jump up and smack him. No, I wanted to jump up and kill him. Just like Knowles had killed others. Preferably with a gun. I would shoot him right between his beady eyes, I thought as he asked more questions. When he was finished, Mr. Dekle walked me out the door. Mr. Yavitz left via the Highway from hell in my mind. Somehow, we survived those atrocious depositions.

Beverly and I compared what took place with Eleanor while she drove us home. Yavitz did not get anything different from what he already knew from police records. We did not want Dale to know what really happened. He just turned nine in April. Dale was so proud of Aunt Beverly and me going to face the crooked attorney. Even though he did not really understand what was going on. Neither did Beverly nor I for that matter.

We picked up Chinese takeout on the way home. Eleanor helped me bring two large bags with three separate dinners into the house. After placing them on the kitchen counter, Dale was right there.

"Mom hurry up. I'm starving. I only had a peanut butter and jelly sandwich a few minutes ago," he said.

He was thrilled when he grabbed the bags and opened them to find one of his favorite meals, fried rice with fried chicken wings. Beverly had Egg Foo Young and I had Shrimp Chow Mein with fried rice.

"Thank you so much, Eleanor, for being there for us today," I said as I hugged her goodbye. Bob was grilling steaks, so she left to be with her husband and children.

June 3, 1977

Honorable George R. Dekle, Sr.

Dear Mr. Dekle:

Yesterday's episode from 2:00 p.m. to 4:30 p.m. at the Associated Court Reporter's office meeting with you and your associate was an experience I shall not forget. I am writing you a short letter to ask this. Is it possible for you to get a copy of the Thursday, June 2, 1977, deposition? I did not ask for a copy from Mr. Sheldon Yavitz, as I did not feel comfortable in

```
that situation and did not put much
trust in him hearing that from my
lips.

Sincerely,

Mrs. Barbara Tucker
```

Mr. Dekle, Sr. never wrote back, so Jack's attorney became my new personal attorney, Mr. Martin Haines III. That same day, I typed a letter to Jack's attorney, hoping for an answer to my question about getting a copy of the deposition.

The months flew by and I just hung in there. I was never subpoenaed by the State vs. Sheldon Yavitz to go up to Perry, Florida for a trial. Thank God. Maybe this was coming to an end!

NEW JOB, AGAIN

I knew God still had a plan for me. My handicapped twin sister, son and I survived. It was over. We all became more aware of our surroundings. We all lived each day to the fullest, helping those in need.

In the beginning of 1978, I applied for a job at Palm Beach Junior College when it was in West Palm Beach. I could not believe who I saw when applying for the job as secretary: my high school Problems of American Democracy teacher. He was one of my favorite teachers. Go figure. God is good. When Mr. Robert D'Angio, Sr. came out of his office and saw me, he came over and hugged me. "Barbara! First off, I glanced at your resume and you are just what we need. You're hired!" Then he went on, "Remember when you were in my class in high school and I yelled out Barbara, look out, as I threw an eraser at Doug?"

"Yes, I do remember. I did not duck, and you clobbered me in the forehead with the eraser. It left a bump on my forehead for a week," I replied.

"Well, Barbara if you had any sense back then you could have sued me."

I am glad I did not sue him, because he would not have hired me. I loved being his secretary. He was a great person with a quick sense of humor that I loved.

Jim Abel came back into my life about six months after getting my job at the college. We had kept in touch with each other, as friends, since our meeting in 1973, when Jim went over to Germany with the Air Force. Apparently, Jim called Beverly and she gave him my work number. Marilyn, my co-worker, answered the phone.

Jim while in USAF - 1977

"Hello, is Barbara Tucker there?" he asked.

"Yes, she is but she's in the other room with her boss. Can I take a message?" she answered.

"I'm Jim Abel calling long distance from a phone booth in Jacksonville."

"Are you the Jim that's in the Air Force?" she asked.

"Yes, but now I'm in the Navy!"

"Wait a minute. I'm going to interrupt them and get her on the phone. Hold on. Don't hang up." She came and got me, I turned red thinking about Jim again. I even got goose bumps, as I grabbed the phone. I hurried to my chair and sat down to talk to him.

"Hi Jim, how are you doing and what's this I hear you're in Jacksonville in the Navy?"

"Listen I don't have much time but wanted to know if I catch a Greyhound bus tomorrow to come to see you, will you be home?' he asked.

"Of course, I'll be home for you. What time do you arrive? I'll pick you up at the bus station." I answered.

"Great, Darling. I'll see you tomorrow at 10 AM at the bus station. Got to go, I love…." as he hung up the phone.

"Marilyn, he's coming tomorrow by bus for the weekend. I'm so excited. Oh, and I think he said he loved me. He hung up before I could ask."

Mr. D'Angio came out of his office to find out what was going on. "What's this I hear? Your young man mentioned love?" he said smiling. Then he got serious. "Enough of this love stuff. I need to get these letters out today," he said as he headed back into his office with me trailing behind him carrying my stenographer's pad and pencil.

I told Beverly and Dale that Jim was coming to visit for the weekend. They were both happy because I seemed so happy. I could not wait for tomorrow to get here. Why was I so excited? Did he really say he loved me?

I got butterflies in my stomach as I pulled into the parking lot of the Greyhound bus station. That is when I noticed Jim from afar waving to me. Damn, he is so handsome, I forgot what a hunk he was. As I walked up to Jim, he grabbed me and lovingly kissed me. As I turned red, I noticed other people walking by.

Jim put his duffle bag in the back seat, and we headed home on the beautiful scenic route along the water. Pulling into the driveway of my home, the front door opened, and out came Dale, running to the car to welcome Jim.

The weekend was wonderful. That afternoon, Jim, Beverly, Dale, and I went to Dreher Park Zoo. The next evening, Jim and I enjoyed a night out after dinner. Jim and I drove over to the beach and parked since Jim had something to tell me. "Barbara, do you really know how I feel? I'm falling in love with you. I haven't been able to get you out of my mind and dreams, ever since you were kidnapped."

"Oh Jim, I know I've fallen in love with you already," I said, as we leaned toward each other and made out. Wow, what a kisser.

The next morning, I drove him to the bus station. With heavy hearts, we said goodbye, promising to keep in touch. As he entered the bus, Jim said he loved me.

"I love you too!"

NEVER SAY NEVER—I'M GETTING MARRIED

Several months went by before Jim came to visit for another weekend. "Remember what we said to each other the last time I was here to visit you Barbara?" Jim said.

"Jim, I never realized you felt that way. Does this mean you truly love me?" I said smiling up into his sparkling blue eyes. He grabbed me and kissed me tenderly letting me know he did love me. I was not damaged goods in his mind, and I would allow him to love and protect me and my family in the future.

The next few months flew by when Jim visited again. We could not get enough of each other.

Jim was nearby when, out of the blue, I decided to play a joke on him. I called my minister to ask if they had an opening for us to get married in June. The minister said, "Yes." He was busy and would call me later that week with details. As I hung up the telephone, I almost burst out laughing.

Jim was beginning to sweat and said, "What did you just do?"

I was so embarrassed, I turned beet red and began to cry.

"Barbara don't cry. I want to marry you. I've loved you for years, but Jack was in the way. Yes, darling let's plan on getting married in June. That will give us about six months," he said. He knelt on one knee, held my hand to kiss it, and asked, "Barbara, will you marry me?"

"YES, yes, yes," I said. I lost all composure. I threw myself into his big strong arms and began crying out with joy!

He adored Beverly and loved Dale. It was a match made in heaven. Jim had left the Navy to join the Air Force, then quit the Air Force to marry me.

I was marrying the love of my life, my soulmate, my friend. Not only was he built like a football quarterback, but most important, he knew how to shoot a gun. He was my hero and would protect me from bad people, forever.

Eleanor picked me up to take me to find a wedding dress at an outlet store. I was nervous and excited. We were like two teenagers looking around for the perfect wedding dress.

"Barbara, what do you think of this one?" she said as she handed me a dress to try on.

"Eleanor, this dress is beautiful!" I said as I came out to show her. It was a sleeveless, floor-length chiffon gown in multiple-colored flowered print with a flowing cape at the shoulders. It was the only dress I tried on. It was so elegant and perfect.

After lunch, Eleanor took me to different hotels to check out for our honeymoon night. She and Bob would give us the hotel room as a gift before we headed up to Ohio with Dale to meet Jim's family for the first time. I had talked to Goldie, Jim's mother, a few times during the months before the wedding. She just wanted to know if I really loved her baby son. I was nervous just at the thought of meeting them.

MARRYING MY SOULMATE

JUNE 21, 1980

The wedding was held at Unity on Flagler Drive in West Palm Beach overlooking the waterfront. Jim was smiling as I walked down the aisle. The wedding dress Eleanor and I picked out was beautiful. My floor length pastel flowered chiffon dress and satin heels made me feel like a princess.

As the wedding began, the pastor tried to get Jim's attention since he was on another planet. My brother-in-law took his false teeth out and smiled at Jim. I gasped in horror, then began laughing. Everybody who saw it began laughing. Jim came back to earth and the pastor said the vows. "Jim, do you take Barbara to be your lawfully wedded wife?"

"I do," he said proudly.

As the pastor finished the ceremony he said to Jim, "You may now kiss the bride."

Jim leaned over and kissed me on the lips. We walked down the aisle listening to my family and friends crying for joy. We were both relieved Jim did not faint.

Afterwards, we went to the reception to eat, dance, and have fun before heading out to the local hotel to celebrate for the night.

The next morning, we headed over to the house to pick up Dale, as we left for our honeymoon in Ohio. Squeaky, Jim's younger sister told Jim on the phone to bring Dale over to stay with them when we arrived. She had two boys around the same age as Dale and they could play together. I was thankful that Jim's sister invited Dale to say with them so we could have a real honeymoon.

Jim was the last of 10 children; one died at birth. The old, quaint, two-story farmhouse was built in 1850 and was very different from the one-story CBS block homes built in Florida back in the 1950's.

Meeting Jim's mother and father for the first time was an experience I will never forget. I pictured in my mind, months before, that they were the stoic couple from the Grant Wood painting "American Gothic," with his dad holding the pitchfork and mother standing next to him. I wasn't even close.

Goldie was 5'4" tall, with hazel eyes, short snow-white hair, and a loving smile like Jim's. She took me in her arms and hugged me, like she had known me for years. Then she took me by the hand and introduced me to those sitting around the kitchen table, gawking at me. First, there was Helen, Jim's oldest sister. She stood up and greeted me with a hug. She was about six feet tall and looked like her brother. Next was Carol, "Squeaky." who was a really skinny, cute girl with shoulder length brown hair. She got the name Squeaky because that is what she did when she was a baby. I thought that was unusual, but then my name was now Barbara Mabee Abel, so I could not say anything. Her hubby, Larry, was there. I just stared at him because he could have been John Denver's twin. Next was Kenny, Jim's brother, and his wife, Donna, whom everybody thought reminded them of me. He looked like Jim, and Donna was beautiful. I would meet the rest of the family the next day since most were working. Squeaky and Larry took Dale home with them to stay for the week and meet their two boys, Mark and Jeff.

On Saturday, a picnic was set up with the entire family at Squeaky's home in the boondocks. Since I was a city gal from Florida everything out in the country amazed me. Squeaky and Larry lived on five acres of land. Her farmhouse was pretty. It was two stories with a large kitchen next to the living room. From the living room windows, you could look out to the neighbors 100 acres of land across the road. Some neighbors raised cows, chickens, and hogs. Squeaky had a cornfield out back. She also had a large garden with strawberries, tomatoes, cucumbers, lima beans, pole beans, and squash.

Goldie and Hubert, Jim's mother and father, rode with us to his sister's home. We were the first to arrive. Helen, Kenny, and Donna came 20 minutes later with cake and fried chicken. Jim's older brothers, Sonny and Lewis, brought their wives Doris and Little Helen. Jack and Rose came with a large ham. Patty and Andy brought potato salad. Charlotte and Richard brought baked beans.

Cee Cee was Jim's niece and showed up to make sure it was okay that I married her favorite uncle. One by one, all the brothers, sisters, and Jim's nieces and nephews arrived. I could not remember all their names at the time. It was a wonderful day.

It was a wonderful day. We played softball after supper out near the cornfields. I changed into my short shorts with a pink, cashmere sweater and sneakers. Jim did not know I was on the Girl's Athletic Team in high school and could play softball like a champ. Everybody was amazed that this prissy young woman with long red fingernails, hot strawberry blonde, flowing shoulder-length hair, blue eyes, and fabulous figure could hit a baseball out into the corn fields then run around all the bases. I cheerfully gazed into family's faces as they gawked at me in wonder.

This is what life is all about: God, family, and friends. We were doing very well. Beverly had her problems with Cerebral Palsy as we both got older, but she was a trooper and still walked with crutches and braces.

As the years passed, everything was drama free. We had a large extended family to visit in Ohio, Georgia, and Florida, at different times of the year when we could get our vacations at the same time. Life was good.

After high school in 1987, Dale met and fell in love with Ginger, who had a baby daughter, Amanda. They married, and a year later had Bobby, another bundle from heaven. Even though their marriage did not last, we still love them.

Later in the 1990's, Dale met and finally found his soulmate, Gloria. She is a beautiful Italian American woman with dark wavy black hair, brown eyes, and a figure like Dolly Parton's. We were so happy for them. They were blessed with a son, Jeremy, and later Mia.

Jim's daughter, Mary Sue, got married in the 1990's. She had four beautiful children—Crystal, Trudy, Amber, and Dustin.

Between two marriages, Jim and I have 10 grandchildren and six great-grandchildren to carry on our legacy. *What a blessing from God.*

AUGUST 1990

Over 500,000 American Troops were deployed to Saudi Arabia as part of Desert Shield in case Iraqi troops attacked Saudi Arabia. On January 15, 1991, Operation Desert Shield became Operation Desert Storm. Desert Storm became the largest air campaign since the conflict in Southeast Asia.

Jim was in the United States Air Force Reserves, stationed at Homestead Air Base in Homestead, Florida. He received notice to serve our country at Shaw Air Force Base in Sumter,

Jim Abel in USAF 1983 with Aunt Nadine

South Carolina the following month.

Our family and friends gave him a going away party over at Jackie's home. Dale was now 23 years old, happily married and was an artist. The most beautiful gift was given to Jim from Dale. He painted an American flag, tank, and jet on the outboard motor of his Jim's Skeeter bass boat that he was taking up to South Carolina to serve our country. We prayed that he did not have to go overseas and fight the war. We were leaving it in God's hands.

The next day, he headed off to Sumter, South Carolina, in his Bronco, pulling his Skeeter bass boat and motor, with the beautiful paintings on it. I could not believe he was taking his boat. But that was Jim. He would be in Sumter near a lake. He had no idea how long this war would last or how long he would be away from us. He would escape occasionally with his boat and fish for fun.

The Air Force put Jim and other reservists up in hotels because there was no room on the base. For the next few months, Jim was working on the base in plumbing and heavy equipment. Luckily, most of the reservists went home early because the war was winding down.

When the war was over and Jim had been home for a few months, he learned from a friend that if he stayed in SC for two more weeks, he would have been shipped overseas.

While Jim was gone, I worked as an Administrative Assistant to the Director of Purchasing at The Breakers Hotel in Palm Beach. When Jim finally came home, he waltzed in the door scaring us. He was home early. We were thrilled to see him. He lifted me up in his arms and gave me a big kiss. Beverly began crying and our dog, RJ, was jumping up and down waiting to be petted. We called Dale and Gloria to tell them Dad was home.

A party was scheduled a week later at The Breakers Hotel in Palm Beach. It would honor all the men and women who served during this war. It was magnificent. All servicemen and women wore uniforms. Their spouses or friends wore suits and dressy dresses.

It was like a gala event for millionaires. We were so proud that this event was for our servicemen and women and their families who served this great United States of America.

Beverly, Jim, and I met our son and his wife in the lobby. Eleanor and Bob got there before us and saved us seats in the ballroom. The ballroom was whimsical. Everything surrounding us was in living colors of red, white, and blue. The chandeliers sparkled from above.

Jim and others were amazed at the ballroom decorated with the United States Flags. Each table had beautiful centerpieces of red, white, and blue carnations with the American flag in the center. Jim looked so handsome in his uniform. I knew later that evening we would be making mad, passionate love again, because he was my hero!

The chefs did a brilliant job with their choices of food that lined several tables at one side of the spacious ballroom. One by one, each table was called to the buffet to get their food. The orchestra was playing in the background, all patriotic songs to make the servicemen and women feel proud to have served this great country. *God Bless America* was sung by a local woman soprano, booming out the song on stage.

It was a magical evening. When it was time for dessert, everybody went to another room. We could not believe the cake the chefs made. It was eight feet by four feet in red, white, and blue sitting on two huge tables. The white cake was decorated with red strawberries, and blueberries to look just like our American flag. It was delicious. Of course, Jim, had to get about six other types of dessert along with the cake. He loves sweets. The entire evening was great.

I WANT TO BE AN ANGEL

DECEMBER 1999

The United Methodist Church of the Palm Beaches was where I performed in plays each year since 1992, when Jim and I joined the church. After joining the choir, I never realized I would be participating in the Christmas Dinner Theatre plays each year. The first time I was in a play, I was petrified. Cheryl, my friend from the choir and neighbor, conned me into being in the plays. Cheryl and I would goof off and be overly dramatic. Sometimes our choir director would get frustrated and tell us to calm down a bit, but we never did.

Practice began in August and went up to the first week in December. It was tedious, but worth seeing strangers faces laughing or crying. The play ran from Wednesday through Friday with a dinner. Saturdays were the matinee performance, with a cookie and punch reception afterwards.

December 1999, I had about five costume changes. I began feeling disorientated and started losing my memory. One scene had 12 angels and when I heard their song it was beautiful. I remember asking one of the sopranos, who was picked to be an angel if I could take her place.

Barbara as the Angel

She asked, "Why do you want to be an angel so badly, Barbara?"

I looked straight at her and said, "Because I won't be here for next year's play."

"Why? Are you moving?"

"No, I'm not moving." I refused to answer because I thought I would be dead. I was an angel with the help of a few friends who knew I was sick and helped me get through the play.

After the play, I began having migraine headaches. They not only made me sick to my stomach, I was dizzy, and when I laid down, I could not move or even cry. I drove myself to a neurologist, who found nothing. Nothing? I knew something was wrong.

A week later, I was cleaning house when my ear felt like it was on fire. A few minutes later, I had a terrible earache. I called my primary doctor and set up an emergency appointment that morning with an ENT. Thank God Jim took off work. We all were very afraid; Jim, Beverly, and I knew something dreadful was going on with my health.

The specialist looked into my eyes, ears, and throat and knew exactly what the problem was. I had an arteriovenous malformation (AVM) in the front part of my brain between my eyebrows. Beverly had cerebral palsy since birth, and I had this since birth. It was not cancer, but it was life threatening. I was told if anything happened out of the ordinary, a slight headache, fever, vomiting, to call an ambulance, and go to the nearest hospital. The ENT called and faxed information about my condition for an MRI to my primary doctor and neurologist.

Two days later, Jim took me to St. Mary's Hospital for my appointment to have an MRI that would take over two hours. Jim kissed me goodbye and left me there with the nurses. They helped me lay down in this massive machine, after putting something on my head to hold it still during the procedure. Then a nurse explained the process. I would have dye put in my arm for the second part of the imaging. It was scary, but I knew it needed to be done.

When the procedure first began, it startled me. The tech asked if I was okay and I answered "Yes." The series of noises began, and I was told not to move an inch. If my nose itched, I would have to tell the staff and they would come and scratch it.

As the clinking and clanking began, it was like a melody. The next series was an annoying rat-a-tat-tat, then loud jarring noises followed next, making me nervous. I willed myself to think of something good. As the MRI machine did its magic over and over with the same harsh noises, I slipped into a trance-like state.

I thought of the stark, white, silky costume with silver sparkling stars on the wings along with the halo perched on my head, making me feel like an angel. I danced and sang with the other angels and wanted this feeling to last forever. When I woke up and realized that I had been dreaming about the time I played the part of an angel in our Christmas play, it made me smile.

When finished, the nurse came over to help me up from the massive machine. She whispered, "Barbara, please get this taken care of soon, Honey. It's nothing to mess with. You could die."

My neurologist that told me I was alright but was scared my husband would sue him if I died. I told Jim earlier to get an attorney if I died. How could a skilled neurologist not have caught an AVM that was life threatening?

I was sent to Dr. Jordan Grable, a famous neurosurgeon who treated patients from all over the world. When Jim and I met him the first time, we could tell right away that he knew what he was doing. The doctor explained the procedure to be done in detail. It was called gamma radiosurgery, also known as gamma knife surgery, and because my AVM was large, it would take about four hours to complete. He then explained that if I got a fever, headache, or eyesight changes to immediately go to the emergency room to make sure I was not having an aneurysm. They scheduled the procedure for two months later, so I would be able to get my affairs in order in case I died.

That weekend, Jim and I went up to Madison, Florida, to be with our friends, Eleanor and Bob. They notified their pastor at church to put us in the prayer.

Sunday, June 25, 2000, our friends took us to their church. Pastor Steve greeted us and led us forward to be seated in the front row seats next to a young couple, Sandy and her husband. "Before we begin the service, I'd like to introduce you to Jim and Barbara Abel from West Palm Beach. Barbara and Sandy are facing brain surgeries, so let's put them in silent prayer right now," he said.

Bob & Eleanor

Just looking over at this beautiful young woman and her husband, caused my heart to be filled with sadness. Not for myself who had lived a long life, but for her. She was so young. Please Lord, let her live a long life, I said to myself.

What a wonderful sermon the pastor gave. Eleanor and Bob told us we were going to another room to have people pray for us. Sandy and her husband were in their early 20s with a small, adorable two-year-old daughter. They would be sitting across the table from Jim and me. Some of the parishioners stayed to lay hands on Sandy and me. It is obvious I always believed in miracles. I was not worried any longer about myself, but about Sandy.

August 20, 2000, Jim brought me to Good Samaritan Hospital for my gamma radiosurgery procedure. Reverend David McEntire, our pastor, met us in the waiting room. He knew a head nurse from church who explained the entire procedure after showing him where the gamma radiosurgery would be performed. He came back out to where I was waiting to be wheeled upstairs for a new MRI and explained in detail what Dr. Grable would be doing. It was fascinating to hear, especially from my pastor. Then he said an inspiring prayer.

Before the surgical procedure was to begin, I was wheeled down the hall of the hospital carrying my new MRI results on my belly. As I put it up to the light, I noticed the spot that used to be the size of a half dollar had shrunk. Of course, I was on some good stuff, so I let it pass until my surgeon told me afterwards that the procedure did not take four hours like expected. It only took two. I survived. Reverend David was there with friends and family for support.

A year later, little did I know, I would be telling Reverend David McEntire another miraculous story from

1974, after I had received a certified letter from a movie company.

NEW DOMINION PICTURES?

FRIDAY, AUGUST 24, 2001

Around 11:30 AM, Airborne Express knocked on the front door. I was doing dishes in the kitchen when Beverly yelled out, "Barbara, somebody's at the front door. Can you get it? I'm lying down."

I walked from the kitchen to the front door, feeling strange. The man was holding a large envelope and asked if I was Mrs. Barbara Abel.

I said, "Yes."

He handed me the envelope and asked, "Would you please sign here?" He then pointed to the receipt on the tablet. After signing the receipt, he said, "Have a great day," and left.

I wondered who in the world would mail me this package from New Dominion Pictures. Since Beverly was lying down in her bedroom, I took the package to the kitchen table, laid it down, and went to the refrigerator to get some iced tea. I sat down at the table, drank a few sips of tea, and opened the following certified letter from New Dominion Pictures, Suffolk, Virginia. It began:

Dear Mrs. Abel:

We would like to inform you that New Dominion Pictures is producing a two-hour cable television special profiling the police investigation into the crimes of Paul John Knowles and his eventual capture. New Dominion Pictures is a television production company producing several series for the Discovery Channel and The Learning Channel including: The New Detectives: Case Studies in Forensic Science, FBI Files, The Prosecutors, and Daring Capers. Our programming always focuses on the work of law enforcement.

We are working with local law enforcement agencies to profile this case including investigators from the West Palm Beach Police Department, the Florida Highway Patrol, and the Federal Bureau of Investigation. Other law enforcement agencies we are working with on this case include the Atlantic Beach Police Department, the Jacksonville Beach Police Department, the Duval County Sheriff's Office, the Duval County District Attorney's Office, the Milledgeville Police Department, and the Georgia Bureau of Investigation.

As our policy, we have changed the victims' names in this story. We would also like to extend to you the opportunity to participate in an on-camera interview.

Please feel free to contact me at our toll-free number.

Best Regards,

Shelly Andrews, Researcher

This letter would change my life, again, having to bring up painful memories of the kidnapping from almost 27 years ago.

After reading this letter more than one time to let it sink in, I burst out crying. The hairs on my arms stood up and I began to sweat. What was happening to me? My anxiety was coming back.

My mind began to have flashbacks like in a movie. I was being forcibly violated once again. The shock of the letter sent me back to that time in 1974. The vision ended with a sawed-off shotgun being aimed at my head as I heard in my mind *BANG, BANG!*

I shook my head to clear it and began to think about what was best for Beverly and me. If we decided to do the interview, we would have to relive our past nightmares all over again. Was it worth it?

My head fell between my arms on the kitchen table as I laid it down to cry again. I jumped halfway out of my skin when a hand touched my shoulder.

"Barbara, why are you crying? What's in that letter? Did somebody die?" Beverly asked.

"No Beverly, we just got a letter from New Dominion Pictures and they are doing a film on Paul John

Knowles. Take it into the living room and read it from your chair. You'll need to sit down," I explained.

After she read it, she said, "No way am I going to participate in an on-camera interview making that bastard out to be a hero. Besides after all these years, why and the hell is somebody doing a story on him? Nope, my answer is no! Call that lady researcher and tell her we won't do it. Period!" she yelled out.

We both were scared to death again, as the memories flooded in front of our eyes, memories we had chosen to forget. It was 27 years later, and New Dominion Pictures was doing a documentary on a Paul John Knowles, the serial killer. We both had to wrap our heads around this news and calm down.

I put the letter away then looked in the cupboards to find peanut butter to make sandwiches for lunch. The buzzer from the stove went off and jolted me back to reality. I turned the timer off, put my oven mitts on to fetch the cookies from the oven. As I opened the door, the aroma of hot baked chocolate chip cookies floated into the kitchen. I baked them for Jim to eat when he got home from work because he loved them.

After lunch, Beverly and I went for a ride to Palm Beach. As we parked, I helped her out of the car and went to the nearest bench to sit down and see the ocean and watch people swimming and having fun. We both needed to get out of the house to clear our minds on that letter we just read.

"Barbara, look out there, look at that good looking man. He's gorgeous. What a tan," Beverly said.

"Yeah, Beverly, you're really looking at the guy's tan," I said with a smile. "Beverly, if you're finished gawking at those hunks out there, let's go home."

Jim, my husband of 21 years, was still at U.S. Foodservice working until around six or seven that evening. He was a truck driver and loved his job. Today he got up at 5 AM and had to work overtime on a run to Miami because his co-worker was out sick.

Jim - US Foods - 2003

We were so proud of Jim. He had retired from the Air Force Reserve in 1993, after serving in Desert Storm. He served in the military for a total of 26 years and is my hero. I had to think of how to tell him about the letter after he ate supper. I made one of his favorite meals of meatloaf with gravy, creamy mashed potatoes, corn, and chocolate chip cookies along with sweet tea.

Jim came home around 6:30 PM. "Honey, I'm here. What smells so good?" he shouted out. I was in the kitchen setting the table for Beverly, Jim, and me for dinner. We had a great meal and Jim was very happy. Afterwards, we went into the living room to wait for our favorite program to begin. We would watch *Frasier* with Kelsey Grammar in about 15 minutes. I finally got my nerve up, walked over with the New Dominion Pictures letter, and handed it to Jim to read before the show began.

He read it and asked, "What are you two going to do? Are you going to be in the show?" By that time, I had enough time to think about helping victims of crime by telling my side of the story in the movie.

I answered, "Yes, I'm going to call them tomorrow and tell them my answer is yes."

Beverly was still thinking and did not want Jim to know she had said no.

After we went to bed that evening, Jim leaned over and said, "Darling, I'm so proud of you and Beverly for all you've been through in your lifetime, dealing with being kidnapped. Do you both really want to go through that nightmare again?"

"Yes, honey, we've dealt with this our entire lives, all three of us, Beverly, Dale, and me. God got us through it in 1974, and He will be with us now, no matter what Beverly and I decide to do about the interview."

Dale was so young, and he suffered so much. It tears me apart just thinking about my courageous son being tied up to Beverly. How did he cope knowing I was taken away by a bad man? I would never ask Dale to be a part of this new chapter of my life. I want to help other victims of crime by telling this story.

"Jim, I have to tell Dale about this soon. That will be the toughest thing to do all these years later. I don't want to bring up bad memories, I need to pray about what needs to be said to my son, Jim. I want Dale to understand this is to help other victims of crime. The story is not about making Paul John Knowles a hero, or me, it's simply to help others who are suffering."

I began to cry and let it all out, as Jim took me in his arms. He let me get it out of my system for the moment. I had no idea how I would get through this. I felt God was making this happen. Beverly could not handle it; she already told me she would not do an interview, ever!

The next day after breakfast, I called the number the researcher gave me. She was not at her desk, so I left word. Beverly and I were finished with breakfast. I was going into my closet to pull out the paperwork I had saved from the nightmare of 1974 up through 1978. All the newspaper articles, subpoenas, letters from the literary agent, attorneys, some had turned brownish yellow. They were 27 years old. What did I expect and why had I saved everything?

As I leafed through the papers, I came across a green scrapbook. When I opened it up I began to tear up. It was a scrapbook Mrs. Thomas, our across the street neighbor, made for me in the '70s. It had all the newspaper articles from the Palm Beach Post and the Miami Herald from Friday, November 15 - December 21, 1974, right after he was killed while trying to escape from the police in Georgia.

As I began going through the box, I lifted a picture that was taken from the West Palm Beach Police Department of me in black and white. Damn, what happened to me? I was beautiful back then. I snapped back into reality when the telephone rang.

Barbara Tucker - 1974

"Barbara, telephone. It's somebody named Sherry," my sister yelled out.

"Tell her I'll be with her in a minute," I replied. I placed the box on top of my bed then took the phone from Beverly and sat down.

"Hello, this is Barbara Abel."

"Good morning Barbara, I'm Sherry Anderson, Researcher for New Dominion Pictures. I will need your e-mail address so we can correspond with what both of us need in the following days for the interview.

"Beverly already told me she does not want to be interviewed and I respect her wishes. We will be setting up the interview date within the following months. We would like you to fly up to Suffolk, Virginia, to be recorded in our studio for New Dominion Pictures. We can pay you $200 for participating. You can at least go out to dinner," she joked. After talking back and forth for about 10 minutes she told me she would e-mail me what was needed.

After getting off the phone, Beverly told me she changed her mind when she heard me say I would get paid $200. Then added, "Do I get $200 also?"

"Beverly that's changing everything, you can't fly up to Virginia. You'd better make sure you really want to be interviewed. You can think about it overnight," I told her.

"No, I've made up my mind, I'm part of this also and want to help victims of crime also, so it's a yes. Call her or e-mail her." she finished with a big smile.

"Okay, I'll e-mail her," I added.

A few minutes later, I was typing an e-mail to Sherry.

Dear Sherry,

Thank you for calling and putting
me at ease over the interview.
Beverly changed her mind and wants
to be interviewed but is afraid to
fly. Can you come to West Palm
Beach and do the interview in a
local hotel? When you called
yesterday, I realized your
producers wanted to tape in our
home, but our family is against it.
We also need our names changed and
the taping had to be backlit, not
showing our faces. Otherwise, we
will not do the interviews. We have
to protect ourselves. Will Beverly
receive $200 also? How long will
the interviews take, and will you
send questions to each of us?

Thanks, Barbara.

Sherry e-mailed back the next morning. She told
me she appreciated our willingness to participate in the
program. She would be speaking with her producer, Mike
Sinclair, about the date for the interviews. They were also
planning on interviewing Eugene Flynn, former FBI
special agent who worked on the case. They had already
interviewed Jim Griffin, James Gabbard, and Greg
Parkinson, all formerly of the West Palm Beach Police
Department.

They were not planning on interviewing Sheldon
Yavitz because the last they heard, he was sent to prison
on a money laundering charge and was disbarred.

I called the church to speak with Rev. David McEntire. His secretary told me he was in a meeting and would call me back within the hour. I asked the office manager if he could fit me in for an emergency appointment. I needed to see him today, if possible. After hanging up the phone, I went to the scrapbook with newspaper articles and picked out one with Paul John Knowles and my picture on it with the headline story depicting me being kidnapped. I never told anyone in the choir or even the pastor about what happened. I only told the United Methodist Church of the Palm Beaches Elizabeth Circle Women's Group. They were my friends and people I trusted not to judge me and tell others.

I prayed to the dear Lord to give me the strength to explain to the pastor what happened and if he would help Beverly and me when they finally set up the interviews. The phone rang; it was Mildred, the office manager, asking me if I could come over now. I told her I would be over in about 15 minutes. I grabbed my paperwork and kissed Beverly goodbye.

"I'll say a prayer for you Barbie," she said as I headed out the door.

Reverend David greeted me as I entered his office. He offered me a seat. I sat stiffly in the chair, took a deep breath, and told him I had been kidnapped in November 1974, by a serial killer. I laid a few newspaper articles on his desk for him to see. I could see the look of sheer surprise and concern on his face.

"Barbara, this is hard to understand. This happened to you in 1974?"

After nodding, I went on to explain we needed a support team. Beverly and I could not do this alone.

He was trying to grasp the sheer horror we must have gone through. I then handed Sherry's letter from New Dominion Pictures to him.

"How in the world did you three survive this? Now, they are asking you both to be in a *Movie of the Week* on Discovery," he said, then added, "Let me look at my schedule for September and October. Tell me the exact date as soon as you can."

After we finished, he prayed over me. We hugged and he told me he would try to be there during the interview. As I walked to my car, I got the uncontrollable urge to cry because I had held this story in my soul all these years. Who would have figured it would come out to haunt us 27 years later?

There was a reason. God knew what was happening. I started the engine and just sat there and began crying. All the hurt and humiliation came flooding back into my soul. I slowly pulled myself together because I believed it was happening for a reason.

After I got home, I told Beverly that Reverend David would try to be there for us during the interview, if possible. Beverly made chicken noodle soup with crackers for lunch. "Thank you, Beverly, I needed to eat," I said.

After lunch, I was curious and e-mailed Sherry.

I went to ask our pastor if he
would be a part of our support
team, he said yes. As soon as you
have a date, I will call him. In
the meantime, how did your company
come up with this story after 27
years?

That afternoon Sherry replied,

As far as the story idea—at the
beginning of this year I was trying
to find good cases for several 2-
hour specials. I consulted a
number of sources such as
newspapers, Internet research,
books, etc. I found a short blurb
on the case in a book titled Blood
Letters and Badmen. It's a
compilation book of various crimes
in American history. I thought the
case sounded interesting but
really didn't know that much about
it. And no one I talked to here
had ever heard of the case before.
We thought it was worthy of
additional research to see if
there was a story there. The more
I found out, the more interesting
it became. We eventually got the
story approved by our executive
producer and the Discovery
Channel. That's where we're at for
now. Sherry

A short time later, Sherry called asking how
Beverly and I were doing. She then wanted my schedule

for September and October so they could set up taping the interview here in West Palm Beach at a local hotel.

I asked Jim and Beverly to help me remember things like doctor appointments. Jim reminded me that I was due for another MRI in September since I had the gamma radiosurgery in August 2000. I had to have them done every six months to show progress. My memory was coming back in bits and pieces. After writing down dates that I could not be interviewed on, in the next few months, I jotted them down and sent Sherry an e-mail the next day.

How could I forget we were supposed to have another class reunion next year? I had to use the calendar to figure out what year it was. It would be our 31st reunion. I needed to have a meeting with our Reunion Committee group. I wrote that on the calendar so I would not forget. Putting together our class reunion for the following year was terrifying me. I could not even remember classmates after pulling out my yearbook. I would figure that out later.

I wanted my good friends from church, Audrey and Lisa, to be with us during the interview. They were in the Elizabeth Circle Women's Group and knew I had been kidnapped and that Beverly was with the murderer for several hours before Dale and I arrived home. I planned to ask them both after church on Sunday.

When I opened up the newspaper clippings and notes I had kept, along with the first manuscript for a book I wrote on the subject of being kidnapped, I became overwhelmed and doubted myself. Why was doubt creeping in all the time? Devil go away!

What was I thinking when I agreed to be in a *Movie of the Week* on Discovery? Saturday, September 15, 2001, was an important date to tell Sherry about. Our choir was recording our first CD and I wanted to be a part of it. So that would not be a good day for the interview.

The toughest thing I still had to do was telling Dale. I should have called him when I got the letter from New Dominion Pictures. I could have told him then, but I felt I needed to tell him in person. I called him earlier to make sure he would be at church on Sunday. I decided to tell him after church. He needed to know.

As soon as I saw Dale at church, I said, "Dale, don't forget I need to talk to you after church, it's important."

Joining the church 1995, Jim, Barbara
Rev. David McEntire, Gloria & Dale

"Okay, Mom. Hurry and get your choir robe on. I'll meet you after church at my van in the front parking lot," he said. He kissed me goodbye on the cheek and headed into church with his wife Gloria. Jeremy, our grandson, was

242

with his other grandparents. Jim, Beverly, Gloria, and Dale sat in the congregation while we sang in the choir loft on stage then listened to Reverend David McEntire do another one of his amazing sermons.

After church, I met Dale who was already in his van. He opened the door and had the motor running to cool us off. "Hi Mom, what's happening?" he said.

"Here Son, it's a letter from New Dominion Pictures. Read it first, then you'll know what I need."

I was watching his face as he turned white. When he finished reading it, he said, "Mom, why are they doing this now? It's been over 20 years. What does Beverly think?" he rambled on.

"Beverly and I know in our hearts that this will help victims of crime. It's not about us or the murderer. Your father (Jim), aunt, and I have already made up our minds. Beverly and I will be taped at a local hotel. We both weighed the good and the bad. I told the research woman that if we were in the movie, we would need our names changed to protect our family. We did not want to show our faces except in shadows."

We both began to cry. Or was it just me? He hugged me and said, "Mom, if you want to bring up the past again, I can't stop you. I know you feel in your heart you'll help other unfortunate victims. Go for it, you have my blessings."

"Thank you, Dale; I know how hard this is for you," I said, wiping the tears from my eyes. "I know you turned to alcohol and drugs when you were a teenager. We both went through the Tough Love Program for over six months after you wound up in jail for fleeing the police and getting caught on I-95 almost crashing your vehicle. I thank the dear Lord that nobody was hurt, especially you, Dale. I just wished I would have opened my eyes earlier when Beverly told me she thought you were taking her drugs, because you had stolen some of her medications. Dale, I understand now why you turned to drugs and alcohol. My God, you were only six years old when the nightmare happened. There were no violent crime therapists to help us. I'm so proud of you today, look how far we've both come, Dale, with our faith in Jesus Christ, our Lord"

"Mom, you don't know everything. I still have issues. God will get us through them," he admitted. I noticed tears streaming down his face. I handed him a tissue to wipe away his tears. We both grabbed each other in a wonderful, embracing, bear hug and cried together knowing God would take care of us.

Jim parked next to Dale's van and held the back door opened as I got into the seat. I was trying not to cry, but the floodgates were already opened. Beverly was wearing her braces and walked with crutches, so she sat in the front seat.

"Honey, what can we do for you? We know how hard that was for you to talk to Dale. Are you and Dale okay?" Jim asked.

"It was very rough for us to talk about, but we both agree, Beverly and I should do the interview. Thanks, for caring so much darling," I added. As we drove home, I silently cried to myself thinking about the talk with my son.

The next day, it was time to organize my thoughts about what happened in 1974. I waited until Jim went to work and Beverly went to lunch with her friend, Betty. I got all the newspapers, letters, subpoenas, and police information from the closet to look over. I was terrified again thinking about having to go through this stuff.

A few days later, Beverly went with Dorothy, our neighbor up the street, to Miami for the day. She left after breakfast. Jim called around 9 AM and told me he had to go to Tampa on his run and would not be home until tomorrow. He would call me later tonight. After Beverly left, I laid my box of stuff out on the bed and started to work.

As I leafed through the articles, paperwork, pictures, and letters from the literary agent, my mind became crystal clear on everything that happened. I remembered it all. Being taken from my home, the radio station scandal, and meeting Burt Reynolds and his friends at his grand opening of the ranch. It all came flooding back into my mind. I was happy, it was coming back. My memory was coming back! I saw the murderer, Knowles, holding the sawed-off shotgun to my head and saying, "BANG, BANG!"

Then I totally lost it. I began sobbing as I fell to the floor near my bed. All the articles were laid out on the bed, as memories came flooding back to me. It was as if the murderer was in the other room.

How would I ever be able to do an interview? I got out of my nightgown so I could take a long, hot shower to clear my mind. "God, please help me so I can help others," I said to Him. I rubbed shampoo into my scalp, scrubbing the fear out of my head.

I stayed home by myself until Beverly came in around 8 PM. She had a ball. They went to the zoo with

Dorothy's grandchildren, stuffed themselves with hotdogs, French fries, and chocolate shakes. She was talking about it when the phone rang. It was Jim checking in.

"Hi darling, how you are doing tonight?" He could read my mind.

I explained that I had pulled all the articles out and went over them and my memory came back.

"Did you remember our truck?" he asked.

"No, I'm afraid I didn't." Jim's favorite truck had to be traded in for a van for Beverly. We talked for about 10 minutes then he said he was going out to get a steak and we said our goodbyes. Jim knew he was the love of my life.

The following Sunday after church, I asked Lisa and Audrey to be a part of our team during the taping of the *Movie of the Week*. I had already told them, earlier about the *Movie of the Week*. They both whispered, they would be honored to be on our support team with Reverend David. "Just let us know the date Barbie!" they said in unison.

Sherry wrote an e-mail on September 26th to let us know they were trying to set up the interviews the week of October 15th. She apologized for the delay in the interviews and said things had become a bit hectic.

On Monday, October 15, 2001, Sherry e-mailed me regarding the interviews. The details of taping were finalized and all questions for each of us were in the e-mail. Beverly and I had only three days before the interviews.

The interviews were set up by Jeff Fine, the director. They were set for Thursday, October 18th beginning at 11:00 AM at the Radisson Hotel on Australian Avenue in West Palm Beach. Then she added, "Barbara Tucker, now Barbara M. Abel, is changed to Deborah Taylor and Beverly Mabee is changed to Darlene Matthews. A few other names were changed also."

Sherry even included a guideline of what outfits for us to wear.

We would be in the background. Who was going to notice what we wore? I finished up reading everything and then printed it all for Beverly to go over. "Beverly," I said, "it looks like we have these sets of questions to go over before this Thursday."

"What? Thursday? That's only three more days," she said.

"Beverly, we don't have a choice. Let's eat our Kentucky Fried Chicken™, and fries first. I'm hungry!" I said as I reached for a chicken wing. After lunch, we settled in our comfortable chairs in the living room to tackle the questions we each received.

"Beverly are you sure you want to go through this? You can still back out," I said before going down this road with questions that would bring all of the terror back for both of us.

"Yes. We made a commitment to help others, and we're both going to do it, Barbie," she answered. "After all, we survived."

RELIVING MY WORST FEARS

I never knew everything that happened to Beverly in 1974. She had been with Paul John Knowles throughout the day and now suffered with nightmares just like I have. I remembered trying to call her on and off that day when working at WJNO.

Now we were facing questions to answer and send back to New Dominion pictures for a *Movie of the Week*. They were taping us in few days, Audrey would pick us up and drive us over to the Radisson Hotel to meet the producer and men who would tape and record. Reverend McEntire and Lisa would meet us at the hotel. It was wonderful knowing our support team would be there for us.

Damn, New Dominion sent us so many questions. This would take hours for us to go over. Nothing we could do but get started. We stopped in between the most bothersome questions to take a break. Beverly was amazed how I just breezed through most of my questions. She knew most of it because I had to let it all out when writing my story. Beverly was my angel who always listened to me. I only did half of my questions in front of her because the others were too much for her to hear.

I had it all planned with Audrey ahead of time. Audrey would bring her home before I would be interviewed on Thursday to spare her feelings. I didn't want her to get too upset.

After a break, I helped Beverly back to her chair. I went over to the computer, telling her I would be typing answers to keep for a rainy day.

"Here we go; I'm starting with question number two," I said.

Q. Please describe what happened after your sister left for work?

A. I did housework and hung up the clothes in the backyard.

Q. When did you first notice someone in your backyard?

A. I was at the back door ready to step in when I asked him who he was."

Q. What did he say to you?

A. He said, "I'm Bob Williams with the IRS."

Q. What was your reaction?

A. Then I went into the house and he followed me. My reaction was fear!

As we went through each question on Beverly's pages, we came to question number 10.

Q. What happened once your sister arrived?

A. I was praying that he wouldn't kill us since he had a gun and knife. When my sister came into the house, I feared for all of our lives. Everything happened so quickly. She came into the bedroom and saw me and came over to the bed and tried to calm me down. I was hysterical. She was really calm, and it helped her son and me. Barbara took Dale out of the bedroom, and I don't know where they went. She came back in the bedroom after my nephew was tied up. Then there was a knock on the door, it was our next-door neighbor. Barbara yelled out for Muffin. My sister went to meet her in the living room. I couldn't hear the rest. Then she left. By that time, Bob Williams told my sister he was taking her with him for insurance. She came over and kissed me and whispered, "Everything is going to be alright," and she told me she loved me!

After she answered all the questions, I printed answers to tough questions then turned the computer off. Beverly was exhausted. I helped her get into her bed so she could take a nap.

I thought we did a good job answering the questions. We only broke down sobbing about 10 different times. How could that monster have done what he did to Beverly that day? How could he have killed so many women, men, and children without the slightest remorse?

Yes, we needed to do this interview and we would. God was with both of us throughout our entire lives. God would not let us down now. I could not imagine Beverly wanting to do this interview and put it all on film for the world to see. She was always more courageous having to live with Cerebral Palsy. This year, I noticed how difficult it had become for her to walk with her crutches and braces.

How she endured each surgery throughout the years had me question myself. If it were me, would I have her bubbly sense of humor through it all? Probably not. I was the serious twin.

Jeff Fine, the producer of the *Movie of the Week*, would meet us at the hotel in a few days. We did not have a clue what we would be getting into. Plus, we did not want to think about it. For the next two days, we went out to a movie or lunch to get out of the house and have fun. The questions had been put away. We talked about them for one day, which was enough.

I had been out of work for over a year due to having gamma radiosurgery for my AVM. It was because I had lost part of my memory. I did not remember Jim's 1988 Ford Ranger truck. He even showed me pictures he had. This might have been a blessing. It probably helped me push the kidnapping incident away from my mind for years, after forgiving the rapist and murderer.

Now, Beverly and I were reliving the entire nightmare once again. I knew the doctor told me it would take time for my full memory to return, so I was thankful for just being alive. I believed that God put Beverly and me in this timeframe to help others who were also unfortunate victims.

We had our support team for taping of the show. It was Reverend David McEntire, Audrey Arthur, and Lisa Pierce from church. Both women were in Christmas plays and Bible studies with me throughout the years. Beverly and I felt confident being interviewed with them nearby.

When Jim got home from work, I called Beverly for supper. The chuck roast with onions, carrots, and potatoes was cooking in the Crockpot™. Best invention ever! I had made strawberry shortcake for dessert.

Jim came home from work exhausted as usual. "Smells good, what we got this evening, Sweetie?" he asked after showering and getting into something comfortable.

"Tonight, we are having homemade chuck roast with your favorite dessert strawberry shortcake. Oh, and decaf coffee." No wonder we were not losing weight. I was a great cook. Then we sat down to eat. After supper, we played Scrabble®. Then Jim went to bed and Beverly and I watched a movie on TV.

How Jim got up most mornings by 4 AM and worked until after 5 PM or longer, amazed me. He drove 20 miles to U.S. Foodservice to pick up his truck to go to work. That is one way. He ran different routes on a weekly basis to Tampa, Jacksonville, Key West, and Miami Beach. He loved his job as a truck driver. It made him feel good.

When he drove out of town into the country, he would call on the phone and say, "Mooooo, the cows are looking back at me Barbie. How's everything back home?"

We would talk for a few minutes. Then I would get off the phone and laugh.

"Hey Barbie, did he Moooo?" Beverly said.

"Yes, of course. That's our Jim. Guess what Beverly? He's naming the cows now," I answered.

She realized how much he loved his job and us. "That's Jim. Gotta love him" she said.

That evening, after supper, Jim took me in the bedroom to make love so we could forget tomorrows taping. Afterwards, I fell into his arms and knew I was blessed.

"Darling, you are the love of my life and I can only imagine what you, Beverly, and Dale went through. God will get you through all this. He always does." As he put his arm around me, I fell asleep thinking of Dale, who was now in his 30s and happily married. He was so proud of Beverly and me. We would tell him when the program would air on the Discovery channel as soon as we found out.

TAPING THE INTERVIEWS

OCTOBER 18, 2001

I was already dressed in the outfit I picked out that morning, a long-sleeved white blouse with blue flowers on the collar and pearl buttons. My linen slacks were dark blue, which matched my new flats.

I helped Beverly get dressed. She wore a cute blouse with a light blue and pink design going through the center and light pink slacks. Her black and white saddle shoes had braces put in them last month.

I had done our make-up to look like the stars we would be. At least it made us feel good because we looked sensational. That is when I remembered, nobody would be seeing us in the movie, because we would be in a darken background. Since we would be filmed in this haze, we had to wear the colors picked from the list they gave us. They were colors that would work well with filming.

Audrey rang the doorbell and we let her in. She was early because she wanted to help us get ready. We were ready and had about 20 minutes before we had to leave. She asked us if we knew what we were going to do or say.

"No Audrey, we don't have a clue what either of us is going to do. We just got the questions three days ago and I only wanted to go over them once," I told her.

"Barbara and Beverly, can I say a prayer before we leave?" she asked.

"Yes!" Beverly and I exclaimed.

"Oh, my God, what a beautiful friend you are Audrey. Praying for Beverly and me to calm our nerves and anxiety by filling our souls with God's spirit is just what we need," I said.

We locked the house and went to the car. Beverly sat in the front seat as it was easier for her to get in. I pushed myself into the backseat and we all buckled up for the drive which was not even 10 minutes from our home. We did not talk much. There was not anything to say. We pulled up to the front of the hotel. The valet helped us all out, then got Beverly's wheelchair from the trunk. She usually walked with her walker, but today she was too nervous. I was not doing much better myself.

Audrey pushed her into the lobby. I followed with my large purse with extra make-up, water, peanut butter crackers, and my stupid cigarettes. I had to have them for breaks. I knew I needed to quit smoking. Now was not the time. It is a shame I did not have a swig of Southern Comfort® before we left.

Jeff Fine startled all three of us as he came from behind a small palm tree in the lobby.

"Good morning, you must be Beverly and Barbara. I'm Jeff Fine, the director from New Dominion Pictures." He introduced his partners, the audio and video men.

Filming Movie of the Week with John, Jeff Fine, & Matt

"I hope you haven't eaten lunch because my team and I are starving."

"No, we haven't eaten lunch, yet, either," I said.

Then Lisa came up from behind and said, "Hi, I'm here!"

"Hi Jeff, this is Beverly, my twin sister. Audrey and Lisa are our friends and support team from church," I added.

"So nice to meet you. We've spoken on the phone once Barbara. Would you all join us for lunch? Our treat," he said.

"We'd love to," we all answered in agreement.

Jeff steered us toward the dining room, and we were all seated at a long table. Beverly's wheelchair was placed over by the wall as she scooted into the booth. The waitress came over and handed us menus. She asked, how we were paying, and Jeff told her he would take care of the bill. Jeff was so polite. He hugged Beverly and me before entering the dining room and was genuinely happy to be interviewing us. He was not like other producers I had met when I was in radio and television ages ago. Most

257

of them thought they were superior to those being interviewed on talk shows. Jeff made us feel special and helped relieve our anxiety.

Lisa had a salad and we three gals had cheeseburgers with bacon, lettuce, tomato, and mayo. French fries and chocolate or strawberry milk shakes. The men had steak and fries with sweet tea or sodas.

I told Jeff that Reverend David was running late but would be coming soon. When we were almost finished eating lunch, Reverend David came in and was introduced. He said he had already eaten so he sat down until we were done. The audio and video men left to set up the room. After eating lunch, we visited for a few more minutes. We had a pleasant time with everyone. I felt more at ease.

"Jeff, will I only take one hour to be interviewed?" Beverly asked.

"Yes, Beverly but do not worry if you mess up. We will stop taping. You can take a break, get a drink of water, or go to the bathroom, whenever you need to. We'll come back and finish taping the same question. You'll do fine," he answered.

Reverend David, Audrey, and Lisa were proud of us. This was all new to us. Beverly and I had no clue what would come from our lips. This documentary was so important to Jeff. He was putting his heart and soul into this project. First, he had to find actors that were around our ages when this nightmare happened. That was just the beginning.

Lisa, Audrey & Beverly - June 22, 2001

Heading toward the elevators, I looked ahead at Beverly being wheeled up to the room by Jeff. She was still smiling and talking with him. I could only pray that her interview would go smoothly. Who was I kidding? I could never imagine the sheer terror and fear in her heart when Paul John Knowles held her captive. I had to shake these feelings loose.

Matt and John opened the door and let us all in. Matt showed me the bed I could sit on, during Beverly's interview. The others could use the chairs to sit on. The bathroom was over to one side of the room. The larger part of the front area had a queen-sized bed and table with chairs nearby. Matt and John had moved the furniture around to make room for the taping equipment. Beverly would sit in her wheelchair and be interviewed. I could see her from where I was sitting.

He set the lighting and used a filtered lens to make us look as if we were partially hidden from the camera. Nobody would see our faces. Then they turned off the lights to darken the room. Our faces would be in the background. Nobody would recognize us, except for our voices. After everything was set up, they let me kiss

Beverly before going into the other room. "Beverly, look at this, we have a famous director to interview you. You'll do great. I love you!" I said.

"I love you too, Barbie," she said as I straightened out her blouse.

I went and climbed onto the bed with pillows to support my back so I would be comfortable. Audrey and Lisa were next to me sitting in chairs. Reverend David said a prayer before beginning and put us at ease before sitting down. Jeff told us we had different names to protect us. The questioning began.

"Please state your name. Please tell us a little background information regarding your personal situation prior to November 14, 1974," Jeff began.

"Darlene Matthews. I babysat for my neighbors and friends."

"How did Knowles enter the house? Did he show you any weapons?" he went on.

"He entered through the back door. He had a bulge in his shirt. He pulled the sawed-off shotgun out. Then he said, 'I just committed a robbery and I need a place to stay because the cops are chasing me, and they know my whereabouts—I have to stay low!'" she told Jeff.

As Beverly was being questioned, I noticed how brave she was. She was not breaking down at all. I thought for sure she would be crying. It did not make sense to me that she was not crying. I was. Audrey handed me tissue from her purse and gave me a bottle of water to drink.

This was just the beginning. Beverly was brief with her answers not elaborating but coming straight to the point.

"How would you describe Knowles? What was his demeanor?" Jeff continued.

"He was mean when he told me to shut up and not yell. Then he said, if I didn't be quiet, he'd kill me. Then in the next instance he was nice," she said.

"What happened next?" he asked.

"He sat on the couch, I was in the chair, and I asked him if he was married. He said, 'Yes, and I have two kids, seven and nine years old.' I then asked when he was going to leave. He said, 'around 12:30 PM.' He then asked me, 'who lives here?' I told him my sister and she has a little boy. I told him my sister worked at WJNO radio as a copywriter and would be home about 5:30 PM. He asked me if she had a car. I said, 'yes.' 'Does she bring it up into the driveway?' I said, 'yes.' About 12:50 PM, he made me go into the bedroom. He made me get on the bed and took his penknife out and made me undress and then he took his pants off and tried to rape me. He couldn't finish because I had a spasm…."

What did I just hear? He undressed her and tried to rape her, but she went into a spasm? Of course, she went into a spasm, she has Cerebral Palsy, you idiot! My mind was not handling this part very well. I do not recall Beverly telling me this part when we went over the questions. The part where he tries to rape her. This was unbearable for me to hear. I was shaking. My entire body felt like somebody hit me over the head with a baseball bat.

Everybody shut the taping down. I got off the bed, ran into the bathroom, shut the door, and sobbed. How am I going to be interviewed when I cannot even hold it together while listening to my sister's story? Reverend David knocked on the door and asked if I was alright. Of course, I was not alright. I want to go home, climb into bed, and put the covers over my entire body, I thought to myself. "I'm okay, just didn't expect that answer," I said as I opened the door.

The next half hour went better. We got through all the questions. Then it was my turn. I told Audrey she could take Beverly home.

That was when Beverly told me she was staying.

"What? You saw what happened to me when I listened to your interview. You've got to be kidding!" I cried.

"No, I'm staying Barbie. You need me, and I am going to stay," she demanded.

"Okay, but if you have to leave before I'm done, Jeff will stop the taping and you can go home with Audrey. Is that a deal?" I asked.

"Okay," she answered.

Jeff, Matt, and John all asked if I was up to this and I told them, "The show must go on. I'll have to be okay."

Beverly's hour was longer than expected, Reverend David came up to me before I was seated for my interview and told me he was sorry but had to get back to church. Lisa had to leave but would stay for part of my taping. At least Lisa, Audrey, and Reverend David were there for Beverly.

"Please state your name. Please tell us a little background information regarding your personal and professional situation prior to November 14, 1974," Jeff began.

"My name is Barbara Abel, oops, I forgot," I said.

"Cut, turn camera off," Jeff said.

"Barbara don't forget your name is Deborah Taylor, simple mistake. Don't worry you'll do fine. Do you need a break?"

"No, I'll remember Jeff. Let's begin again," I stated as the camera started rolling again. "My name is Deborah Taylor, I worked at WJNO radio in the Palm Beaches as a copywriter. I loved my job creating exciting commercials along with recording them. I guess you would call me a ham!"

"When did you first realize that something was wrong on that day?"

"I was calling home every few hours trying to get ahold of Darlene, my handicapped twin sister. She never answered the phone that day. Normally, she would call me to let me know if she was going out with friends. We always checked up on each other. This day was different. I felt a cold chill down my spine. Something was wrong, but I couldn't pinpoint it at the time. I was busy trying to write several commercials and the time whizzed by."

"Please describe what happened when you pulled into the driveway. What time did you return? Was it dark yet? Was there anything unusual about the house? What did your son do?

The lights were not on in the living room. I felt shivers go up my arms and the pit of my stomach began aching. Something wasn't right. It was around 6 PM and it was getting dark. I don't know what happened as I opened the front door with my key. Dale was telling me he'd go find Aunt Beverly as he ran in ahead of me. Everything happened so fast. There was a man beside me. He put his hand on my shoulder and said—what did he say? I forgot. I forgot.

The cameras were turned off as I struggled to remember.

Why was I rambling on and on? I could not control my thoughts, as the tears spilled once again from my eyes. I was hurting!

I did not want to tell Jeff the truth. It was too painful. My heart was beating, the palms of my hands became sweaty, and there was a vision ahead of me on the blank wall. It was like I was watching a movie. Only I was in the movie with the murderer. It was not 2001. It was as though I had been transported back to Thursday night, November 14, 1974, as my thoughts wandered back to the nightmare again.

As the cameras began to roll, I began talking about the abduction.

As I bent over to get a drink of water from the kitchen sink, my hands began to shake. Something was not right; I felt a presence behind me. The hot air breathing on my neck made me look down and see a sawed-off shotgun. Then a man's voice yelled in my ear, 'Don't turn around or I'll kill you.' The glass shattered to the floor and I turned around to face—nothing.

Oh no, I thought to myself, as my hands went to my face and I burst out crying, because the nightmare was here again. I shook my head to clear it and noticed I was being taped, as Jeff came over to me.

Jeff was worried and said, "Barbara? Barbara are you alright? Matt, go get Barbara a drink of water."

As Matt went to the cooler to grab a bottle of water, I looked over at Beverly and she was okay. I gave Beverly a look to let her know I would be okay in a few minutes. Matt handed me the bottle of water and walked into the bathroom with me to have a cigarette break together. He mentioned how good I was doing, then said, "Barbara, don't worry about having to stop at certain questions that make you remember the horror. You are helping others. You and Beverly are so brave."

We hugged and I thanked him for understanding as we walked out to continue the interview. I went and found my chair among the cables on the floor.

Audrey came over to me after I sat in the chair. She kneeled on the floor next to me and grabbed my hand. She was crying. I was crying.

Everybody was scared for me and wanted to take away the pain I was feeling.

"Barbara, are you okay honey? You are so brave to be doing this interview. Remember when I always kid you and call you a ditzy blonde? I'll never call you that again, never!" said Audrey, as she got up off the floor. "Oh my God, I do not know how you and Beverly survived the most horrific experience of one's life and still have any brains in tack. You are both survivors with the Grace of God. I'm shocked and blown away at how brave you are."

Jeff asked, if I was ready to tape again and I nodded.

"Please describe what happened when you left the house in your Volkswagen. What were you thinking during this time?"

He took me to my car and said, 'we're going to Georgia together.' I said, 'Well you don't need me. Then he said, 'Yes, I do because you are my insurance policy.' When we were driving along, he heard the news on the car radio, and he started getting agitated. That's when I thought, oh no, this man has more than one personality and this other side started to scare me. Whatever came out of our mouths while driving was nothing but small talk. He asked me what I did, and I told him I worked in radio. 'And what do you do in radio? I heard you're a writer or something,' he asked. I said, 'Yes, I am a copywriter.' He said, 'This is good. Yes, this is good.' He pressed me about my writing skills. He said, 'So you can write a book.' Then I said, 'Sure.' 'Good, that's what is probably going to happen. You're going to be able to help me write my story.' He then said, 'I'll tell you later what it's all about.' So, I started talking about the weather, or anything that would come into my mind to get his mind off the newscast. It worked. I had to keep his mind occupied while driving from West Palm Beach to Ft. Pierce, Florida, which was almost 70 miles.

"Please describe what happened when you arrived in Ft. Pierce," The interviewer asked.

We arrived in Ft. Pierce and he noticed a motel, kind of on a hill overlooking the highway. He said, "We're going to stay here for the night. I'm just too tired. Then we'll head out in the morning to Georgia. Don't forget we're married. I'll think of a name when we get to the front desk. We're newlyweds!' I thought to myself, Was he crazy? We weren't newlyweds. First off, I would never stay at an old motel like this, I'd stay in a luxurious hotel with all the good stuff. It would have to have a spa area for a massage. 'Barbara, we're here' the madman said bringing me out of my thoughts and back to the present. 'What are you thinking?' John asked. 'Oh nothing, just that we're newlyweds?' I answered.

As the interviewer continued to ask questions, I answered as best I could. It was now 27 years later.

Can you remember exactly what happened to you 27 years ago? Can you describe what the next few hours were like? Was Knowles watching the news on television? What was his reaction? How did you become aware of what crimes Knowles had committed? What was your reaction? How would you characterize Knowles during the time you spent in the hotel room with him? What did you think might happen to you? What prompted you to finally admit that Knowles had repeatedly raped you? During your ordeal, what thoughts went through your mind regarding how you were going to get through this?

After answering a grueling 37 questions, one for each hour of captivity, I was exhausted. I realized that Jeff could only use a few questions for the documentary. I wondered, which ones he would use. I was glad the interview was over. When I glanced up and saw Beverly she looked just as exhausted as me.

Jeff, Matt, and John thanked Beverly and me for being so wonderful in answering such tough questions. We both felt pretty good for not breaking down, too often. I had survived with God's will. I know I must have smoked a pack of cigarettes that day because I was so uptight. I never smoked that much unless I was doing my bills.

Jeff wheeled Beverly all the way to the lobby while Audrey and I followed. Jeff hugged us goodbye then said he would be in touch with us as soon as the movie was finished. Hopefully, the movie would be ready to air on the Discovery Channel before March 2002.

As Audrey was driving Beverly and me home, I asked Beverly, "Why didn't you cry?"

She answered, "Because if I cried, I'd never stop!" "You don't think that tore me up listening to you answer those questions, Barbie? I wanted to cry, but with my spasms, I never would have made it."

What a trooper, I thought to myself. She had to survive that along with other challenges in her life and always came out smiling in the end. I wanted to be more like her. I did not want to be so serious. I knew I needed to work on that one.

As the weeks and months went by, Sherry Anderson, research developer for *Movie of the Week,* and I kept in touch by e-mail, letters, and cards. Our busy lives just kept us moving on.

THE AIRING

Jim got a promotion at work; we were so proud, and we all went out to dinner at the local steak house. Beverly and I ordered filet mignon, baked potato with butter, sour cream, chef's salad with ranch dressing along with sweet tea. Jim got their famous prime rib with seasoned potato fries, salad, and sweet tea. For dessert, we shared their special chocolate seven-tiered cake. It was a wonderful evening. We would have many more to celebrate.

The next couple of weeks was vacation time. We decided to go away from West Palm Beach and all the excruciatingly painful memories from the past months. Still not knowing exactly when the *Movie of the Week* was to be aired on Discovery Channel, we headed toward Ohio to visit family and have fun.

Beverly, Jim, and I needed to get away from the madness. The alarm clock went off around 6 AM. We packed the night before and were ready to pick up a quick sausage, egg muffin and coffee on the road. Cheryl, our friend, who lived up the street, would babysit our cat, Honeybun. Our beautiful female Springer Spaniel, RJ, was put in the kennel the night before. Our puppy was not happy!

Jim drove from West Palm Beach to Madison, Florida. We visited Eleanor and her husband at their beautiful 15-acre ranch for one-day, before heading up to Ohio to be with Jim's family. Eleanor and I took time to walk outside and sit on the porch to talk about the *Movie of the Week* and how I truly felt about everything. I told her how worried I was about Beverly taking so long to express her true feelings about the kidnapping. I could not hold anything back from my best friend.

After supper at Eleanor's, we played games and went to bed early. Beverly and I stayed in one bedroom together and Jim slept in the other room on the queen-sized daybed. The next morning, we headed to the great Smokey Mountains. I drove four hours, then we stopped for lunch. After lunch Jim drove all the way into Gatlinburg, Tennessee. On the way, Beverly saw a sign about *The Incline Railroad*. Jim said, "This is vacation time, let's go check it out!"

"Yeah, we get to go on a train," Beverly chimed in.

We found the entrance in St. Elmo, Tennessee. Jim parked, got out, and bought our tickets. Then we put Beverly into her wheelchair and walked up the sidewalk to enter the train. After being seated, I looked out the window. It was straight up the mountain. No curves, no stops. Fear rose up into my belly. Luckily, I had not eaten much. The train started up slowly at a snail's pace. Then whoosh, the train went faster and faster. I got more anxious as the train climbed straight up into the sky. I closed my eyes in terror. I was about to scream bloody murder but could not manage to even get a slight squeal from my throat. As we reached the top, the conductor said, "Everybody it's time to get off."

As my knees wobbled and I struggled to exit the door onto a platform, I looked down from where we came. I got dizzy and sat on a step. They had an observation deck, food service, and a gift shop nearby. Jim had already gone ahead of me, wheeling Beverly in her wheelchair. A few minutes later, Jim came up to me and asked why I was sitting on the steps.

"I'm not going back on that damn train. I refuse to go back down this mountain."

"Wait a minute. You're scared? Why? It was fun, Beverly wants to go on it again," he finished.

"I'll be damned if I'm getting back on the stupid train. GET THE CAR!"

As he wheeled Beverly over to the steps, they started laughing at me. It took 10 minutes for them to convince me to get back on the train. Jim told me if I did not scream bloody murder on the train, he would take us to a special restaurant for supper. That was a stupid statement. We had to eat anyway.

After having my tizzy fit, I sat in the seat and made myself look out the window going back down the mountain. It was kind of fun. Why was I afraid on the way up? It took 10 minutes to get down and we could see the Great Smokey Mountains from 100 miles away. We could also see four different states. It was awesome. I felt stupid. This would not be the last time I had to deal with fear.

Jim's family was having their annual reunion. Beverly and I got to meet over 140 relatives. That was a bit overwhelming. During the next few weeks, we went on picnics, traveled to Pennsylvania to see the Amish country, and had so much fun visiting with Jim's brothers and sisters by themselves.

After two weeks of fun with family, it was time to go home. On the way from Ohio to Florida we were able to meet a variety of different personalities through the people at restaurants, stores, or parks. People are fascinating!

After we arrived home, I turned on our computer and read what felt like a million-and-one emails, most of which I deleted. Suddenly I saw an email from Sherry, at New Dominion Pictures. The email included the date the *Movie of the Week* was to be aired on the Discovery Channel in our area. It would be Sunday, May 19, 2002, at 9 PM. The title would be *Deadly Pursuit*. Sherry mentioned that this *Movie of the Week* would air in the United States and overseas reaching millions of viewers.

The next day, after picking up RJ, our Springer Spaniel, at the kennel, I had a lot of laundry to do. Jim went back to work and had to spend the night in Tampa that first night back from vacation. While he was away, I needed to call our family and friends to tell them the documentary/*Movie of the Week* would be aired. Those that lived out of Florida had to find what the Discovery Channel was on in their area.

I talked at great length with Dale for the past few months about his feelings at the time we would be interviewed. He had worked through some of his own fears throughout the years. Later on in life, pastors, who he trusted, helped him. God was with all three of us when the kidnapping happened, and God is with us today. Beverly, Dale, and I had to let go and let God do his magic with each of us in order to heal us throughout the years. We had to do our part by keeping our faith.

WATCHING THE MOVIE OF THE WEEK

SUNDAY, MAY 19, 2002

Sunday came and since the program aired at 9 PM, Jim had to go to bed early. U.S. Foodservice needed him to be at work the next day at 1 AM. He was scheduled to go to Jacksonville and stay overnight. Sherry would mail us a few videos after it the show aired on television first. Those were the rules in TV at the time.

That evening, I kissed Jim goodnight and wished him well the next day. Then I pulled two comfortable chairs over to the middle of the living room so Beverly and I could watch the movie together. I made popcorn. She had a Pepsi®. I made myself a stiff drink of Southern Comfort® with a twist of lemon. My cigarettes were nearby. Then I turned the television on to find the Discovery channel. Right before the documentary movie began, the phone rang. I jumped.

"Hello?" I said.

"Hi Mom. Are you ready to watch the movie with me?" Dale said.

"Yes son, we're as ready as we'll ever be," I answered.

"Mom, how's Bev doing?"

"We're going to be fine honey. Just call in between commercials if you want," I added.

The documentary began with the opening scene.

"Palm Beach, Florida is a vacationers' paradise. Its upscale resorts and beautiful beaches attract tourists looking for adventure and romance."

As Beverly and I watched the beginning of movie we said together, "I forgot he picked up a woman, in Palm Beach and tried to take her to the woods and rape her."

As the actor was running from the police and made his way to West Palm Beach, then finding a carport to leave his car in, Beverly realized that is when he ran near our house and saw her hanging clothes on the line.

"Barbara, he lied to me and told me, his name was Bob Williams and was with the IRS. But it was too late and there was nothing I could do, as he led me into the house."

"Beverly, I know this. If it's bothering you this much, I'll turn the TV off," I said.

"No, turn the volume up a little," she added.

That entire scene was about Beverly. How he took her into the house. How he threatened her life with the shotgun.

We both gasped as we saw Beverly being interviewed in the movie. We leaned toward the television set in awe of the words that came from her mouth.

"If you scream or anything, I'll just blow you away," he said, *"Whose here with you, who stays with you?"*

And Darlene Matthews said, *"My sister works at a radio station...."*

I knew the documentary was awful for Beverly to see herself in this movie on TV. I knew deep down it was bringing back the terror she felt. We were not even to the first commercial break. I sipped my stiff drink and wished I could pause the damned TV show. I would have to swallow my pride and keep watching for both our sakes as the scene showed the actor tying her up.

Then Darlene continued, *"I didn't think he'd leave before my sister came home, because he needed a way to get out. To go from our house to the next crime he was going to do, he had to have that car."*

Clearly, the movie was bothering Beverly. We watched the next scene during which the actor playing Knowles was waiting for me to arrive home.

The movie then showed the actor playing Knowles leading my son, Dale, and me into the bedroom with his shotgun. I saw myself for the first time and it was surreal. I began to talk on screen:

And everything just happened so fast. There was a man beside me. He put his hand on my shoulder and said, 'Don't turn around or I'll kill you.' I wasn't crying then, I was calm. It was so unreal to me. I said, I just cashed my paycheck. I have money in my bedroom drawer. I'll give you the money and keys to my car.' I said, 'Just don't hurt us.'

Watching this TV special made my heart flutter in fear. That was me in the movie. ME! Did I really say that? That is right, Jeff, the Producer, told us they would need to edit some of what both of us said during the taping. Finally, a commercial break.

"Beverly what do you think of the movie so far? Are you okay?" I asked.

"Yes. I can't believe we're both in this movie. Most of it so far is true."

The phone rang and scared us back into reality.

"Hi Mom and Bev. How are you two holding up?" Dale asked.

"Hi Son. Beverly and I are amazed so far, but they haven't gotten into the real murder spree yet. We're sure that will bother us the most," I added.

"It's on-again Mom. Call you soon," he said as he hung up the phone.

"Damn, I'm still in this scene Beverly!" I yelled out, surprised.

The following scene in the movie depicted the actor Knowles leading me outside to my Volkswagen.

I heard my voice. *"He said, 'We're going to Georgia together.' I said, 'Well, you don't need me, please let me stay with Beverly and Dale.' And he said, 'Yes, I do, you're my insurance policy.'"*

Then the movie showed when Dale untied himself and got loose, then went next-door to get our neighbor to help. Beverly got dressed before the police came to our home.

Detective James Gabbard from the West Palm Beach Police Department was in the movie explaining about taking a hostage and kidnapping someone along with tying up two individuals and leaving them behind. Obviously, it was a very serious situation.

"Beverly," I said, "Detective Gabbard helped us back in 1974. He was a wonderful man." They called in the FBI hostage negotiator Agent James Cavanaugh on screen in the next scenes. "I know him also." They are both good people, I thought to myself.

During the next commercial break after speaking to Dale for a minute, I went to get another drink. This show was nerve racking, but fascinating at the same time. We still had not come to the crimes Knowles had committed yet. For now, my feelings were in check.

The commercial break was over and I was seated, after taking a big sip of my drink. Beverly had more popcorn put in her dish. I had not touched mine yet. I was just smoking and drinking.

When the movie began again it was stressful watching because neither Beverly nor I never thought much about who Knowles had murdered back in 1974. Even though I had seen file folders of those murdered by Knowles flung onto the desk at the police department, I blocked them from my mind for years. It was way different now, watching this documentary, seeing Beverly and me in the background during certain scenes talking about our experiences being with a serial killer.

The movie continued with the FBI explaining about putting out a nationwide alert for the car with the license tag that was involved in a kidnapping. As he went on to explain Knowles profile, a frightening image was portrayed. They were now dealing with a multiple state serial killer. That was the reason the FBI was called in.

As the movie progressed, it showed proof of a murder in Jacksonville Beach, Florida. The woman had been murdered in her bedroom and her car was stolen.

With the evidence that Paul John Knowles was a murderer, police intensified the manhunt.

The following scene depicted the actors driving to an unknown destination. Then, I realized it was my words coming from the TV.

"Whatever came out of our mouths while driving was nothing but small talk. He asked me what I did, and I told him I worked in radio. 'And what do you do in radio, I heard you're a writer or something?' he said. I'm a copywriter. 'This is good. Yes, this is good. So, you can write a book?' I said, Sure! He said, 'Well, that's what's probably going to happen. You're going to be able to help me write my story. I'll tell you later what it's all about.'"

Next one of the detectives said: *"As the search began to widen, investigators began to fear for her life. When we first heard of the kidnapping of Deborah Taylor, we had learned enough about Paul John Knowles to feel there was not going to be that much hope of finding her alive."*

On the next commercial break, I called my son and asked how he was holding up.

"Mom, this is pretty bad. How are you guys doing? Mom, I love you. Tell Aunt Beverly the same," he said as he hung up the phone.

As the movie played, the murder spree was revealed. First, a woman in Jacksonville, FL had been murdered. One murder led to finding two young girls in Jacksonville missing and also found dead. This was explained to me in the West Palm Beach Police station that Sunday in 1974. I had flashbacks of police, FBI, and other law enforcement agents throwing their folders on the table. My mind replayed visions of dead bodies in various positions from separate folders and the lives that had been taken by a madman.

I snapped back to reality when James Cavanaugh, FBI from Palm Beach said in the movie, *"This guy is all over the board doing, all types of crimes, but his trail he left behind was a very distinct trail, so we would know where it was ...."*

The movie showed more of Knowles tying me up again and getting agitated.

"He began talking and telling me how many he had killed. Maybe it was two, 12, or 35. I just kept blocking it out of my mind. When he started talking about murdering someone, you could just see the evil in his face. It was like seeing Dr. Jekyll and Mr. Hyde. I mean just that fast, he would trigger off into another person. I knew I had to keep my wits about me...."

I did not tell anyone the truth during our interview for the program that Knowles let me know, more than once, that he had killed 35 people. Only because, at the time, I did not want to believe it.

Beverly and I could not believe the words coming from the FBI agent's mouth on TV. Something to the affect that they had little hope of finding Deborah Taylor alive. Deborah Taylor was me!

"Beverly, what are you feeling now?" I asked as the scenes went up north to another person or persons that had been murdered.

"Barbara, how come he didn't kill us?"

"It's only because God didn't want him to at the time."

"Did I tell you when you came in the door that night with Dale, that John or Paul, whatever his name was, had the shotgun to my head and was ready to blow my brains out?" Beverly said, her voice quivering. "By the way, I am feeling horrible, but now we're okay because we are alive and watching this movie."

As the movie went to commercial break, the phone rang again. It was Dale.

"Mom, Beverly, he killed those people and you're alive. I never wanted to know that. I am so glad you are both alive. I love you both. I'm sorry to keep calling but I have to know you're both okay. Wait until Dad gets to watch the video. He'll flip out! Shows on again," he said as he hung the phone up.

I had nightmares in 1974, about what really went on in Beverly's and Dale's minds after Knowles was captured by the police. I made them both talk to me about what they were going through. I guess they never really answered me truthfully. I thought Dale was too young for me to think he knew anything, except hearing his mother being taken away by a bad man. I must have blocked it out of mind. Years later, I was made aware of what Dale really went through and it was heartbreaking. What a monster Knowles was. Beverly held most of the bad stuff in also. Throughout the years she would blurt something that happened to her like it happened yesterday. We were upset because we did not receive help from a psychiatrist or psychologist the weeks after it happened. We knew that this movie would be a vivid reminder of what happened so many years ago. With our belief in God, we had gotten through life by forgiving the monster Knowles had become.

The documentary ended with Knowles being captured and later being killed on December 18, 1974, by

Georgia Bureau of Investigations (GBI), Agent Ron Angel and Douglas County Sheriff Earl D. Ray. The film depicted Knowles being taken from jail and in their custody, to show them where the gun was hidden in the woods nearby. He tried to escape from the police car and was shot to death.

After being rescued from the Ft. Pierce motel, I was told by one of the FBI agents that I had Stockholm syndrome. No wonder I was mixed up in my mind. It is a psychological condition where after a period of being held captive the hostage—me—begins to sympathize with their capture, Knowles, as a means of enduring the violence. When I was debriefed in Ft. Pierce's FBI office, the FBI and police believed about 30%-40% of what I said. I remembered at that time, while being questioned, that I had taken the glass Knowles had drunk from and washed it in the bathroom sink. I remembered hiding the room keys, postcard, and torn parts of sheet used to tie me up, under the bed. Now, I had a name for what I had done as the guilt poured out of my soul then, STOCKHOLM SYNDROME. I had never heard of it before the kidnapping, but it made sense to me now.

As the movie ended, I called my son to ask him how he was holding up.

"Mom tell Aunt Beverly that you two are amazing! How you both endured such terror and physical abuse is mind boggling. I realize Mom, that I'm a Christian and am so glad we all have Jesus Christ, our Lord and Savior in our lives. I'm so proud of both of you. I wish I were there to hug you both. Let me say goodnight to Beverly," he said.

"Dale, what did you think of the movie?" Beverly asked. "I'm so glad we called each other during the commercial breaks. I know you love us Dale, I heard you telling your mom."

"Aunt Beverly, you can't imagine what went through my mind while watching this program. I told Mom, I'm so proud of you for being so courageous throughout the years. Aunt Beverly, you've been through so much during your lifetime and you always smile. I've got to get to sleep, I have a house to paint in the morning. I love you."

"Goodnight Dale, we both love you too," said Beverly just before hanging up the phone.

I wonder what life will bring next, I thought to myself as I headed toward bed. After getting into my negligee and slipping in between the cool satin sheets, Jim turned around and hugged me telling me everything would be alright. I fell into a deep slumber. I knew we all were survivors.

SPEAKING OUT FOR VICTIMS OF CRIME

February 2010

As the years passed after the *Movie of the Week – Deadly Pursuit* aired on television back in 2002 our lives turned back to normal. Or did they?

Michele was like our daughter and now part of our family since her parents moved to the Carolinas, a year ago. Beverly and Michele both were born with Cerebral Palsy and were friends throughout the years. In 2010, Beverly moved into a nursing home, due to complications with her

Beverly & Michelle - 2017

health. She ended up never being able to live at home again. She lost the use of her legs due to a severe infection and was not able to have therapy in the hospital because she was too weak.

Beverly's wonderful spirit and great sense of humor, along with believing in God, got us all through her illness. Her favorite saying is "If life gives you lemons, make lemonade." That is our Beverly.

My darling husband turned the heater on in our house before leaving for work at three in the morning. After all these years, Jim was still a truck driver at U.S. Foodservice, and loved his job. A note for Barbara was on the kitchen table saying: I have to go to Key West on Carl's run since he has the flu. That means I have to spend the night, sorry. I'll call you later. Love Jim.

After dressing warmly and eating breakfast, I went outside. The wind whipped me in the face and I lifted my collar for protection. It was around 60 F, but felt like 50 F. I realized this was not Ohio where the temperatures plummet down into the teens, but for Florida, it was *COLD*. Thank heavens, I had jeans on along with my favorite pink cashmere sweater, matching pink shoes, and short, black, faux fur coat.

December traffic was always crazy in Florida with northerners leaving the snow to hit the beaches and clog up our streets. I finally got onto I-95, hitting the accelerator to get up to 60 mph then noticed people whizzing by me going over 80 mph—to where? Who needs to go that fast? I glanced down at my speedometer and was shocked to see that I was driving 85 mph! I eased my foot from the accelerator to get off the exit I needed to take to get to the supply medical store.

The medical supply store was pretty far from I-95, I remembered, as I calmed down and headed to the store. Jim made his famous peanut butter cookies for Pete, the owner that I brought with me. I had called earlier to ask him if he had walkers and he told me to come in and pick out what I wanted.

After parking close to the door, I entered and noticed Pete at the counter. He waved me over and I handed him the cookies.

"Oh, thank you so much. Tell Jim I really do appreciate his cookies," he said. Then he took me over to the walkers.

There were so many for me to choose from, until I noticed the shiny red walker. "I'll take that one. Let me get my credit card first," I told him.

"Barbara, you can't have that one, it's a display model. I'll get one from the back and put it together for you," he added.

"Okay, thanks Pete," I said as he headed toward the back of the store.

"Hello, I'm Myra and this is my husband, Neil. I noticed you're buying a walker. Is it for someone in your family?" a woman asked.

I turned around. The woman who spoke to me was stunningly beautiful. Her long black hair flowed past her shoulders. Her pretty dark brown eyes with long eyelashes were to die for. Who was she? I thought.

I really was not in the mood to talk. I was in a hurry to buy the walker, then stop by the nursing home to visit Beverly and have lunch.

"Yes, it's for Michele who has Cerebral Palsy and is like a daughter to me," I answered.

"Since we're both stuck here waiting for our supplies," she said, "I'd like to introduce myself. I'm Myra Goldick and have a talk show, which perhaps Michele might be interested in being interviewed on. It's called *Dancing on Our Disabilities*. Dancing is of a spiritual nature, a figure of speech. We embrace our disabilities and we dance with our hearts and our minds."

Afterwards Myra handed me her card. I thanked her and said, "I'll ask Michele if she'd like to be on your program and get back with you."

"Thank you, Barbara. Oh, here comes Pete with your walker. It was nice talking with you and have a good day," she said.

After meeting Pete at the counter and paying for the walker, I said goodbye to everyone. Neil, Myra's husband, got a few words in while we chatted. He was almost as tall as my husband who is 6'6" tall. Neil was thinner and in good shape, like my Jim. I noticed how he looked at his wife, with adoring love in his eyes.

I went to the nursing home with lunch for Beverly and me: hamburgers, fries, and chocolate shakes. What a woman Beverly was, always making nurses, aides, and me laugh. I would shoot myself if I had to go into a nursing home, I thought to myself.

When I got home, I decided to go to the computer and look up the site Myra had on her business card. The card had already impressed me. Her website was amazing. Myra was not only a famous talk show host on

Dancing on Our Disabilities, but she also had another program, *"Never Say Impossible."* I learned on her site, that Myra was not only a talk show host, speaker, and author, she was also a professional artist.

My mind was going a mile a minute thinking about Michele telling me she did not want to do any interview unless she was paid. My having been in radio and television for over 15-years, I knew you do not get paid for interviews unless you are already famous. I realized, at that moment, that I had to e-mail Myra and let her know Michele's answer. I waited a few days so I would not appear anxious.

As I sat at my computer trying to think of what to type to Myra, I quietly prayed. God, why did you bring this woman into my life? Why were we at the medical supply store that same day with nobody in there but Myra, Neil, the employees, and me, why? Then it hit me, and my fingers sailed through the keys on my computer. I typed about being kidnapped by a serial killer, Paul John Knowles on November 14, 1974, for over 37 hours. I re-read it and pushed the send button. Then immediately regretted pushing the button. Oh no, I thought to myself, she will think I am a crazy person and never call me after leaving my phone number on the e-mail message.

The following Sunday evening, Myra called. "Hello, is this Barbara?" she asked.

"Yes, it is" I answered. After talking back and forth for over an hour she learned about my being kidnapped and the book I have been writing for over thirty years. Then she asked me if I would be on her talk show *Never Say Impossible.* I agreed, and she told me she would send interview questions for me to answer. We would record the show in January. I never knew her past, or the book she wrote about her own personal life. It would all fall into place and make sense later. Nothing made sense now. I agreed to be on a talk show. What was I thinking? I could not be on a talk show. What would I say? Oh yes, I forgot. She would send questions for me to answer then put them together for the show.

January 16, 2013

Myra called me on the phone and put me at ease before we recorded the entire 50-minute phone interview. The interview was stopped if I sneezed, coughed, or had to take a break. She called me the next day to tell me the date it would air. Myra changed my name to Diane Tailor, similar to the *Movie of the Week* with New Dominion Pictures, in order to protect my identity.

After the *Never Say Impossible* show aired on the Internet and my friends, family, and church members had a chance to listen to it, I was so proud to help victims of crime. That was the beginning of my speaking, to help those who have suffered abuse. The following year, I had a speaking engagement with Myra downtown in West Palm Beach, for an event at the local library. Myra asked questions we already had gone over. I was amazed. I was not scared like I was the night before, stressing over the thought of speaking in front of other people. Myra was a professional and made me feel important that day by putting me completely at ease as we did the interview.

After the interview was done, people came up to me and thanked me for telling my story. That was what gave me the courage to speak at local church events all by myself, without Myra. God had put Myra in my life to help me know I was stronger than I realized and that my story needed to be told, because I was a survivor.

FORTY-FIVE YEARS LATER

JUNE 2019

I had been writing my book and was almost to the end of a chapter, which took me back to when the horror began in 1974. It was tearing me up, but I believed that my story needed to be told.

I was getting discouraged and almost gave up finishing my book when Jim, my loving husband said, "Don't give up honey, you've come this far. God will give you a sign."

After tucking my arms around my loving hubby that night, I whispered in his ear, "Honey, do you think He will really give me a sign?"

"Yes, I do, because God got you this far," he said, as we both drifted off to sleep.

The next evening after supper, the phone rang. I picked it up and a voice at the other end said, "Hello, are you Barbara Tucker?"

"Barbara Tucker. How would you know my name?" I said.

"Barbara are you the Barbara Tucker that was kidnapped by serial killer, Paul John Knowles?" he asked.

I almost dropped the phone or pushed my call block button when my curiosity got the best of me and I said, "Yes, this is Barbara." Forty-five years later, it was happening again.

Jeremy Campbell was a reporter-journalist from WXIA in Atlanta, Georgia. "We are working on a documentary about the tragic events that took place at the hands of Paul John Knowles in 1974. We believe that there are some victims' families that never got the closure they needed," he said.

Why did God throw this person in my life after 45 years?

After talking for several minutes Jeremy asked, "Barbara, I would love for you to be interviewed. Thank you for taking part in our report. Barbara, you inspired me. I'd been struggling to find the light—and now I'm convinced that with you, we have it. Goodbye for now, I'll call you in a week after you and your family make a decision and then I'll set up a date after checking my schedule."

"When you have a minute, would you send me an e-mail detailing what the documentary is about?" I asked, after giving him my address.

"Sure, I'll get that out in a few hours." As he hung up the phone on his end, I stood there holding the phone as Jim took the phone from me and hung it up.

"Jim, Darling, what have I agreed to?"

"Honey, it's always in God's hands. You're supposed to do the interview."

That night after falling asleep, the nightmares began again. I was running for my life this time. The crazed killer was after me again. Running in slow motion, he grabbed my shoulder as I noticed the sawed-off shotgun. Damn, it was the serial killer, Paul John Knowles—it cannot be—he is dead.

Jim was startled awake by my sobbing uncontrollably. "What's the matter darling?"

"It's happening all over again. I don't know if I can do the interview. What did I get myself into?"

The next morning, I read Jeremy's e-mail:

As you requested, we are working on a documentary about the tragic events that took place at Paul Knowles hand in 1974. We believe there are victims' families who have not yet gotten the closure they need. We will highlight the fact that out of Knowles' 35 claimed murders, only 18 have been linked to him...and help the families of the others get answers. We have a few dates that we're available. Let me know what's best for you, Jim and Beverly. I'll call you next week after you decide. - Jeremy Campbell, WXIA, Atlanta

A week later Jeremy called and we both agreed that July 2, 2019, around noon would work for both of us. Jeremy would bring Matt Livingston, Audio/Video Tech to set up and record. We would keep in touch if anything else was needed before their flight in July.

Dale, my son, Mary Sue, Jim's daughter from his previous marriage, and Beverly were getting excited about the upcoming interview that would be in three weeks. The weeks passed quickly. Trying not to dwell on the interview was difficult for me because I was not the young woman in radio and TV anymore. I was a great-grandmother and proud to be one.

July 2, 2019 – Interview

That morning I dressed in a pretty black and white top with white slacks and black flats. Jim made a quick breakfast and we ate. "Honey, are my eyelashes glued on straight?" I asked Jim.

"Of course. You look great," he said, as he leaned down to give me a kiss on the cheek.

Jeremy and Matt called from the airport around 10:30 AM. I was nervous and excited because I never allowed anybody, in all of these years, to tape in our home.

A short time later, Jim called out. "Barbie, they're here," as he headed to the front door to open it.

Jeremy came in first and we hugged. "It's so good to finally meet you in person" I said. He was not as tall as his friend, Matt. They were both good looking. One was married, the other had a girlfriend. I liked them and could not wait to get the interview underway. I went into the bedroom to freshen up as I heard furniture being moved. Jeremy, the famous reporter was moving a chair into the middle of the living room.

"I can't believe there's popcorn under that chair!" I said in shock. Jeremy came from behind with the vacuum

Jim brought out from the bedroom, plugged it in and went about cleaning under the chair. We all laughed then got situated to begin taping. Matt had already set up the camera and lights. Jeremy moved a chair from the kitchen. He sat several feet away in front of me to do the interview.

"How long will you be taping?" Jim asked as he headed out to play games on the computer. "About 45 minutes, one-hour tops," Jeremy said.

My stomach was in knots. I had this same uneasy feeling the first time I recorded my first commercial when I was a young girl in radio. The butterflies calmed down when Jeremy asked the first question.

Barbara, I'll start by asking about the events of 1974 – as much or as little as you want to share about it. Next, I'll ask about how the experience has shaped your life after all these years that followed. When we spoke over the phone before, I sensed a real light coming from you. I'd like to hear about how you've kept your light strong, your faith strong…and your advice for others out there who have survived trauma. I have a feeling that's where the magic of this conversation lies.

The taping began as Jeremy asked, "Tell me about the events of 1974 after being forced from your home by serial killer Paul John Knowles."

If I would have met Paul John Knowles at a nightclub, I would have gone out with him. He was good looking. For an instant, I thought it was my ex-husband." Then I continued, "I knew immediately something was wrong. Paul John Knowles said, 'Don't turn around or I'll shoot you.' Then I turned around and couldn't believe what happened next. I walked him through the house. Then I went into the bedroom where Beverly was. She had a sheet tied over her face and blood dripping from her gag....

I could not continue. I was overwhelmed with emotion and bad memories.

A few minutes later we continued with the interview. "Barbara, you're putting in more than I expected. That's a good thing," said Jeremy.

Next Jeremy asked how the experience shaped my life in the years that followed.

For many years, Beverly and I led pretty normal lives. Our lives were changed, the moment we received the letter from New Dominion Pictures. They were doing *The Movie of the Week – Deadly Pursuit* that aired on the Discovery Channel for over four years. Beverly and I had buried our thoughts about being held hostage and my kidnapping and rape for years. It was deep in our subconscious minds.

In my mind, we both were living our lives to the fullest, making others laugh, while we cried inside, never forgetting the numbness in our souls. Even though Dale, my son wasn't in the *Movie of the Week*, he had to face his own demons. But God was with all three of us during our lifetime.

After the interview was over, I was drained. I needed a drink of water. Jim came over and hugged me then said, "Darling, I didn't hear your interview, but I know it will turn out great. I'll hear it when the show is completed in a few months."

"We're having lunch here, after we go see Beverly at the nursing home for a half hour. I know your flight isn't until four this afternoon so we'll have time to do both," I said to Jeremy and Matt.

On the ride to the nursing home, we made small talk. Jim parked the car and we all headed toward the door.

Carla, the bookkeeper, was there filling in for the receptionist that left for lunch.

"Hi Barbie and Jim. I'm so glad you came today," she said.

Jeremy and Matt followed us in. "Carla, this is Jeremy Campbell and Matt Livingston from WXIA, Atlanta," I said.

It was so much fun walking down the halls introducing Jeremy as the famous WXIA reporter and Matt audio/video personality. When we arrived at Beverly's hallway, we saw her sitting in her wheelchair at the end

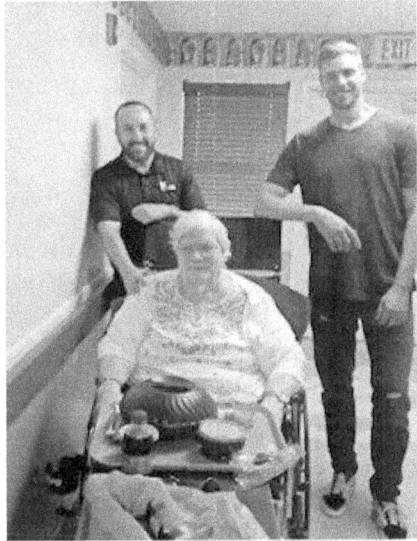

Jeremy Campbell, Reporter
Beverly & Matt Livingston, A/V Tech

of the hall eating her lunch. As we got closer, Beverly yelled out, "Barbie, you're here!"

She was so excited to meet Jeremy and Matt, we stopped to take pictures of them together and Beverly felt like a princess. As Jim wheeled Beverly back into her room, he put her next to Mary Jane, her roommate. "What a pleasure to meet you two!" Mary Jane said.

"Mary Jane has been Beverly's roommate now for three years. They're beginning to think alike," I said. I was not surprised that the administrator, physical therapist, aides, and a few nurses came by to visit while the famous men where there.

"Can I have your autograph, Jeremy?" Beverly asked.

"Sure. Have Barbara e-mail me a reminder and I'll send it to you in a few weeks."

It was a good visit and Beverly was very happy. When we were ready to leave, everyone hugged each other. Now we were ready to return to my house. Beverly and Mary Jane talked about this day for a long time.

When we got back to the house, I asked everybody to go into the kitchen and sit at the table for lunch. Jim heated up my Mama's famous Mac' N Cheese on the stove. I brought out the two platters of food I had prepared earlier. "Shrimp, wow, that's my favorite food!" Matt said as I placed it near him. Next, the platter of apples, grapes, cheeses, rolled deli meats, and small breads were laid down on the other side of the table. Everyone got their own sodas before sitting down to eat.

We talked about where each of us were from, other small talk, then I asked, "How long will it take to finish this program?"

Over lunch, we discussed the time frame. "Hopefully, it will be done by the end of the year," Jim said between bites of Mac' N Cheese. "We have a few more interviews to be done I'll let you both know in plenty of time to tell your friends and family."

Matt went out to take a call and came back to tell us that they had to catch an earlier flight back to Atlanta due to a problem on one of the shows. We visited for another half hour then Matt took his audio/visual equipment out to the van. "Don't forget you can come back anytime for my tacos," Jim said as we walked them to their rented vehicle.

After getting back in the house, I grabbed Jim and hugged him with all my might. "I'm so glad I married you, honey. I'll need you to get me through this next venture when the show actually airs."

Little did anyone know that Beverly would be dealt another blow in her life. She had been feeling exhausted for over a month. After the interview in July, Beverly told me her breast hurt and it was hot. I had the nurse come to her room and she told me she had set up a meeting to have an ultrasound done as soon as possible. Beverly could not stand up to have a mammogram so the following week the ambulance service took her to my oncologist who examined her and did an ultrasound plus a complete exam. He told Beverly that she had inflammatory breast cancer but needed to find out what stage it was. I was then asked by the doctor to come out into the hallway. I asked the nurse to please get Jim.

The doctor took me in the hallway and said, "I'm sorry to tell you this but it has spread and I need to do a biopsy to find out what stage it is in."

Damn, how much more can Beverly go through in life? I thought to myself trying to squelch back the tears.

The following week, after being in shock over the news, Beverly went to JFK hospital to have a biopsy. Jim and I, along with Dale and his family, visited Beverly at the nursing home as often as we could.

The following Monday we went back to the oncologist's office to get the news and see if she could be saved. I made the mistake of reading up on the Internet about inflammatory breast cancer and the different stages. In the stark office, as we waited for the doctor, we knew in our hearts it was not going to be good news. The doctor came in and confirmed our fears. Beverly's cancer had spread and it was stage IV. The chances of living were slim to none, due to the fact it had already metastasized to several parts of her body. Jim and I went over to Beverly and just hugged each other as if we would never see our Beverly again. We had to snap ourselves out of that mood. The doctor even hugged Beverly as she cried out, "WHY ME?"

We were all devastated as we followed the ambulance back to the nursing home. "Barbara, am I going to die?" she asked after she got situated in her bed at the nursing home.

"Yes, we are all going to die, but let's not get ahead of ourselves. It's God's will Beverly, not mine," I said with tears streaming down my face. Jim and I went over to the bed and leaned over and held her as we all cried. This was the nightmare I never wanted to face. I did not want to lose my beautiful twin sister, Beverly. There was nothing, NOTHING we could do but pray at this time. As Jim and I held her in our arms, our life together flashed before my eyes. At the house, we had one large bag packed for hospital visits. The other large bag was packed with games and fun stuff when we visited weekly at the nursing home. This had been going on for 10 years! Now I was losing part of myself.

"Barbie, quit crying, I'll be fine. I'm not dying today," she said. We kissed goodbye and Jim grabbed me by the hand to take me to the car. We were all in shock. Jim loved Beverly almost as much as he loved me. But of course, in a sisterly way. How would I tell our children, Dale and Mary Sue? I had to get a grip on my emotions and do what was needed to be done.

When we got the news, we realized nobody knew how long she had to live. So, we would live the following weeks and months having our family and friends call or visit as often as possible. In the past, I used to always complain to her friends to not take over so much food. She needed to lose weight. Now, I was telling them to take whatever she liked to eat over along with gifts of small stuffed animals or dolls.

Every time Jim and I visited Beverly we made sure we did not bring up cancer unless she wanted to talk about it. We had her come home by transport more often, until she was not strong enough to travel. It was always a joyous occasion when she came home and our family and friends stopped by to visit.

Friday, November 15th, 2019

Jim and I just finished shopping at Sam's Club. We had not stocked up on groceries for over two months due to wanting to be near Beverly. While driving home from Sam's I said, "Jim, we have to drop these groceries off at home then see Beverly today."

"Okay Honey, I know your sisterly intuition that God gave you and Beverly. We'll just go now. The groceries can wait," Jim said.

When we got to her room, she was loopy, not on the planet. I got a nurse to come in immediately who explained it was the new medicine the doctor prescribed.

"Take her off of that crap, it's making her crazy," I said to the nurse, as I went over to hug my sister and tell her everything was going to be alright.

"Don't leave me Barbara—Don't leave me!!!" she shouted out to me. My heart broke in two. Fifteen minutes later she fell asleep knowing we would be there in the morning to visit for the day. Saturdays we always had the most fun because there were not that many workers on duty and it was calmer.

Saturday, November 16th, 2019

Jim and I were dressed to visit Beverly at the nursing home. I felt uneasy and told Jim, Beverly was not answering her phone. Then I called the nurses' station. "Barbara, is this you? We're trying to get ahold of you...Beverly's being rushed to JFK Emergency Room. She took a turn for the worse this morning and can't speak."

I thanked her and told her we would head to JFK immediately. Jim heard the phone conversation and grabbed our bags with water and food along with needed paperwork and headed for JFK.

While driving to the hospital I called Dale and told him to meet us at the hospital. "Mom, I'm working," he started to say.

"Dale, please get your stuff done and meet us there as soon as you can. Oh, and be careful driving son."

When we arrived, they had Jim and me go to a section of the hospital that was strictly for patients near death. I was told that only one of us could go in to see Beverly. Jim told me to go first. I went in the large room. It held a few chairs, a desk and along the wall, in the back of room, was a bed with Beverly in it. "Oh my God, Beverly, I love you!" I shouted out as I walked up to her bed with hoses in her nose, machines hooked up on both sides of her. She lay there with her eyes closed and it looked as if she were in a coma.

A woman came up to me and put her arms around my shoulders, as she guided me out the door to explain what was happening. "Beverly is in a coma and dying. We've called in Hospice to take her there later in the day. We're keeping her here for the next few hours to observe her and make her comfortable with the meds. Didn't you say she was allergic to morphine because it made her go crazy?" she asked.

"Yes, but if that's what she needs so she won't be in pain, give it to her," I said. "I need my husband Jim, he's six feet six and waiting in the waiting room, I told the nurse. Or was it the doctor? I don't know. I didn't care. I wanted my husband.

"You can go out into the waiting room and we'll have your husband come in," she said.

"Oh, no, I'm not leaving my sister, and I need my husband—NOW!" I screamed out.

"Calm down, I'll have the nurse go get him for you."

When Jim came in the room, he was speechless as he walked over to her bed and laid his hand over hers. He just stood there and looked at her not knowing what to do or what to say.

A few minutes later Dale and his wife, Gloria came in. You could see the sheer panic on each face as they glanced over Beverly's bed saying beautiful words and not knowing if she could hear them or not. About a half hour later, another doctor and group of nurses came in to check on Beverly. We all went out in the hallway not having a clue what to say to one another. We were all trying to deal with the moment. One moment at a time. Jeremy, Dale's son and our grandson, came in and

Gloria, Dale, Mia, Barbara & Jeremy 2019

saw Beverly and lost it. He loved his great aunt.

Jeremy left the room to compose himself, then came back a few minutes later. Jim offered everybody a peanut butter and jelly sandwich. Beverly's favorite! I could only stomach half of it along with gulps of water.

Another hour had gone by after each of us went to Beverly and said whatever we thought she would love to hear. Every hour from 11 AM until late afternoon it was the same over and over again: nurses or doctors coming in to check Beverly while we stood or sat wondering what was next. I remembered Beverly's favorite song and told Dale and Gloria it was *Amazing Grace*. "Let's all sing it Mom," Dale said.

"*Amazing Grace! How sweet the sound that saved a wretch like me! I once was lost, but now I'm found; was blind, but now I see...Twas' grace that taught my heart to fear...*"

We were surrounding her bed, some holding her hands, and tears flowing from our eyes when Beverly

ONE SURVIVOR

actually moved her finger. She did! She could hear us singing. We sang the song again knowing God was in the room with us.

After singing, the nurse came in to tell us that the ambulance was on its way to JFK to pick Beverly up and take her across town to Hospice. We were told to go eat supper first because it would be over two hours before she would be settled in at Hospice.

Jim and I followed Dale and Gloria up to North Palm Beach to eat at the Outback Steakhouse. Jeremy had his car and met us there. After being seated Dale ordered appetizers while Jim and I ordered meals. Jeremy had lost his appetite and did not want to eat. The waitress forgot Dale's meal. A few minutes later we noticed Dale doubling over in excruciating pain due to a bad backache. He asked his son to go to Publix to buy some Aleve® to help the pain. While Jeremy was gone, Jim and I told Gloria and Dale that we would go to Hospice by ourselves. Dale needed to go home and take care of himself. After supper we said our goodbyes and left for Hospice.

We called Reverend Patti, who was still at church, and met her 20 minutes later at the Dunkin Donut shop near Hospice. She came with us to Hospice. I was trying to keep my composure and hugged Jim before entering the front door. The front of the building was surrounded by beautiful palm trees. Inside we were greeted by the receptionist, who took us into the foyer that was soothing with comfortable furniture and subtle lighting. Afterwards, the head nurse helped us with paperwork then called another nurse to take us to see Beverly.

"My God, she's still in a coma," I said to Jim and Reverend Patti.

307

"Barbara, she can still hear us, Reverend Patti said. Let's all let her know we're here and then say what you want. After you talk to her. I'll say a prayer and we can leave. She's going to meet God soon."

After we each told Beverly what was in our hearts and Reverend Patti said a lovely prayer, we headed out to go home. I stopped at the door. "Is it okay if I go back in and say something else to Beverly?" I asked.

"Sure. Take your time Barbara," Reverend Patti said. Jim hugged me knowing I needed strength.

I walked up to her bed, put my hand in hers and said,

Okay damn it. Let go and let God do his magic. We've already told you that Dale, Gloria, Jeremy, Mia, along with Michele, and your roommate Mary Jane and all of our families and friends are fine with you meeting God. It's time Beverly for you to meet your Glorious Maker. Beverly, Jim, and I will be okay. Especially ME, Beverly! You will be in my heart forever. Oh, by the way, remember when we promised whoever goes first, you or me—we'd save each a mansion in Heaven? Well, you're first and you have to save us a mansion in Heaven—But I swear to you Beverly—I will NOT clean it!

I leaned over to blow her a kiss. I left the room, almost losing my balance and falling out the door. That would have been a sight Beverly would have loved. Ah, the drama queen does it again—what a performance!

We said goodbye to the nurse on duty and left for home. We hugged Reverend Patti goodbye and thanked her again.

"Barbara, it's going to be alright. When God decides to take her to Heaven whether it's soon or in a few weeks, you'll be okay."

When we arrived home, I went to get my pajamas on and get comfortable before turning on a funny movie to relieve the tension of the day.

Sunday, November 17th, 2019

Beverly passed away peacefully that morning at 12:07 AM. We got the call around nine in the morning. I called Dale and Mary Sue in Georgia. Afterwards I called Reverend Patti. After church services that afternoon, Reverend Patti and Reverend Phyllis came to the house and said we needed to set the funeral services up as soon as possible because Thanksgiving was right around the corner. The following Monday, Jim and I went to All County Funeral Home and finalized her funeral arrangements. It was a very pleasant experience because she was in Heaven and all we had to do was give her the best, modest funeral in town. We picked out loving memory cards and brought along 30 pictures with Beverly in them to make up a DVD to be played at her Celebration of Life Service in our church's chapel.

Friday, November 22nd, 2019

CELEBRATION OF LIFE

Church service at

United Methodist Church Palm Beaches – Chapel
4:00 PM

Reception to follow in the Gathering Place.

The church service in the chapel was amazing. Since I wrote the eulogy for my sister. I was excited to tell her how I felt in a very humorous way. It took me three days to get my funny self together while writing. Everything was happening so fast. I called everybody I could think of to tell them about the service. It took six days to set up the funeral, service and do my eulogy. Only God could do that for me. Reverends Patti and Phyllis came over to our home and saw all the stuffed animals, dolls, etc. that Beverly had collected over the years. They took about 30 of them and had them set up in the Chapel when Jim and I arrived. Stuffed animals were in every pew. Before the service began, I went into the choir room and put on my choir robe. I wanted to sing along with the choir later during the service.

Choir members, Donna and Cary sang Beverly's favorite song, *Amazing Grace,* in perfect harmony. I thought the service was being recorded. Unfortunately, it was not. But my memories will last forever. Eleanor and her new husband, Larry, Jim, and I, along with Audrey were in the front row. Dale, Gloria, Jeremy, their young daughter Mia, and Michele sat behind us. Some people wept uncontrollably because of the DVD showing pictures on the screen of Beverly's life. Music played along with the video.

When it was the choirs turn to sing, they began walking up from the back of the church. I got out of my seat and joined them. They told me to sit down but I refused. I wanted to sing with them. The music began and we all sang *I Want Jesus to Walk with Me*. It was beautiful.

Afterwards, Reverend Patti introduced me. I began the eulogy for Beverly. "As most of you know, I am Barbara Abel, Beverly's twin sister. She was older by two minutes because I kicked her out first." I ended with the story about Dale's wedding to Gloria when Beverly took my wig and threw it on the ground. Fifteen minutes later, the final words were, "Well you were first and you promised to ask for my mansion in Heaven—only I'm NOT cleaning it." The audience broke out in laughter. "Damn Beverly, I was good, listen to them—and you already knew I was your favorite drama queen!"

Reverend Phyllis and Reverend Patti wound down the service. Cary, our choir director, had a recording of Beverly's favorite fun song that he began playing, *Oh, happy day, oh happy day, when Jesus washed, when Jesus washed my sins away*. As the music played, I got out of my seat in the front row, walked up to Rev. Patti and we both walked down the aisles and met in the center, singing together as everybody in the chapel got up, stood, and sang with us to the end of the song.

As the weeks went by, I began to heal and remember the wonderful life Beverly shared with Jim and me. She is in her mansion in heaven still watching out for me. And YES, I once again survived with God's help.

EPILOGUE

There is so much pain and suffering these days. Every time you turn on the news you hear bad things. In March 2020, a shooter killed four people, including a police officer, and injured two others before taking his own life at a local gas station. Then along comes the Coronavirus from China and we are devastated at the lives that were lost. Especially, the elderly in nursing homes in a few States that allowed people with the virus in hospitals to be sent to nursing homes that did not have staff or knowledge to handle this pandemic.

Just when we thought everything was getting better, another black man is murdered right in front of our eyes on the nightly news by a monstrous police officer. The resulting riots around the country were appalling. What about the black, white, or Asian police officers who were murdered? It is one thing to peacefully stand up for one's rights, another when vicious, hateful groups ruin it. I never thought we would see it in our lifetime. The hatred among groups that do not care anything about the United States of America.

Why do we have a few bad police officers? Were they not vetted or trained properly? What is happening to other people that kill for fun? Is it mental illness, being abused, the Internet, violent games, or joining gangs to feel better? The answer could be all the above. With millions of dollars being spent throughout the decades, the problems have not gone away and appear to be getting worse.

We, as American citizens, need to be mindful of others around us. If something seems out of place or odd, you overheard something suspicious, or see a crime it is your duty as a citizen to act; you need to call your local police department. Use Crime Stoppers, tip lines, do it anonymously, or block your caller ID if you must (I have included some of the federal tip lines in the resources section). If possible, record a video and take pictures for evidence of what you see, but do not get yourself hurt or do anything unlawful to take them. Another option: if you feel your complaint is not being handled, you can try contacting your local news media outlets to see if any of them might be interested in the story.

Even if you despise your police, do not do it for them, do it for the victim instead. That victim could be your neighbor's sister or your sister's new boyfriend you have not met yet. Remember each police officer is a different human being and the chance of meeting a bad one is extremely low; however, if you do not want to meet the officer in person, do it anonymously or tell the dispatcher you do not want to be contacted.

Something has to be done to help others by holding the bad guys and bad law enforcement officers accountable for their actions. We should be grateful to live in this great United States of America. We will come together as a nation, through all of this turmoil, ahead of the game, by getting back the good values that have been lost along the way. We will all survive!

My story was written to help victims of crime. Other victims may feel alone and that no one else ever experienced a plethora of feelings and emotions that happen during and after their assault. During my kidnapping and repeated rapes in 1974, the police were untrained to offer professional counselling, few psychologists were experts in the field of working with victims of violent crimes, no one ever suggested getting some mental health. Fortunately, that has changed. If you have been a victim, see a properly trained psychologist or social worker at least once and become a survivor. Understand you must have love and hope in your life. I chose to forgive, a long time ago, in order to survive, but it was through God being in my heart that I managed to survive all these years.

WHO WAS PAUL JOHN KNOWLES AND WHY I MAY HAVE SURVIVED?

NOTE: This chapter is for those ONLY interested in knowing more about Paul John Knowles. It is not for everyone and it will not change the memoir by Barbara Mabee Abel.

It is written by the editor, a retired Florida law enforcement officer from Metro-Dade Police Department, now known as Miami-Dade Police Department and later the Palm Beach County Sheriff's Office during the early 1980's to the mid 1990's. The research of Paul John Knowles was conducted by the editor using law enforcement training, practices, and the opinions are those of the editor in this chapter, including current psychological and physical forensic interpretations.

Nevertheless, this story is solely about Barbara Mabee (Tucker) Abel and not Paul John Knowles. However, the information about Knowles may help you understand his motivations, mindset, antisocial, and social behaviors, and those effects on Barbara. He is one of the most psychologically intriguing serial killers to study. However, we will never know the whole truth as to all the victims he may have killed, his underlying motives, reasons for his actions, and how they came to be. Unfortunately, we will never know the answers we seek and the ability to use that information to identify and stop potential killers in the future.

Paul John Knowles was born April 25, 1946, near Orlando, Florida and lived in the Jacksonville area. He was known to his family and friends as PJ. According, to his brother, Clifton, they were a very poor family, living in a three-room home. Their parents had the bedroom. There was a kitchen. The living room was where the five siblings stayed. And there was an outhouse. Clifton spoke of his father's severe beatings as "whoopings" that left lasting bruises. The children should have been removed from the parents and put into foster home early on for their safety, though it never happened. PJ was his father's favorite target of his whoopings. His mother, Bonnie was kind to PJ, but subservient to her husband. PJ was close with his mother and it seemed that she was truly the only woman figure that accepted him in his life. His father, Thomas Jefferson Knowles, desperately wanted a girl and he tormented PJ (Campbell & Livingston, 2019). PJ wanted to be a man's man and to show off his masculinity, around 8-9 years old he started getting into legal trouble. In 1954, he started his juvenile record for petty theft, burglary, and later grand theft auto.

Paul John Knowles

Thomas Knowles relinquished PJ to the State of Florida and PJ started a long stint in the infamous Arthur G. Dozier School for Boys, later becoming the Florida State Reform School. The Dozier School, in the panhandle town of Marianna, FL, was known for its violence, correcting its students/inmates by beatings, whippings, rapes, and even killing them. In a visit from then Gov. Claude Kirk in 1968, when corporal punishment was finally outlawed, Kirk declared it "a training ground for a life of crime (Montgomery & Moore, 2019)."

The school opened in 1900 and was segregated until 1966. It was finally closed in 2011, after numerous investigations and inspection failures. During subsequent investigations over 100 identified graves were found on the 1400-acre property; however, more horrifying was more than 75 unmarked graves that have been identified as of 2019, and the search continues.

According to Tampa Tribune reports, Montgomery and Moore (2019), "For 109 years, this is where Florida has sent bad boys. Boys have been sent here for rape or assault, yes, but also for skipping school, smoking cigarettes, or running hard from broken homes. Some were tough, some confused and afraid; all were treading through their formative years in the custody of the state. They were as young as 5, as old as 20, and they needed to be reformed." But it was far from a reform school and often much worse than adult prisons.

PAUL JOHN KNOWLES

By the time he turned 19, he was convicted of kidnapping a police officer. He was sentenced from one to five years and was paroled in November 1967 (Campbell & Livingston, 2019). He was convicted and sentenced for breaking and entering in 1968-1971. In 1971, he was sentenced to three years for another breaking and entering, however, he escaped in November 1972. He was returned to prison; an additional three years was added to his sentence for the escape and resisting an officer during his capture. It ran concurrently with his previous sentence.

Paul John Knowles became a pen pal with and eventually engaged to Angela Covic, while incarcerated in Raiford prison, now known as Florida State Prison. Raiford was known for being the worst prison in Florida. Knowles convinced Covic to hire and pay for an attorney for his upcoming parole hearing in May 1974. She hired Sheldon Yavitz, the famed Miami attorney to the South American drug cartel. Yavitz was successful in getting Knowles released on parole with the stipulation that Knowles would leave Florida and serve his parole in California.

Knowles flew to San Francisco to marry Angela Covic, a recently divorced cocktail waitress. The week before Knowles arrived, she saw a physic who warned that a dangerous man would be coming into her life and to be careful. When Knowles arrived, Covic started to feel different towards Knowles and after three days she told Knowles to leave.

Knowles claimed his killing binge started that night by stabbing three people in San Francisco, before he flew back to Jacksonville. However, those three killings were never tied to Knowles. Once back in Jacksonville, he got into a bar fight and was arrested again.

Knowles started crisscrossing the United States from Florida, to Connecticut, to Washington, Nevada, New Mexico, including a 40-state, 20,000-mile killing spree, according to Sandy Fawke. Fawke was a British reporter that met Knowles in a bar in Georgia, in early November 1974. She founded him good-looking and charming, and travelled for several days with him to South Florida. She stated that Knowles was unable to perform sexually and passed it off as too much alcohol. Fawke never had a clue that Knowles was a serial killer. Knowles most likely saw her as someone that could write his story and make him famous. Fawke accepted him and was kind, something Knowles relished. He never committed any crimes during their encounter; therefore, she was not a witness that needed elimination.

Charles Marchman, an attorney from Macon, Georgia, believes that Knowles perpetrated the 35 murders he claims to have committed. Knowles did not identify all of the victims killed from being paroled from Raiford prison in May to his capture on November 17, 1974. To this day, there could be upwards of two-dozen more unidentified victims unaccounted to Knowles doing. If all the police departments across the country succeeded in proving the cases they want against Knowles, Marchman says he would have been convicted of up to 150 killings. But most of those cases never could be proven. Nonetheless, there are still a number of open cases, in 37 states during Knowles's 6-month killing spree.

Both Marchman and Yavitz agree many of Knowles crimes were linked to sex—to women who rejected his advances and to homosexual men that he raped and killed. Knowles could not become erect when raping women, but could with his male victims. He performed necrophilia on some of his victims, especially children. Knowles would probably have been diagnosed with antisocial personality disorder, intermittent explosive disorder (IED), borderline personality disorder, hypomania, gender dysphoria, sexual deviance tendencies, and dissociative identity disorder among other diagnosis.

Knowles did not have a clear modus operandi. He killed by strangulation, stabbing, and shooting his victims. His victims ranged from seven to 63 years old. They were people he picked up as hitchhikers, from bars, strangers he befriended found near campgrounds, just seen walking down the street, burglary victims, and so on.

They were male, female, heterosexual, homosexuals, and virgins. He would rape them alive or have sex after killing them. This all made it difficult for law enforcement to determine, which victims were tied to Knowles.

With today's technologies and forensics, Paul John Knowles would have never had a chance to kill in the numbers he did. He stole many of the victims' cars and credit cards. Credit cards were slow to process in 1974. The card was put into a machine and several copies were made of the card. Those copies might take up to a month to be turned in by the merchant to the processing company and another couple of weeks to process. It would take a court order to have the copies pulled by the different card companies and could take several more weeks before the law enforcement agency had the information.

Today, law enforcement can get a court order and have the information from a sale within a few hours. Tracking of the suspect is now almost instantaneous; additionally, they can request to have a continuous live tracking of new purchases, within a few minutes.

In 1974, DNA was in its infancy and not used by law enforcement. Today, DNA is a fairly quick process, tying victims to suspects and followed up by having warrants issued for the suspect's apprehension.

Changes in victim's rights, services, and mental health have changed drastically since Barbara's kidnapping and rape. Law enforcement would get preliminary information of the crime, such as urgent information to apprehend a suspect, the victim's name, date of birth, and contact, and a brief statement to what happened. Today, a rape kit and medical exam would happen prior to any formal statements ask by the police. At the hospital, a victim receives information, along with available mental counseling, a follow-up contact, and many information pamphlets on different victim services and advocacy groups. Finally, when the exam is complete, the victim would give a formal statement to all necessary law enforcement agencies. Today's detectives have an abundance of training dealing with victims, especially not re-victimizing them all over again.

Paul John Knowles After His Capture
...suspect in as many as 35 murders

Between Knowles' capture in mid-November 1974 and his death a month later, he was interview by a court appointed psychiatrist. The following is an excerpt of the transcript of that interview.

DR: If you had to live your life over again, what would you do?

PJK: If I had to live life over again—I wouldn't. You know?

DR: You wouldn't do what?

PJK: I wouldn't live it again.

DR: It's been that bad?

PJK: There's no way I could go through another year of it. I fully intended to—be shot before I was arrested.

DR: What's the worst thing that ever happened to you in your life?

PJK: The worst? I was born, to be truthful.

DR: You mean from the time you were born; you've been that bitter against life?

PJK: Well, I look at it like this, I was a hell of a lot better off before I was born than I am or have been since I was born.

DR: Well, let me ask you something else, what's the best thing that ever happened to you in your life?

PJK: Nothing. I mean so—Nothing good so far. I'm a criminal, and I've been a criminal since I was a little kid.

DR: You really are saying that you believe you have a criminal mind?

PJK: Well, it's been through the road. My life has been more involved in the criminal sense than the average. I realized there was a lack of—maybe not a lack of love, but a lack caring. So, I had no doubt that they (his parents) loved me, but they just didn't give a damn.

DR: Well, if you love somebody, how can you not give a damn?

PJK: It's possible. Perhaps they did give a damn—but they just didn't know how to show it.

Further discussion and the topic came to his father's beating him. And what Knowles did after one of the severe beatings.

PJK: For three days I partied. You know just rode around town, went to the shooting galleries, penny arcades, and stuff like that. Just whatever.

DR: Didn't go home?

PJK: No sir. Just sleeping in the woods—you know? And then they caught me and they sent me home and the next day I was at school, and they called me across the street to the police station, and they started talking to me and that was when they take me up there (Dozier School).

Yavitz spoke of Knowles as a fatalist and that Knowles placed a great deal of value on his own life. He was afraid of dying. He was extremely afraid of dying by the electric chair stating to Yavitz, "I don't want to be electrocuted. I don't want them to fry me. That's a bad way to die." Florida's death penalty was carried out at that time by *Old Sparky*, the State's electric chair. Knowles continued, "I don't want to be hung either—I'd take poison. But I want you (Yavitz) to do whatever it takes to keep me alive."

Knowles' conversations with the state appointed psychiatrist and Sheldon Yavitz shows a very conflicted man. Possibly it was the different personalities speaking. Nevertheless, conflicted.

While Knowles was being investigated and awaiting trial and just before his death, he sent Yavitz an envelope. It did not contain any tapes, just on the outside was written, "15th and 16th" referring to the November 6, 1974, killings of Carswell Carr and his 15-year-old daughter, Mandy. Carswell was stabbed multiple times soaking his mattress through and the strangulation of Mandy and necrophilia with her body (Campbell & Livingston, 2019).

Knowles sent one final letter to Angela Covic dated December 14, 1974, and it was mailed the day before his death. It was received by Covic on Christmas eve and was released by Sheldon Yavitz. She would have already known his fate. The letter read:

> I am very content within myself and having a tremendously good time. I am watching the human comedy evolving around me. As a matter of fact, two cops just came to the door and peeked in through the little screen-covered hole in my door.
>
> I couldn't help but laugh at that, I mean like you should see the ridiculous looks on their faces when they peek in.
>
> They look like spectators at a carnival or a zoo. Ha! The jailers aren't so bad, it's the detectives and other cops that come in off the street, expecting me to look like Godzilla's twin brother or something.
>
> I swear! And when I don't start tearing the door off and beating on the walls they don't know what to think. It just freaks them out when I just sit and laugh at them or smile and then ask them how they are doing.
>
> This case will go down in history. It has been predicted that I will turn out to be the most

```
henious   [sic]  murderer  in   the
history   of   crime.  Big   Deal
(Douthat, 1974).
```

So why did Barbara Tucker, her twin sister, and son survive since Knowles believed you never left a witness alive? Barbara would say it was her faith in God. As a former law enforcement officer, I believe she is alive because she played into his needs and wants at that moment. He needed someone to write a book to make him famous. The Casanova Killer had a goal—to be the nation's number one serial killer. He wanted to be more famous than Clyde Barrow (1931-1934, 13 victims, nine that were law enforcement), Manson (1969, the Manson family murdered eight victims), the Zodiac killer (late 1960s - early 1970s, five confirmed victims, possibly 20-28), and more after his death like Theodore Bundy (1974-1978, seven victims but claimed 30), BTK (1975-2005, 10 victims), Son of Sam (late 1975 – early 1977, killed six and wounded 10) Jeffrey Dahmer (1978-1991, 17 victims), and all received more notoriety than Knowles.

Barbara never showed fear or very little towards him, even from the beginning when he told her not to turn around in the kitchen, when he was holding a shotgun, and she still turned around. She sat down with him in her Florida room and talked calmly with him. She was willing to go with him instead of her son, then pretended to be friendly and keeping him at ease on the drive to Ft. Pierce. She thought clearly enough to keep him driving on surface streets rather than Interstate-95. She went into survival mode and she played his game.

Barbara made him think she really liked him and maybe even loved him. The one thing Knowles wanted more than anything was to be accepted, cared for, and loved. I am sure during Barbara's abduction, there were many questionable moments wondering if the other person was pretending or was it for real. But if he thought there was really a possibility that she might love him, was he willing to lose that chance of his lifetime or was she just a witness needing to be killed? We may never know what he was thinking the moment he left the hotel. He did seem conflicted by returning to the room several times, until he made the error of forgetting the room key.

I believe that Knowles thought a disabled person and a six-year-old were either unable to be witnesses mentally or he planned on returning to kill them soon after disposing of Barbara's body, until he realized she was valuable to him. We do know when Yavitz met him in Milledgeville Jail, there was a discussion to escape and return to kill Beverly, Dale, and Barbara because these witnesses were still alive.

ACKNOWLEDGEMENTS

First and foremost, I want to thank my sister, Beverly Mabee for being there every step of my life, knowing every detail and emotion I have dealt with. If not for Beverly making me promise her that I would finish writing this book, getting into the hands of others, and helping them—victims of crimes—as her last wish, it may have never happened.

My darling husband, Jim Abel, you are always my anchor and soulmate. You made this book happen by never letting me give up on myself. How you have put up with me all these years is a mystery. I think they call it LOVE!

My son, Dale, thank you for becoming the man you have become by overcoming adversities in your own life, by fighting your own demons and finding the Lord. You are an amazing Warrior for our Lord, Jesus Christ in helping others less fortunate.

Mary Sue and Michele, daughters, who helped me with many words of encouragement and who are always with me or just a phone call away.

My sister, Jackie who passed away in 1997 from cancer, was an integral part of my writing. Gary, my brother, Ylwa, his wife, and their children, David, Shawn, and April for believing in me, I am grateful.

Omah, Tara, Barbara, and Terry were there in times of joy and sorrow. This book would not have been possible, if not for the many people who supported and inspired me.

The nurses, aides, office workers at Consulate Healthcare of West Palm Beach where Beverly, my twin, was until she went to Heaven after a bout with cancer. Especially, to Beverly's roommate, Mary Jane, I truly appreciate you.

Cary Collins, our choir director, and our wonderful choir for putting joy into my life.

I thank William who first drafted a few book covers.

Shermaine, Shawn, Pam, and Phillip along with members of our UMCPB church giving me encouragement to continue throughout the years.

A special thanks to Reverend. Kent Crow, who gave me the courage to speak at church and Celebrate Recovery.

Reverend Phyllis and Reverend Patti guided me through some rough patches when my sister passed away and I wanted to give up writing, again.

Eleanor, Cheryl, and Bill you have helped me explain my thoughts, organize them, and amend my book. You have provided numerous hours of love and attention to this project.

A grateful thanks to Reverend David McEntire, Audrey and Arthur Rao and Liza Pierce for being there in some of my most dreadful times. Beverly and I thank you for supporting us during the filming of the Movie of the Week back in 2001 which aired on the Discovery Channel for over four years titled "Dangerous Pursuit."

I would like to thank everyone in the Senile Old Broadcasters club, better known as the S.O.B club for their backing.

The Forest Hill High School class of '61 reunion committee who encouraged me to continue with my dreams of helping victims of crime.

A joyous thanks to Fredrick "Fred" T. Joss, a fellow author known as Joss Tallman, who introduced me to the person who would get my book to press. That person was Laurel L. Galvan, my editor, cover creator, and publisher. She has become a friend throughout these months of struggling to finish this book. I thought it was finished when I submitted it to her and boy was I in for a shock. Her infinite patience with me, superb graphic, and editorial skills made this possible.

For anyone who helped along the way that I inadvertently missed, thank you!

VICTIM LIST & TIMELINE

Knowles victims need to be remembered. They were everyday good hardworking people like us. Who knows what these victims would have contributed to society if their lives were not so senselessly extinguished? As an honor to their families and their lives, they are listed here. **Bold name** are the murdered victims.

Angela Covic

MAY 1974 - John Paul Knowles claimed to have **killed three people in one night**. After being rejected by a woman named Angela Covic, Knowles said he took to the streets of San Francisco and murdered three strangers. Police have never verified his claims.

MAY 1974 – Knowles returns from California and gets into a knife fight at a bar, injuring the bartender. Knowles is arrested and jailed.

JULY 26, 1974 – Knowles escapes jail, again.

JULY 26, 1974 - **Alice Henrietta Curtis, 65,** is robbed in her Lima, Florida home. Knowles is a novice robber. He binds and gags Curtis to keep her quiet. She chokes to death on the gag.

AUGUST 1, 1974 Part 1 - **Lillian Annette Anderson, 11**, and sister, **Mylette Josephine Anderson, 7,** are reported missing from Jacksonville, Florida. Knowles claimed he killed both girls, but neither body has never been found. Knowles said he dumped the bodies in a swamp. Police do not think he committed this murder even though he claimed to have killed them. Knowles said he was acquainted with the Anderson family, and was spotted by Lillian and Mylette. Knowles said he killed them to make sure they would not say that they had seen him.

PHOTO CREDIT: The Anderson Family

AUGUST 1, 1974 Part 2 - **Ima Jean Sanders, 13,** decides to hitchhike. Knowles claims he picked her up, sexually assaulted her, and strangled her in Peach County, Georgia. Knowles claimed he returned to the body later, and buried the jawbone.

PHOTO CREDIT: Sanders Family

AUGUST 2,1974 - **Marjorie Howie, 49**, is murdered in her home in Atlantic Beach, Florida. Howie is sexually assaulted and strangled with a nylon stocking. Knowles stole her TV.

AUGUST 23, 1974 - **Kathy Sue Woods Pierce, 24,** is found strangled on the bathroom floor of her home in Musella, Georgia. Knowles used a telephone cord. The case is not pursued by police.

SEPTEMBER 3, 1974 - **William Vernon Bates, 32** and John Paul Knowles start drinking together. Knowles binds and strangles Bates with electrical wire. Bates's car, credit cards, among other things, were stolen. Bates is not immediately found.

SEPTEMBER 12, 1974 - Emmett Alexander Johnson, 62, and **Lois Mildred Clendenen Johnson, 59,** stop at a truck stop in Ely, Nevada. Knowles shoots and kills them both. They are not noticed.

PHOTO CREDIT: Johnson Family

SEPTEMBER 18, 1974 - Emmett Johnson's body is found in the camper where he was killed. Lois Johnson is also found, partially nude, under a table.

SEPTEMBER 21, 1974 - Charlynn Hopkins Hicks (Charlynn Hicks), 42, stops her car at a rest stop. She is abducted and sexually assaulted by Knowles. Hicks is strangled with pantyhose. Her body is dumped in a nearby wooded area in Seguin, Texas.

SEPTEMBER 23, 1974 - Charlynn Hicks' body is found. **Ann Dawson**, a beautician went missing from Birmingham, Alabama.

SEPTEMBER 29, 1974 - **Ann Jean Dawson, 49,** was last seen leaving Pinson Lounge in Birmingham, Alabama on September 23. She was with a man "about 30, with red hair, about six feet tall and weighing about 170 lbs." Her body was never found. Knowles said they traveled together for a few days before he killed her. He says he threw her body in the Mississippi River.

OCTOBER 16, 1974 - **Karen Marie Wine, 35,** and her daughter **Dawn Marie, 15/16,** are murdered in their home in Marlborough, Connecticut. Both are bound, sexually assaulted, and strangled with a nylon stocking. They were robbed. The robbery included a small tape recorder of no resale value.

Dawn Wine

PHOTO CREDIT: Newspaper archives

OCTOBER 18, 1974 – Knowles traveled to Woodford, Virginia. He breaks into the home of **Doris Evelyn Hosey, 53.** Saying he will not kill her, Knowles demands a gun and some money. Hosey gives the

337

killer her husband's rifle. Knowles shoots Hosey with the rifle, wipes off his fingerprints, and leaves the gun by her body.

PHOTO CREDIT: Newspaper Archives
Doris Bruce Hosey

MID-OCTOBER 1974 – **Debbie Griffin**, a hitchhiker in Bibb, Georgia, went missing. (See November 2, 1974)

OCTOBER 23, 1974 (approx.) - Still driving William Bates' stolen car, Knowles picked up two hitchhikers in Key West, Florida with the intention of killing them both, but his plan went awry when a policeman stopped him for a traffic violation. Unaware of who he was dealing with, the officer let Knowles go with a warning. Shaken by the experience, Knowles had mercy on his victims and dropped them off in Miami, Florida. He contacted his lawyer shortly thereafter.

OCTOBER 24, 1974 – Knowles meets with his attorney, Sheldon Yavitz, at the bar of the University Inn, Miami, FL and proclaims he is a mass murder. Yavitz advises him to tape his detailed confessions to the murders that he remembers and give him the tape(s).

OCTOBER 26, 1974 – Knowles meets with his attorney, Sheldon Yavitz and turns over the tapes in a sealed envelope and told him not to open it until his death. Knowles wanted Yavitz to write a book about Knowles killings and to make him famous. Yavitz was instructed to split the profits of the book between himself and his mother. Yavitz failed to inform him that a criminal cannot profit from a movie or book, and the proceeds would be dispersed among victims' families that made a claim to Knowles' estate.

NOVEMBER 2, 1974 - **Edward Hilliard** and **Debbie Griffin** were hitchhiking near Milledgeville, Georgia. Knowles claimed he shot Hilliard and left the body by a tree. Knowles claimed he raped Griffin. Her body was found in 1975.

PHOTO CREDIT: Hillard-Griffin Families

NOVEMBER 6, 1974 - **Amanda "Mandy" Beth Carr, 15,** is killed in her home in Milledgeville, Georgia. Knowles strangled her with a silk stocking. Reports say Knowles failed in his attempt at necrophilia. Her father, **Carswell Hall Carr Sr.**, is also killed. Knowles bound and stabbed him 27 times with scissors and a butcher knife. He was mutilated. His car and credit cards were stolen.

NOVEMBER 7-13, 1974 - British journalist Sandy Fawkes, met Darrel Golden (Paul John Knowles) in a bar in Atlanta. She traveled with him to Florida, not knowing he was a wanted man. She left him days later as she prepared to return to London on November 16, 1974. She found out the next day that he tried to rape a friend she had introduced him to, and reported him to police.

NOVEMBER 14, 1974 – Part 1 - Susan MacKenzie, said she did, vaguely know Fawkes. She was the wife of one of the journalists (Sandy Fawkes' acquaintance) Fawkes had gone out drinking with the prior night. Mrs. MacKenzie says that when he was driving her to the hairdresser this morning, he pulled the car off the road and asked her to make love to him. When she refused, he pulled a gun on her. Susan managed to get out of the car, despite Knowles grabbing her by the hair, and called police from a nearby pay phone.

NOVEMBER 14, 1974 – Part 2 – Knowles was pulled over by a West Palm Beach Police squad car. Knowles pointed the shotgun at the officer and Knowles escaped, though police now knew the make and model of his car.

NOVEMBER 14, 1974 – Part 3 – Knowles ditched the car and was on foot when he saw Beverly Mabee, 31, putting clothes on the line. Mabee had Cerebral Palsy. Knowles forced her into the house and attempted to rape Mabee, while he waited for Mabee's twin sister, Barbara Tucker, 31, and her son, Dale, 6, to come home that evening. Knowles kidnaps Tucker and takes her to a Ft. Pierce, FL motel.

NOVEMBER 15 - 16, 1974 – Knowles held Barbara Tucker captive and repeatedly raped her. Knowles wanted to leave for Georgia with Tucker, but locked himself out of the motel room and left without her early in the morning of November 16, 1974.

NOVEMBER 16, 1974, Part 1 - **Florida Highway Patrol Trooper Charles "Charley" Eugene Campbell, 35,** spots a stolen car. He attempts to arrest the driver, Knowles, but is overpowered. Knowles steals the police car and takes Campbell hostage, driving over state lines.

Photo Credit: FHP
Trooper Charles Campbell

NOVEMBER 16, 1974, Part 2 - Knowles uses police sirens to pull over **James Meyer**, a Wilmington, DE businessman. He steals Meyer's less-conspicuous rental car, taking him hostage along with Campbell.

PHOTO CREDIT: Meyers Family

NOVEMBER 16, 1974, Part 3 - Knowles takes his hostages **Campbell and Meyer** into the woods in Pulaski County, Georgia. He handcuffs them to a tree, then shoots both men in the head. Knowles flees, crashing through a police roadblock. He loses control and crashes, but still manages to elude police.

NOVEMBER 17, 1974 - Knowles is captured by an armed civilian who is close to, but outside, the police search area. David T. Clark, a Vietnam Veteran, walks to a nearby pastor's home with Knowles to use the phone, but the pastor refuses to open the door. Clark takes Knowles to another house and asks that they call police. Knowles is taken into custody.

NOVEMBER 21, 1974 - The bodies of **Trooper Charles Campbell and James Meyer** are found handcuffed to a tree in Pulaski County, Georgia by a hunter. They have been shot.

NOVEMBER 28, 1974 - The decomposed body of 32-year-old **William Bates** is found in Lima Ohio, in a wooded area near his home.

DECEMBER 18, 1974 - Police transported Knowles to where he said he hid some guns. En route, Knowles freed one hand from his handcuffs with a paperclip. Knowles attacked Sheriff Earl Lee and Georgia Bureau of Investigation Agent Ronnie Angel in the car. He reached for the Sheriff's gun. Agent Angel shot Knowles three times, killing him. Just as Knowles predicted his life would end.

DECEMBER 30, 1974 - A coroner's jury ruled the shooting of Knowles was justifiable self-defense.

FALL 1975 – **Debbie Griffin**'s body was discovered in the woods in Bibb County, Georgia. Griffin's body was found almost a year after her murder, a few miles from Hillard's body.

APRIL 1976 - The skeleton of a young girl is found. She cannot be identified until 2011, the police announce she is **Ima Sanders**.

NOVEMBER 29, 1977 - Newspapers report that the body of **Ann Dawson** was found earlier that month. She was identified through dental records.

DECEMBER 21, 2011 - Investigators use DNA to link the slaying of **Ima Sanders** to Paul John Knowles.

RESOURCES

Myra Goldick, radio producer of two popular Podcast shows ran for five years. "Dancing on Your Disabilities and "Never Say Impossible were cancelled after Myra retired. In 2013 Barbara was interviewed by Myra on one of her two podcasts: "Never Say Impossible". This show was about people who overcame adversity in difficult situations, in both their personal and business lives. How each survived their challenges and came out winners. https://myragoldick.com/

TIPLINES

National Suicide Prevention Lifeline 1-800-273-TALK (8255)

https://www.suicidepreventionlifeline.org

Youthline – Text teen2teen to 839863 or call 1-877-968-8491

YouthLine is a free, confidential teen-to-teen crisis and help line. Contact us with anything that may be bothering you. No problem is too big or too small for the YouthLine!

Teens are available to help daily from 4-10 pm PST
(adults are available by phone at all other times!)

**Majority of crimes are considered local
jurisdiction and should be reported to the local
police department who enforces the laws of that
state, county, and city. If they determine it is a
federal crime, they will turn it over to the proper
federal organization.**

The United States Department of Justice

https://www.justice.gov/actioncenter/report-
crime

This is an excellent website to report tips of
Federal crimes. This website is the best place to
start. It will direct you to each Federal law
enforcement agency for the type of crime or
information you would like to leave in your tip. If
you cannot find it here than look at the tip lines
below.

ATF -
https://www.justice.gov/actioncenter/report-
crime

Crimes involving alcohol, tobacco, firearms, or
explosives

ATF TIPS: Anonymous tips may be submitted to
ATF through the ReportIt® mobile app, available
on both Google Play and the Apple App Store, or

by visiting www.reportit.com. The app allows users to submit tips about crimes that involve firearms, violent crime, explosives, and arson.

> Arson hotline - 888-ATF-FIRE (888-283-3473)
>
> Bomb hotline - 888-ATF-BOMB (888-283-2662)
>
> Illegal firearms activity - 800-ATF-GUNS (800-283-4867)
>
> Firearms theft hotline - 888-930-9275
>
> Explosives theft or loss - 800-461-8841
>
> Other crimes involving alcohol, tobacco, firearms, or explosives - 888-283-8477

FBI Tip Line https://www.fbi.gov/tips

General Public

Members of the public can report violations of U.S. federal law or suspected terrorism or criminal activity as follows:

- Terrorism
- Counterintelligence
- Cyber Crime
- Public Corruption
- Civil Rights
- Organized Crime
- White-Collar Crime
- Violent Crime
- WMD (Weapons of Mass Destruction)

Contact us online

- Use our **Online Tips and Public Leads** form to report information on criminal activity and suspected terrorist threats
- Report cyber-crimes by filing a complaint with our **Internet Crime Complaint Center** go to https://www.ic3.gov/complaint/default.aspx

Contact us via telephone or mail

- Contact your **local FBI office** go to https://www.fbi.gov/contact-us/field-offices
- Call **1-800-CALLFBI (225-5324)** for the Major Case Contact Center
- Call **(866) 720-5721** to report fraud, waste, and abuse involving disaster relief to the:
  National Center for Disaster Fraud or write to NCDF
  Baton Rouge, LA 70821-4909

ICE Homeland Security Investigations (HSI) [https://www.ice.gov/tipline]

Individuals across the world can report suspicious criminal activity to the **ICE Homeland Security Investigations (HSI) Tip Line** 24 hours a day, seven days a week. Highly trained specialists take reports from both the public and law enforcement agencies on more than 400 laws enforced by ICE HSI.

What types of crimes should you report to the ICE HSI Tip Line?

- Terrorism
- Cyber Crimes
- Drug Smuggling
- Money Laundering
- Human Trafficking/Smuggling
- Human Rights Violators
- Import/Export Violations
- Child Pornography/Exploitation
- Document and Benefit Fraud
- Gang-related Crimes
- Intellectual Property Rights Violations
- Worksite Enforcement

If you would like to report suspicious criminal activity:

Call 866-DHS-2-ICE (866-347-2423) (from U.S. and Canada)

Online go to **https://www.ice.gov/webform/hsi-tip-form**

TTY for hearing impaired **only**: TTY para personas con discapacidad auditiva **solamente**: (802) 872-6196

Call 802-872-6199 (from other locations around the globe)

U.S. Marshals Service -
https://www.usmarshals.gov/tips/index.html

The U.S. Marshals Service (USMS) relies on you to provide us with tips on wanted fugitives, non-compliant sex offenders, and threats to the judiciary.

The U.S. Marshal's Service has two ways to submit tips. Online through your Internet browser at https://www.usmarshals.gov/tips/index.html

Or by Mobile Device Tip Submissions

To submit a tip on your phone, download the USMS Tips app from your mobile provider's marketplace. When you submit a tip using the USMS Tips mobile app, you can choose to receive push notifications to stay connected with us.

U.S. Secret Service
https://www.secretservice.gov/contact/

The Secret Service is recognized for the physical protection it provides to the nation's highest elected leaders, visiting foreign dignitaries, facilities, and major events. Today, Secret Service agents, professionals, and specialists work in field offices around the world to fight the 21st century's financial crimes, which are increasingly conducted through cyberspace. These investigations continue to address counterfeit, which still undermines confidence in the U.S. dollar, but it is credit card fraud, wire and bank fraud, computer network breaches, ransomware, and other cyber-enabled financial crimes that have become the focus of much of the Secret Service investigative work. Secret Service field offices continue their investigative work and are ready to combat a new wave of COVID-19 related cyber-enabled fraud.

Time-sensitive or critical information should NOT be sent via email. Please contact your nearest field office by telephone if you need immediate assistance.

U.S. Secret Service

245 Murray Ln SW - BLDG T-5,

Washington, DC 20223

202-406-5708

Counterfeit Notes should NOT be sent to this address. Please send all counterfeit Notes to the appropriate controlling Field Office by using the Find a Field Office function below.

https://www.secretservice.gov/contact/

Podcast on Knowles

https://www.listennotes.com/podcasts/all-killa-no-filla/all-killa-no-filla-episode-TbjlyB4dNS3/

https://www.listennotes.com/podcasts/serial-killers/the-casanova-killer-paul-tAJUV271Ml4/

https://www.listennotes.com/podcasts/parcast-presents/s5-love-the-casanova-killer-_6ogCuvZwAQ/

https://www.listennotes.com/podcasts/parcast-presents/s5-love-the-casanova-killer-Nvj8e2Gol6t/

https://www.listennotes.com/podcasts/redrum-blonde/casanova-killer-paul-john-CrX-Wcw0Gjy/

https://www.listennotes.com/podcasts/killer/case-014-paul-john-knowles-ReHmT7xBi6X/

https://www.listennotes.com/podcasts/crime-binge/episode-9-paul-john-knowles-WT0rplR2xn5/

https://www.listennotes.com/podcasts/southern-disgrace/the-one-where-you-dont-buy-nJOgxILZvp4/

https://www.listennotes.com/podcasts/which-murderer/21-s2-episode-21-charming-VLclTKfa4u0/

https://www.iheart.com/podcast/409-serial-killers-28186923/episode/the-casanova-killer-paul-john-29783838/?keyid%5B0%5D=Serial%20Killers&keyid%5B1%5D=%E2%80%9CThe%20Casanova%20Killer%E2%80%9D%20-%20Paul%20John%20Knowles&sc=podcast_widget

REFERENCES

11Alive. (2019). The Casanova Killer's Victims.
https://www.11alive.com/gallery/news/investigation
s/casanova-killer/casanova-killers-victims/85-
b97d65f9-6069-43a4-a0c1-9ee421433d9b

Campbell, J., Livingston, M. (2019) *Serial killer
documentary | Meet the Casanova Killer called
'more brutal than Bundy'* [Video]. YouTube.
https://www.youtube.com/watch?v=kaeRLHJidOo

Davids, C. (2014, January 29). Capturing Paul John
Knowles: exclusive photographs from the arrest of
"The Casanova Killer." *Asheville Oral History
Project*
https://ashevilleoralhistoryproject.com/2014/01/29/c
asanova-killer/

Douthat, B. (1974, December 27). 'Content – having a
good time' Knowles wrote from jail. *The Miami
News*.

Montgomery, B., Moore, W.A. (2019, August 18). They
went to the Dozier School for Boys damaged. They
came out destroyed.
https://www.tampabay.com/investigations/2019/08/1
8/they-went-to-the-dozier-school-for-boys-damaged-
they-came-out-destroyed/

Morganthau, T. (1974, December 19). Knowles had a goal—to be the nation's no. 1 killer. *The Miami Herald.*

Serial Dispatches. (2019, December 18). Knowles, Paul John. https://serialdispatches.com/serial-killer-paul-john-knowles/#timeline

Sympton, R. (1976, May 22). Contempt in Georgia jail, he won't bend. *The Miami Herald.*

Weinman, S. (2019, April 4). Sandy Fawke: The reporter and the serial killer. https://crimereads.com/sandy-fawkes-the-reporter-and-the-serial-killer/

www.ingramcontent.com/pod-product-compliance
Lightning Source LLC
Chambersburg PA
CBHW061000280326
41935CB00009B/780